D1757887

Political Evil in a Global Age

Hannah Arendt is widely regarded as one of the twentieth century's most powerful political theorists. The purpose of this book is to make an innovative contribution to the newly emerging literature connecting Arendt to international political theory and debates surrounding globalization.

In recent years, the work of Arendt has gathered increasing interest from scholars in the field of international political theory because of its potential relevance for understanding international affairs. Focusing on the central theme of evil in Arendt's work, this book weaves together elements of Arendt's theory in order to engage with four major problems connected with contemporary globalization: genocide and crimes against humanity; global poverty and radical economic inequality; global refugees, displaced persons and the 'stateless'; and the destructive domination of the public realm by predatory neoliberal economic globalization. Hayden shows that a key constellation of her concepts – the right to have rights, superfluousness, thoughtlessness, plurality, freedom and power – can help us to understand and address some of the central problems involving political evil in our global age. In doing so, this book takes Arendtian scholarship and international political theory in provocative new directions.

Political Evil in a Global Age will be of interest to students, researchers and scholars of politics, philosophy, sociology and cultural studies.

Patrick Hayden is Senior Lecturer at the School of International Relations at the University of St Andrews, UK.

Routledge Innovations in Political Theory

1 **A Radical Green Political Theory**
Alan Carter

2 **Rational Woman**
A feminist critique of dualism
Raia Prokhovnik

3 **Rethinking State Theory**
Mark J. Smith

4 **Gramsci and Contemporary Politics**
Beyond pessimism of the intellect
Anne Showstack Sassoon

5 **Post-Ecologist Politics**
Social theory and the abdication of the ecologist paradigm
Ingolfur Blühdorn

6 **Ecological Relations**
Susan Board

7 **The Political Theory of Global Citizenship**
April Carter

8 **Democracy and National Pluralism**
Edited by Ferran Requejo

9 **Civil Society and Democratic Theory**
Alternative voices
Gideon Baker

10 **Ethics and Politics in Contemporary Theory**
Between critical theory and post-marxism
Mark Devenney

11 **Citizenship and Identity**
Towards a new republic
John Schwarzmantel

12 **Multiculturalism, Identity and Rights**
Edited by Bruce Haddock and Peter Sutch

13 **Political Theory of Global Justice**
A cosmopolitan case for the World State
Luis Cabrera

14 **Democracy, Nationalism and Multiculturalism**
Edited by Ramón Maiz and Ferrán Requejo

15 **Political Reconciliation**
Andrew Schaap

16 **National Cultural Autonomy and Its Contemporary Critics**
Edited by Ephraim Nimni

17 **Power and Politics in Poststructuralist Thought**
New theories of the political
Saul Newman

18 **Capabilities Equality**
Basic issues and problems
Edited by Alexander Kaufman

19 **Morality and Nationalism**
Catherine Frost

20 **Principles and Political Order**
The challenge of diversity
*Edited by Bruce Haddock, Peri
Roberts and Peter Sutch*

21 **European Integration and the
Nationalities Question**
*Edited by John McGarry and Michael
Keating*

22 **Deliberation, Social Choice and
Absolutist Democracy**
David van Mill

23 **Sexual Justice / Cultural Justice**
Critical perspectives in political theory
and practice
*Edited by Barbara Arneil, Monique
Deveaux, Rita Dhamoon and Avigail
Eisenberg*

24 **The International Political Thought
of Carl Schmitt**
Terror, Liberal War and the Crisis of
Global Order
*Edited by Louiza Odysseos and Fabio
Petito*

25 **In Defense of Human Rights**
A non-religious grounding in a
pluralistic world
Ari Kohen

26 **Logics of Critical Explanation in
Social and Political Theory**
Jason Glynos and David Howarth

27 **Political Constructivism**
Peri Roberts

28 **The New Politics of Masculinity**
Men, Power and Resistance
Fidelma Ashe

29 **Citizens and the State**
Attitudes in Western Europe and East
and Southeast Asia
Takashi Inoguchi and Jean Blondel

30 **Political Language and Metaphor**
Interpreting *and* Changing the World
*Edited by Terrell Carver and Jernej
Pikalo*

31 **Political Pluralism and the State**
Beyond Sovereignty
Marcel Wissenburg

32 **Political Evil in a Global Age**
Hannah Arendt and International
Theory
Patrick Hayden

Political Evil in a Global Age

Hannah Arendt and International Theory

Patrick Hayden

Routledge
Taylor & Francis Group

LONDON AND NEW YORK

First published 2009
by Routledge
2 Park Square Milton Park Abingdon Oxon OX14 4RN

Simultaneously published in the USA and Canada
by Routledge
270 Madison Avenue, New York, NY 10016

Routledge is an imprint of the Taylor & Francis Group, an informa business.

© 2009 Patrick Hayden

Typeset in Times New Roman by
Value Chain International Ltd

British Library Cataloguing in Publication Data
A catalogue record for this book is available from the British Library

Library of Congress Cataloging in Publication Data
Hayden, Patrick, 1965–
    Political evil in a global age : Hannah Arendt and international theory /
Patrick Hayden.
        p. cm. — (Routledge innovations in political theory ; 32)
    Includes bibliographical references and index.
    1. Arendt, Hannah, 1906–1975. 2. International relations.
    3. Globalization—Political aspects. 4. Good and evil. I. Title.
    JC251.A74H439 2008
    172–dc22
                                                                    2008034101
ISBN: 978-0-415-45106-2 (hbk)
ISBN: 978-0-203-88253-5 (ebk)

For Katherine and Zoë

Contents

Acknowledgements   x
List of Abbreviations   xi

Introduction   1

1   Violating the human status: the evil of genocide and
    crimes against humanity   9

2   Superfluous humanity: the evil of global poverty   32

3   Citizens of nowhere: the evil of statelessness   55

4   Effacing the political: the evil of neoliberal globalization   92

Notes   122
Bibliography   129
Index   141

Acknowledgements

I wish to thank the friends and colleagues who provided generous advice and support (as well as healthy scepticism) at key points in the genesis of this book. Chamsy el-Ojeili, Anthony Lang, Nicholas Rengger and Paul Voice each read various chapters and took the time to discuss my ideas critically. Thanks also to Richard Beardsworth, Antonio Franceschet, Patricia Owens, Steven Roach and John Williams, who read or talked about portions of the manuscript in some form and provided perceptive suggestions as I worked to clarify my arguments. The Carnegie Trust for the Universities of Scotland provided a grant that funded some of the research carried out in support of this project. Thanks are also due to Heidi Bagtazo for taking an interest in this book and helping to bring it to fruition at Routledge. My greatest debt is to my wife, Katherine, whose sacrifice, determination and encouragement made completion of this book possible. Finally, I express my gratitude to my daughter, Zoë, whose demands, questions and humour keep me grounded daily in the reality of natality.

Abbreviations of books by Hannah Arendt

AJ	*Hannah Arendt/Karl Jaspers: Correspondence 1926–1969*
BPF	*Between Past and Future*
CR	*Crises of the Republic*
EJ	*Eichmann in Jerusalem*
EU	*Essays in Understanding*
HC	*The Human Condition*
JP	*The Jew as Pariah*
JW	*The Jewish Writings*
LK	*Lectures on Kant's Political Philosophy*
LMT	*The Life of the Mind, Vol. 1, Thinking*
LMW	*The Life of the Mind, Vol. 2, Willing*
LSA	*Love and Saint Augustine*
MDT	*Men in Dark Times*
OR	*On Revolution*
OT	*The Origins of Totalitarianism*
OV	*On Violence*
PP	*The Promise of Politics*
RJ	*Responsibility and Judgment*

Introduction

> The atrophy of the political realm is one of those objectively demonstrable tendencies of the modern era.
>
> Arendt 2005

> The sad truth of the matter is that most evil is done by people who never made up their minds to be or do evil or good.
>
> Arendt 1978b

This book examines the occurrence of political evil in an increasingly globalized world, using the work of Hannah Arendt (1906–75) as its focus and point of departure. 'Evil' has assumed a remarkably high profile on the international stage over the past seven years (see Lu 2004; Jeffery 2005; Rengger and Jeffery 2005). From the destruction of the World Trade Centre in New York City on 11 September 2001, to the 'War on Terror' unleashed in response by President George W. Bush, to the subsequent naming of an 'axis of evil' and the US military invasion of Iraq, the rhetoric of evil has in recent years assumed a familiar if somewhat infamous place within political discourse. Although this is a book about political evil, it does not necessarily welcome this particular recent turn towards the invocation of evil. For the most part, this invocation is little more than a self-serving abuse of the term that demonizes the 'other' and focuses 'exclusively upon a single enemy' in order to 'justify a hundred lesser crimes of our own' (Judt 2008). In short, the grand return of evil as an international political issue fails to grasp the post-metaphysical lessons about the origin and nature of historical atrocities of which Arendt was well aware.

If this is the case, why employ the language of political evil? Why not appeal to less controversial terms, such harm, oppression or injustice? Why not avoid the language of evil entirely? I think two fundamental and decisive answers can be given to these questions. The first of these is expressed clearly in the work of Paul Ricoeur. In his essay 'The Political Paradox', written in the immediate aftermath of the 1956 Soviet invasion of Hungary, Ricoeur argues that political evil is a problematic of power insofar as political power is paradoxical: power may be used for both the progress and perversion of human freedom. Yet to recognize the reality of the 'evils of political power' is not the same thing as declaring politics to be evil (Ricoeur 1965: 248). Rather, it is to identify the specific ways that power may turn to violence through particular decisions and actions that result in profound dehumanization or 'alienation'. The difficulty posed by political evil, as Ricoeur proposes in very Arendtian fashion, is that the political condition of human existence is inseparable from, and indeed constituted by, power. Power is the essence of the political and of the 'grandeur' and 'splendor' of politics. But it is this same 'splendor' that is 'eminently prone to evil' (*ibid.*: 256). It is a mistake to believe, then, either that politics as a whole is corrupt and malevolent, or that it may be finally cleansed of power and its vices; both despairing pessimism and sanguine idealism often tend to produce the very abuses of power that prompt their anti-political 'moods' (see PP: 97). For if power is inherent to the political condition of human existence, then the divide between political freedom and political evil is '*internal* to all political power' (Ricoeur 1965: 259). Consequently, the answer that Ricoeur provides us with is that, as a matter of collective responsibility, we are confronted with the unending task of exercising a 'political *vigilance*' with regard to our political decisions and actions (*ibid.*: 261). But this vigilance is dependent on a 'lucidity' with respect to the reality of the evil specific to political power. Denying the persistent reality of political evil leads not only to an evasion of politics, but to an evasion of our humanity as well (*ibid.*: 260–61).

The second answer is suggested by George Kateb, a thoughtful commentator on Arendt's work. Kateb admits that many people 'recoil' at the word evil, and find it to be 'melodramatic', 'lurid', or an 'exaggeration'. It also carries a great deal of metaphysical baggage. Yet Kateb replies, rightly I believe, that there are certain 'deeds or policies or conditions or systems' that are so wrong – wrongs of the worst kind – that they 'deserve the utmost condemnation' (Kateb 1992: 199). So while we should certainly exercise caution when using the term, nevertheless it should be retained precisely because it expresses the 'utmost condemnation' in a way that words such as oppression or injustice cannot do. What does Kateb mean when he refers to 'the worst wrong'? He defines evil as 'the deliberate infliction (or sponsorship or knowing allowance) … of suffering of great intensity … and of death … done for the sake of advancing purposes and defending commitments that have nothing to do with strict self-defense' (*ibid.*: 200). Injustice and oppression almost certainly will be components of political evil, but by themselves do not necessarily rise to the level of evil – hence the boundaries between these political phenomena may not always be clear. Yet whereas injustice and oppression involve the denial of some or even many 'personal and political rights', political evil entails 'the *obliteration of personhood*' on a 'scale of action that usually only political agencies and forces are capable of' (*ibid.*: 201–02; emphasis added). The second answer that I will appeal to, then, is that the concepts of oppression and injustice, although invaluable and appropriate when analysing many political wrongs, are not quite 'weighty' enough to convey the ultimate wrong of engaging in the large-scale, systemic 'obliteration of personhood'.

Ricoeur and Kateb thus give us very good reasons for using the concept and language of political evil today. Obviously there are some disadvantages to doing so: the metaphysical or religious associations may be so complete that some people simply cannot bring themselves to think of evil in a secular, historical, political sense; the temptation to exploit and abuse the term (for what are, paradoxically, often manifestly evil ends) remains great; the battle over which definitions of evil are 'right' may never end. But we should not lose sight of the fact that so many people utilize conceptions of evil in their accounts of politics, and arguably strong agreement about how political evil should be properly understood has developed in the post-Second World War discourse of human rights (*ibid.*: 202). Further, our thinking about political evil probably can avoid certain disadvantages if we attend to Ricoeur's and Kateb's – as well as, we shall see, Arendt's – insight that good and evil cannot be counterposed in any simple way. In the end, I think that the concept of political evil is a necessary and potent tool for both critique and change, given the reality that political activity is 'eminently prone' (Ricoeur) to the 'obliteration of personhood' as a 'matter of policy' (Kateb).

Following the insights provided by Ricoeur and Kateb, the present volume explores the reality of the obliteration of personhood through several perversions of power that plague contemporary political activity on a global scale. The particular understanding of political evil adopted in the book rests upon what Arendt calls 'superfluousness' – the distinctively political problem of dehumanization associated with the deliberate infliction of large-scale degradation, exclusion and, ultimately, dispensability or disposability from political life of increasingly larger numbers of people. The prevalence of superfluousness in the world today, I will argue, reveals the occurrence of political evil that is fatal not merely to human life, but to human status and political existence itself. Superfluous people are not only oppressed or treated unjustly, they are made expendable from a properly human world. For Arendt, the expansion of superfluousness throughout the modern age also diminishes politics and the political realm. Although drawing much-needed attention to shameful forms of injustice and oppression, the explosive growth during the past 10–15 years of literature devoted to the topic of global justice has been markedly unwilling to confront the vexing issue of political evil.[1] The work of Arendt, who both engaged deeply with and initiated a critical rethinking of the problem of evil, runs counter to this trend. If only for that reason, it is easy to see 'why Arendt matters' (Young-Bruehl 2006).

Arendt's concern with evil in the political realm, from the state to the international level, pervades her life and thought. From the time of her 'turn to the political' following the burning of the Reichstag in February 1933 (EU: 4–5), Arendt became increasingly convinced that 'the precondition of any modern political thinking' is recognition of the 'incalculable evil that men are capable of bringing about' (EU: 132). There has been considerable debate, however, since the appearance of her book *Eichmann in Jerusalem* (1963), as to whether Arendt's thinking about the origin of evil in the world changed, in particular whether she rejected the concept of radical evil in favour of the concept of the banality of evil. In *Eichmann in Jerusalem*, Arendt conceptualized the 'banality of evil' in order to describe the concrete origin of evil that seemed to defy conventional assumptions about the nature of evil individuals and their actions. For some, this concept represented a profound and regrettable shift in Arendt's thinking. Gershom Scholem, for instance, viewed it as betraying Arendt's 'profound analysis' of radical or 'absolute' evil in her earlier book *The Origins of Totalitarianism* (1951) (JP: 245). In her response to Scholem, Arendt admitted that her conception of evil had indeed changed in some way:

> You are quite right: I changed my mind and do no longer speak of 'radical evil'. ... It is indeed my opinion now that evil is never 'radical', that it is only extreme, and that it possesses neither depth nor any demonic dimension. It can overgrow and lay waste the whole world because it spreads like a fungus on the surface. It is 'thought-defying,' as I said, because thought tries to reach some depth, to go to the roots, and the moment it concerns itself with evil, it is frustrated because there is nothing. That is its 'banality'.
>
> (JP: 251)

Yet to presume that for Arendt the banality of evil supersedes the notion of radical evil overlooks both the nature of political evil as she conceived it, and the enduring place of extreme evil in her thought. Radical evil and evil as banal are distinct, though complementary, aspects of extreme evil as a whole (see Bernstein 1996: 137–53). In other words, as Richard Bernstein notes, 'the phenomenon that she identified as the banality of evil *presupposes* [the] understanding of radical evil' (Bernstein 2002: 218). To put the matter most simply, radical evil refers to the way in which life is 'thoroughly and systematically organized with a view to the greatest possible torment' of large numbers of human beings (OT: 574), while the banality of evil points to the singular and most terrifying condition of the modern human character that makes the appearance of radical evil possible – thoughtlessness and an uncritical reliance on conventional attitudes as a shield against reality. For this reason, Arendt's concept of the banality of evil does not refute the idea of radical evil, but instead illuminates how radical evil typically originates in the modern political domain. Therefore the thesis of the banality of evil can assume its full implications only when considered as inseparable from Arendt's analysis of radical or extreme evil. But why is it that Arendt 'ceased to speak' of radical evil in one sense, and how exactly should we understand the relationship between radical evil and evil as banal?

Arendt's theoretical engagement with the problem of radical evil can be seen as a reaction to Immanuel Kant, who claimed that evil is the outcome of what a person freely wills, and not the expression of a necessarily evil human nature. It is Kant's position that a person may will action either from respect for the moral law, or from sensible inclinations that deviate from or 'corrupt' such law. What is crucial for Kant is that if the notion of evil (and of ourselves as moral beings) is to make any sense, then evil acts must have their source in the subjective grounds (or maxims) of the autonomous will; good or evil is the result of what a person freely wills (Kant 1960: 23–40; see also Kant 1978: 241–46). While all human beings are capable of doing both good and evil, only individual agents can choose either good or evil maxims, and thereby become either good or evil persons. Kant further distinguishes between different degrees of the propensity to do evil: first is the general frailty or 'weakness of the human heart' in observing adopted maxims; second is the occasional 'impurity' of 'mixing unmoral with moral motivating causes'; and third is the exceptional 'wickedness' or 'perversity of the human heart' that comes from adopting maxims that consistently affirm non-moral incentives over moral ones (Kant 1960: 24). This highest degree of the capacity for evil is radical in that it exhibits a 'cast of mind' whose disposition is 'corrupted at its root' and which 'corrupts the ground of all maxims' adopted by such a person (*ibid.*: 29, 32). The radically evil person *freely and unfailingly* chooses 'the law of self-love' in preference to the 'moral law' (*ibid.*: 31–32).

In *The Origins of Totalitarianism*, her first substantive attempt to analyse political evil, Arendt argues that the traditional explanation for radical evil breaks down in the face of the unprecedented crimes committed by the Nazi regime. Whereas Kant (and others before him, such as Augustine) had conceived evil as having its origin in desires and behaviours that contradicted conventional social morality – lust, greed, dishonesty, envy – the great atrocities of totalitarianism, culminating in genocide, were produced only because vast numbers of dutiful, rule-following citizens failed to question or challenge social convention. The worst horrors imaginable were produced by the masses of 'good' respectable citizens of respectable society, not by the perverted or demonic few. This meant that the Western moral and political tradition could not provide the intellectual and normative resources needed to grasp the concrete experience of the 'overpowering reality' of political evil (OT: 591–92). For Arendt, this shift in thinking about the origins of radical evil from abnormality to normality is epitomized by the transformation that occurred when control of the Nazi death camps passed from the SA (*Sturmabteilung*) to the SS (*Schutzstaffel*). According to Arendt, many of the SA personnel were 'criminal and abnormal' elements who carried out brutally sadistic forms of torture as an expression of the hatred and resentment they harboured for others. In contrast, however, 'the real horror began' under the SS administration as the 'old spontaneous bestiality gave way to an absolutely cold and systematic destruction of human bodies' (OT: 585). At this point the camps were no longer an outlet for recognizably abnormal pathological behaviour, rather 'they were turned into "drill grounds," on which perfectly normal men' were trained to become calculating and efficient bureaucrats of systematic mass murder (OT: 585; see also EU: 240). This phenomenological difference stands at the heart of Arendt's disagreement with Kant's account of radical evil.

The inability to uncover any further explanatory depths below the surface of extreme political evil led Arendt to distinguish her understanding of radical evil from Kant's. On the one hand, radical evil is 'thought-defying' because there is nothing more to it than the horror of what appears; there is no metaphysical depth beneath it that will enable us to rationalize its extreme nature. Simply positing the existence of 'sinful' or 'corrupt' motives shifts our attention away from the enormity of radical evil as a political fact that tears apart the fabric of reality, to supposedly deeper inclinations that can be classified as the 'abnormal' characteristics of a few exceptionally wicked individuals. To adopt the latter approach is to sanitize radical evil, to contain it to an individual source, and ultimately to ignore the extent to which radical evil becomes socialized. In one sense, then, it is a mistake to speak of radical evil, if by that is meant the hidden depths or 'roots' of evil that are restricted to a few extraordinarily perverted individuals who operate beyond the margins of normality and respectable society.

On the other hand, this does not mean there is no such thing as radical evil at all. Arendt is clear that the kinds of crimes committed by the Nazi regime exemplify extreme evil. Yet what is crucial to the radical nature of this evil is that it 'appeared in connection with a system in which all men have become superfluous in some way' (OT: 612). The core of Arendt's concept of radical evil, then, is that it 'has to do with the following phenomenon: making human beings as human beings superfluous' (AJ: 166). In their systematic attempt to eliminate human spontaneity, individuality and plurality, totalitarian regimes were not liquidating simply individuals, but rather the very idea of humanity itself. All human beings, including the leaders of totalitarian regimes themselves, were treated as completely superfluous and dispensable. As Arendt suggests, 'perhaps what is behind it all is ... that an organized attempt was made to eradicate the concept of human being' (AJ: 69). Making humanity superfluous, on the basis of the most mundane motivations and socially acceptable modes of obedience, is the key to thinking about the appearance and functioning of political evil on the modern political landscape. Consequently, Arendt does not abandon the concept of radical evil *per se*. Rather, she holds that evil acts are wrongs of the most radically extreme kind, but appealing to the pathological natures of abnormal individuals is inadequate to explain radical evil as a political, systemic phenomenon. As Arendt recalls about the Eichmann trial in her last book, *The Life of the Mind*:

> I was struck by a manifest shallowness in the doer that made it impossible to trace the uncontestable evil of his deeds to any deeper level of roots or motives. The deeds were monstrous, but the doer – at least the very effective one now on trial – was quite ordinary, commonplace, and neither demonic nor monstrous. There was no sign in him of firm ideological convictions or of specific evil motives, and the only notable characteristic one could detect in his past behaviour as well as in his behaviour during the trial and throughout the pre-trial police examination was something entirely negative: it was not stupidity but *thoughtlessness*.

> (LMT: 4)

Many of the themes raised in the preceding discussion are addressed at greater length in the chapters that follow. But the preceding considerations demand that I note briefly three further crucial aspects of Arendt's views regarding political evil. First, while Arendt's concerns regarding the dehumanizing functions of political evil were prompted by the horrors of totalitarianism, her conception of superfluousness as complete dehumanization cannot be limited only to the case of totalitarianism. Indeed, although totalitarianism proved itself to be the 'one supreme and radical evil' of the twentieth century, compared with which all other political evils appeared to be 'lesser', Arendt insists that this type of comparison is actually 'meaningless, because this may be true of all evils in our entire history' (EU: 271). She continues:

> Yet all historical and political evidence clearly points to the more-than-intimate connection between the lesser and the greater evil. If homelessness, rootlessness, and the disintegration of political bodies and social classes do not directly produce totalitarianism, they at least produce almost all of the elements that eventually go into its formation. … The natural conclusion from true insight into a century so fraught with danger of the greatest evil should be a radical negation of the whole concept of the lesser evil in politics, because far from protecting us against the greater ones, the lesser evils have invariably led us into them. The greatest danger of recognizing totalitarianism as the curse of the century would be an obsession with it to the extent of becoming blind to the numerous small and not so small evils with which the road to hell is paved.
>
> (EU: 271–72)

With this in mind, my intent has been to confront and examine some of the most disturbing forms of political evil that either have been relegated to a 'lesser' status, or to which we have become completely blind, especially in comparison with the current obsessive focus on the supposedly single 'great' evil of terrorism. As a further development of Arendt's position on political evil, a second feature of her overall political thought that I have sought to emphasize is that the problem of political evil is a cosmopolitan concern. While each political evil assumes a concrete form within specific historical circumstances, the spectre of such evil haunts the political mode of existence characteristic of the human condition, and therefore humanity itself. The problem of political evil is never merely parochial, it is always universal. One of the core lessons to be taken from Arendt's work is that plurality and humanity form an indissociable unity. The destruction and dehumanization of a particular group of people is, at the same time, an assault on the very idea of humanity itself; similarly, humanity exists only through the robust plurality of those diverse individuals and peoples out of which it is composed. Genocide, for instance, is a crime directed both at a particular people and at the human status.

Finally, the third aspect of Arendt's views in which I am particularly interested, and which colours the other two, is that her attitude toward all of the above exhibits a bracing sense of ambivalence. Whatever cosmopolitan sensibility runs throughout her probing life and work – manifested in her critique of sovereignty and nationalist essentialism, her attempt to reconceptualize a politically effective approach to human rights, her plea for transnational solidarity and collective responsibility, and her passionate affirmation of human equality and dignity – it remains chastened by an equally marked suspicion of moral and political idealism, the abuse of power disguised by cynical assertions of universalism and commonality, facile political prescriptions based on dogmatic certainty, and failure to appreciate the complexity of political action and its frequently unexpected consequences. This ambivalence is central to Arendt's thought inasmuch as it expresses a mode of rejecting absolutist distinctions while remaining open to the unpredictability of the future and of our plural world. I believe that Arendt's approach to the problem of political evil shows both her affirmative side and her darker side, both her unwavering commitment to hope and her willingness to face up to the unspeakable horrors that pervade the world. For that reason, I refer to her simultaneous acceptance of the tragic side of human affairs and affirmation of the possibility of resisting evil for the sake of human dignity as 'cosmopolitan realism'. Looking into the ways in which we render vast portions of humanity superfluous can demonstrate how blinded we have become to the occurrence of political evil in our globalized world. Confronting these evils directly can help give expression to Arendt's deep concern for, and dedication to, the human capacity for freedom and the power to begin something new, by acting *with* others rather than against them (see HC: 180).

1 Violating the human status
The evil of genocide and crimes against humanity

In October 1945, 24 Nazi leaders, bureaucrats and architects of the Holocaust were indicted by the International Military Tribunal for Nuremberg, charged with war crimes, crimes against peace and, for the first time in history, crimes against humanity (Schabas 2001: 6). The Nuremberg trials exposed to the world the still-emerging details of the Nazi regime's attempt to eradicate entire groups of human beings from the earth, and prompted a revolution in international law and politics. Subsequently, *ad hoc* international criminal tribunals were established to prosecute those accused of atrocities in the former Yugoslavia and Rwanda, and most recently a permanent International Criminal Court (ICC) was established in order to take legal action against individuals accused of the gravest war crimes, crimes against humanity, and genocide. Given these developments, it might seem that the international community is, finally, making good on its promise that 'never again' should genocide be allowed to occur. Clearly, this promise has yet to be fulfilled, as numerous examples – from Bangladesh and East Timor, to Cambodia, Rwanda and now Darfur – attest. In all these cases, the failure to prevent or halt genocide can be described, as has been widely said about the Rwandan genocide, as the triumph of evil. Yet how are we to understand the relationship between the concept of evil and the legal category of crimes against humanity? Further, how are we to make sense of the promise 'never again'? What is at stake, morally and politically, in making such a promise? Finally, how can reflecting upon evil and promise-making be brought to bear on the existence of the ICC?

A number of commentators have suggested that the establishment of the ICC is a cosmopolitan moment in our globalizing world (Ralph 2003; Franceschet 2005; Roach 2005). Its appearance seems to mark the successful realization of certain cosmopolitan ideals and practices. While some backers of the ICC might regard its creation as evidence of the progressive 'enlightenment' of humankind, this chapter adopts a different approach, and argues instead that the ICC is best characterized in terms of *cosmopolitan realism*, that is, a critical cosmopolitanism shorn of historical and moral idealism. This approach is adopted for several reasons. Most importantly, I contend, the creation of a cosmopolitan 'regime' leading to the establishment of the ICC has been motivated more by the terrifying experience of political evil than by the triumph of enlightened moral consciousness, that is, by the horror that humanity inspires rather than by Kantian awe at the 'moral law within' (Kant 1997: 133). Further, the cosmopolitan law underwriting the ICC can be properly understood only with constant reference to the phenomenon of political evil, in two ways: first, as a way to make the historical experience of evil intelligible; and second, as a way to subject the perpetrators of evil to political judgement and legal accountability. From this perspective, the ICC should be regarded as the latest effort to juridify evil.[1]

The basis for this chapter comes from Hannah Arendt's claim that while the 'shrinking of geographic distances' throughout the twentieth century made humanity 'a political actuality of the first order', it also rendered 'idealistic talk about mankind and the dignity of man an affair of the past simply because all these fine and dreamlike notions, with their time-honoured traditions, suddenly assumed a terrifying timeliness' (OT: 303). For Arendt, the major weakness of the cosmopolitan tradition has been its tendency to succumb to idealistic illusions while neglecting the cruel realities of political life. Thus, while Arendt's political theory exhibits a strongly cosmopolitan sensibility – although Arendt does not call herself a cosmopolitan theorist – it is a sensibility conditioned by an uncompromising willingness to face up to the moral and political horrors of modern life, the 'dark times' of political evil that shake our sense of reality and threaten our capacity for judgement, responsibility, and action. Following Arendt's lead, this chapter argues that a critical and realistic cosmopolitanism must start from, and respond to, the lived reality of the shared experience of extreme political evil.

My reading of Arendt's cosmopolitan realism implies that the process of translating horrifying atrocities into politically intelligible and legally sanctionable crimes provides a new juridical idiom for resisting evil actions. This commitment, however, cannot escape from the condition of normative ambivalence that necessarily accompanies moral and political confrontation with evil. Cosmopolitans can seek to eradicate evil through moral perfectionism, or accept the capacity for evil while resisting it whenever possible, but not both. This, I think, means that we can support the aims of the ICC and resist pernicious threats to the human status, but to do so responsibly requires accepting rather than dismissing normative ambivalence in the global age if we wish to remain in touch with reality and not succumb to the dangerous illusions of cosmopolitan idealism.

Following from this, I suggest that what most distinguishes cosmopolitan realism from other versions of cosmopolitanism is that it begins from, and continually refers back to, the shared experience of extreme evil. While it regards the formal juridification of evil as necessary in order to achieve justice, it refuses to lose sight of the fact that the most egregious of international criminal acts – genocide and crimes against humanity – nonetheless are acts of evil, the meaning of which is irreducible to the category of criminal transgression. The juridification of evil is necessary for mechanisms of justice, but by itself is insufficient to grasp the political and existential significance of the elusive experience of extreme evil. For this reason, cosmopolitan realism is predicated on recognition of the ineliminable human capacity for evil as a political reality, the risk of which the juridification of evil cannot dispel altogether.[2] It also exposes an inescapable paradox at the heart of the juridification of extreme evil: that the occurrence of evil can be eliminated *completely* only by generating further acts of evil against humanity. Political responsibility, as a necessary supplement to the juridification of evil, requires understanding and acceptance of this paradox.

To illustrate this argument, this chapter draws primarily on the work of Arendt, supplemented at points by that of Ulrich Beck. The first section discusses the necessity of bringing evil 'down to earth' in response to the experiential horizon of the twentieth century, and employs Arendt's conception of extreme evil in order to show that the 'problem of evil' is best understood not as a problem in the traditional metaphysical sense, but as a political problem of the age of genocide. The second section addresses the issue of juridification as a process of translating extreme evil into politically intelligible and legally sanctionable crimes. Here, I explore how the doctrine of crimes against humanity provided a new juridical idiom for extreme evil, which is then used to illuminate Arendt's understanding of cosmopolitanism from a distinctively realist perspective. The third section connects the preceding discussion to the argument for cosmopolitan realism advanced by Beck as a way to view the ICC as a manifestation of reflexive modernization in contemporary global politics, and thus as a form of cosmopolitanization that political action realistically can take in resisting evil actions. The fourth section considers the implications of the paradox of extreme evil for cosmopolitan responsibility and solidarity, and relates this to the ICC's first case in Uganda and then back to the burden imposed by the promise 'never again'.

Thinking about evil in the age of genocide

Adam Lebor recently suggested that in the post-Cold War era the United Nations has been, and remains, at least passively complicit 'with evil' (2006: ix–xiv). From Srebrenica to Rwanda and Darfur, the United Nations repeatedly has chosen not to act to prevent or stop genocide, despite possessing knowledge that genocide is being committed and having the means to intervene. As Lebor's discussion makes clear, 'complicity with evil' can occur either through aiding and abetting perpetrators or through refusing to deter them when in a position to do so, and in the case of modern genocide these two sides of complicity have become deeply intertwined. While Lebor insists (2006: 5) that his account of the UN's complicity with evil should not be taken as a blanket condemnation of the institution – and even less so of the ideals it embodies – it points nevertheless to an ambivalent relationship between a defining moral discourse of our era and the extant organization of power, ethics and politics in the international system. In the post-Holocaust age, 'evil' has become synonymous with genocide and crimes against humanity, and this familiar public discourse has helped to justify the idea of an international legal and political order predicated on the suppression of such evils, irrespective of territorial borders. In practice, however, the categorical promise to 'never again' allow such evil to go unchallenged has been betrayed with astonishing regularity.

The basic dilemma of the post-Holocaust era remains unresolved: can the international community successfully stop genocide and crimes against humanity, or are its efforts doomed to inevitable failure? But there is a flaw in this question that arises from a misconception of the evil at stake, and thus of a paradox that confounds the effort to eliminate evil. This flaw is dangerous in that if one admits the inevitability of failure, then it may seem reasonable to not make the effort at all; yet if one accepts the possibility of success, then this may license the emergence of new forms of evil in order to combat some pre-existing evil. In either case, evil persists. There is a way to negotiate this paradox but only, I contend, if we both accept the persistence of evil and act to reduce the risk of its occurring needlessly. This means also accepting the normative ambivalence within which international efforts to prevent, suppress and punish genocide and crimes against humanity will remain, inasmuch as this ambivalence is a reflection of the place of evil in the human condition.

We can better understand the normative ambivalence that arises from efforts to condemn the most egregious atrocities through a consideration of how evil can be conceived in the age of genocide. Much of the philosophical canon is predicated in the idea that evil is a 'problem' to be neatly solved. Philosophers and theologians have long struggled with the problem of theodicy, of how to reconcile the existence of evil with belief in a benevolent and perfect God (Bernstein 2005: 2–3). I do not wish to rehearse the various and usually elaborate attempts to explain (or justify) evil when viewed as a metaphysical conundrum (see Neiman 2002; Morton 2004; Cole 2006). I would only like to suggest that, given the historical and metaphysical rupture symbolized by Auschwitz, we cannot rest content with debating the problem of evil in purely religious or philosophical terms. Rather, evil has become a concrete, lived experience that defines, in large part, the self-understanding of our age – the age of genocide (Power 2002). Because of this experience, Arendt was to argue that the problem of extreme evil as a *political* phenomenon forms the background against which all attempts to understand the contemporary world and our responsibilities within it necessarily must be made (EU: 134). The political question that arises concerns the meaning of the modern human condition inescapably framed within the horizon of once 'unimaginable' acts and actors that have now become all too human. The search for the unassailable truth of how to reconcile good and evil in a transcendent order and thereby rid the earth of evil (if only through redemption) is now replaced by a more worldly yet no less challenging question: What is the meaning of the great political evil that confronts us as humans today and what ethical, political, and legal responses can be offered?

Arendt is perhaps the foremost thinker of the postmetaphysical meaning of evil in relation to the age of genocide.[3] While Arendt was deeply knowledgeable of theodicy and the traditional problem of evil (see LSE; Kohn 1996: 151–52), her concern with evil was motivated primarily by the political catastrophes of imperialism, totalitarianism and the Holocaust. In struggling to make sense of modernity's darkest moments, Arendt sought to shed evil of its supernatural connotations by treating it as a political phenomenon mediated not through divine or demonic forces, but through the actions of ordinary individuals and the power relations of social institutions within which these actions are inscribed. In *The Origins of Totalitarianism*, Arendt argues that neither Christian theologians nor Immanuel

Kant (who coined the phrase 'radical evil') were able to conceive the reality of radical evil in the body politic; the former because it 'conceded even to the Devil himself a celestial origin' and the latter because, even though he 'at least must have suspected the existence of this evil' he nevertheless 'immediately rationalized it in the concept of the "perverted will" that could be explained by comprehensible motives' (OT: 591–92). Arendt believes that the phenomenon of radical evil only suspected by Kant became the distinctive reality of modern society, as witnessed by the deliberate fabrication of an 'earthly hell' in the 'concentration camps and torture cellars' perfected by the Nazis (EU: 383). In the Nazis' political regime, the totalitarian belief that 'everything is possible' was given material expression, with the result that when 'the impossible was made possible it became the … absolute evil which could no longer be understood and explained by' the malice, insanity or character defects of a few monstrous individuals (OT: 591).

Arendt's controversial and frequently misunderstood notion of the 'banality of evil', presented briefly in *Eichmann in Jerusalem*, exemplifies her intervention into the narrative of the Holocaust and Nazi atrocities. With this concept, Arendt departed from Kant's explanation of 'radical evil' according to which the doer of evil deeds was wicked, monstrous or demonic, towards a more nuanced account of 'extreme evil', which emphasizes that terrible atrocities are committed even when 'evil motivations' are absent, precisely because such atrocities are 'normalized' within powerful political regimes and social discourses (JP: 417). Arendt argues that the traditional approach that locates evil either in the extrahuman or the sub-human merely reduces evil to a sterile scholastic problem, which makes it possible to shut our eyes to the material reality and political significance of the systematic extermination of millions of people (OT: 592). Arendt thus sought to change our perspective on evil and give expression to its unique character as something made concrete under historical circumstances.

What constitutes the 'horizon of experience' for the world after Auschwitz is knowledge that 'killing is far from the worst that man can inflict on man' (MDT: 127). The most extreme evil on earth is not merely violent death at the hands of others, but the 'historically and politically intelligible preparation of living corpses', that is, the planned transformation of human beings into non-humans which precedes their extermination (OT: 576). To be clear, Arendt is not suggest-ing that the mass killing of human beings carried out by the Nazi genocide is not evil. What she is suggesting, however, is that the *meaning* of this atrocity is located in the experiential space opened up between the actual killing itself and the pre-paratory dehumanization coldly and systematically carried out beforehand. How can we make sense of the moral and political abyss that exists between murder on the one hand and the 'fabrication of corpses' on the other? More than death itself, complete dehumanization – the loss of personhood and exclusion from a human world – is the most terrifying possibility we can now too easily imagine.

Arendt's postmetaphysical definition of evildoing 'has to do with the follow-ing phenomenon: making human beings as human beings superfluous' (AJ: 166). Actions are evil insofar as they produce the systematic destruction of people's human status by means of rendering their particularity, that is, *who* they are as unique human beings, superfluous. The logic of superfluity – what Arendt (OT: 384, n. 54) referred to as the 'modern expulsion from humanity' – is not merely to kill people, but completely to dehumanize them, to strip them of all dignity and to treat them as nothing more than manipulable and expendable matter. Superfluous people are those cast out of a common world through the destruction of their political, legal, economic and moral status. Arendt's view of extremely evil acts involving superfluity, and frequently consistent with ordinary or 'banal' society-wide attitudes and moral codes, is intended to shift our thinking to the question of what it means to be human. The answer to this question rests upon the fragile interrelationship of the human condition of plurality and having a place in the public world shared with others. Political evil typically entails a double process of superfluity – destroying the fact of plurality in the pursuit of an ideal of homogeneous 'Man' (as opposed to the lived reality of heterogeneous 'men'), and denying individuals moral, juridical and political standing as unique persons within a community founded on reciprocal recognition of equal status. The result of such a process of dehumanization is an assault on the very idea of 'humanity' itself. Seen in this light, Arendt rightly emphasizes that we are human not solely because of our physical birth, but also because of our belonging with others politically in a world we create together between us; we become human on the basis of the natality of our second, 'political' birth (HC: 176). Properly speaking, then, genocide is an evil act because it seeks to efface humanity as the active coming together of a plurality of persons within a commonly shared world.

In sum, the crucial feature of extreme evil in Arendt's account is that it is a form of political action that takes aim at the human status as such, in its relentless drive to deprive individuals *qua* politically recognized human beings from having a place in the world. Moreover, Arendt thought that one of the most terrifying characteristics of political evil in modernity is the fact that it often can be committed on a 'gigantic scale' on the basis of the most petty and all-too-human motives (RJ: 159). Arendt's notion of the 'banality of evil' has been frequently criticized, and just as frequently misunderstood. With this concept, Arendt simply brought to our attention that it is best to conceive of evil actions not as external manifestations of innately corrupt properties of human nature, but in terms of the concrete social, ethical and political actions of specific individuals, even if the motives for these actions are often mundane (JP: 245). For instance, although Eichmann seemingly was motivated by the most banal careerism, he nevertheless intended to coordinate the transportation of millions of innocent people to their deaths and acted so as to make this happen. His actions were evil despite the absence of 'demonic' motives; to put it another way, he *did* evil without *being* evil. Arendt's argument also drives home the point that attributing the magnitude of extreme evil to a few deviant 'others' serves to obfuscate the fact that so many people just like 'us' are required for such evil to happen (EJ: 276). In order to accomplish the extreme evil of genocide, it is necessary for a broad spectrum of society to accept and facilitate the crime as a 'normal' or acceptable political goal. Arendt insists that because evil occurs on a collective, political plane, it requires a political response of articulating institutional arrangements and a juridical discourse for inscribing political evil within a global legal order, such as with a permanent International Criminal Court (EJ: 270–72). But in doing so, we must remain aware of the normative ambivalence that, Arendt cautions, conditions such endeavours.

Facing up to extreme evil: towards cosmopolitan realism

Susan Neiman stresses that the problem of evil 'is fundamentally a problem about the intelligibility of the world as a whole' (Neiman 2002: 7–8). The appearance of evil actions threatens our trust in the world and disrupts our sense of reality through which we interpret, understand and interact with the world in which we live. In Arendtian terms, evil destroys the social or public roots of 'common sense', the shared measure of human experience through which we have a place in the world with others (LK: 27; RJ: 138–43). Evil thus provokes an ethical crisis in that it may jeopardize our ability to judge and to act; ethical paralysis, if not outright nihilism, can be a destructive effect of evil actions. This provides a way to understand normative responses to evil as attempts to render intelligible the seemingly unintelligible, to make orderly the potentially chaotic, and to reconstruct a sensible world – however precarious – from the reality fractured by the experience of evil. Thus evil is both interruptive and inaugurative, as it ruptures our sense of the familiar while opening up new possibilities for the world to take on new meaning. As Arendt concludes, no matter how much the Holocaust constitutes an epochal break, it is still 'historically and politically intelligible' (OT: 576). As such, it gives rise to the collective demand for moral judgement, responsibility and accountability sufficient to its reality; in short, both reality and justice must be restored. The intersubjective reconstruction of common sense is an expression of resistance to the occurrence of evil, which 'arises out of incidents of living experience and must remain bound to them as the only guideposts by which to take its bearings' (BPF: 14). Here I want to focus on the doctrine of crime against humanity as a historical construct that helps us to make extremely evil actions morally intelligible and thereby to hold perpetrators accountable within a collectively defined juridical framework. This juridification of evil is a core commitment of cosmopolitan realism imbued with a sense of the desolation woven into the fabric of late modern political life.

One of the most prominent recent attempts at juridifying and resisting extreme evil is the ICC. The preamble to the 1998 Statute of the ICC (the 'Rome Statute'), which entered into force in 2002, articulates the Court's rationale retrospectively and prospectively, in terms of the 'unimaginable atrocities' of the twentieth century and the potential for further such atrocities to 'shatter' the 'delicate mosaic' of the world's plurality (Rome Statute 1998: 7). The Rome Statute and the ICC were preceded by several other significant developments in international criminal law, most notably the formation of the *ad hoc* International Criminal Tribunals for the former Yugoslavia (established in 1993) and for Rwanda (established in 1994), and the earlier Nuremberg and Tokyo International Military Tribunals. Shoring up these institutions were doctrinal developments, including the adoption of the

Charter of the Nuremberg International Military Tribunal (1945), the UN Charter (1945), the Universal Declaration of Human Rights (1948), and the Convention on the Prevention and Punishment of the Crime of Genocide (1948).

The idea of 'crime against humanity' attempts to translate the sense of extreme evil into juridical discourse, and thereby to make it more recognizable, rationally comprehensible and 'familiar'. The expression 'crime against humanity' first appeared in a joint declaration issued by the French, British and Russian governments in 1915, condemning the massacres (the term genocide was not yet in use) of Armenians by the Turkish government.[4] Yet it became a justiciable crime within international law only at the time of the Nuremberg trials, when the Nuremberg Charter referred to crime against humanity as a type of war crime committed against civilian populations (in this case, on the part of the German state against its own citizens).[5] Developments subsequent to Nuremberg indicate that the predication of crime against humanity upon the 'war nexus' has been removed, and it is now defined as a crime by state or non-state actors against any civilian population, which can take place in either peacetime or wartime (Ratner and Abrams 2001: 54–58, 67–68). Furthermore, the Rome Statute codifies a notable expansion of the acts constituting crimes against humanity, adding torture, rape, enforced disappearance and apartheid to the list enumerated by the Nuremberg Charter (Rome Statute 1998: 9–10). Functionally, the doctrine of crime against humanity is designed to bring evil within the purview of the rule of law and prosecutable crimes, so that perpetrators may be held accountable for 'the great evils they visit upon humankind' (Robertson 1999: 375). As such, it is an indispensable component of the universal juridification of extreme evil into a criminally liable act (see May 2005).

The prescriptive translation of 'evil' into juridical discourse is necessary in order to carry out the demands of justice, but we should not lose sight of the fact that the phenomenon of extreme evil and its effect upon our sense of reality cannot be exhausted by its conversion into the legal figure of 'crime against humanity' (Vernon 2002: 249). This is reflected in the philosophical difficulties attendant on the attempts to introduce and articulate the category of crime against humanity (see Ratner and Abrams 2001: 47–79; Altman and Wellman 2004). That which the crime is intended to identify and interdict exceeds the posited crime itself as the most serious moral and political wrong: whether expressed as St Augustine's (1972) 'degradation', Kant's (1960) 'wickedness' or Raphael Lemkin's 'barbarity' (Power 2002: 21–22), the evil translated into the legal doctrine of crime against humanity signals its presence insofar as it 'shocks the conscience of humanity' (Bassiouni 1999: 42). Laurence Thomas avers that crime against humanity denotes 'a level of callousness that embodies the very essence of evil itself' (Thomas 2003: 205). As Arendt points out, extreme evil is to be identified specifically with the calculated attempt to make the human status embodied within particular people superfluous, thereby to exterminate humanity by 'refusing to share the earth' with a particular group of people (EJ: 268).

Nevertheless, Arendt expressed reservations about the limitations of legal concepts to convey fully the experience of evil translated formally into the doctrine of crimes against humanity: 'We attempt to classify as criminal a thing which, as we all feel, no such category was ever intended to cover', she writes (OT: 568–69). 'What meaning has the concept of murder when we are confronted with the mass production of corpses?' In a letter to her friend and mentor Karl Jaspers, Arendt reiterates her desire to demythologize those who commit atrocities and thus avoid reference to 'satanic greatness' when thinking about the evil perpetrated in the Holocaust. Yet she insists on the irreducible difference between 'a man who sets out to murder his old aunt and people who … built factories to produce corpses' (JP: 69). She holds that while murder is intended to destroy a particular in-itself, crimes against humanity are intended to eradicate the universal 'concept of the human being' without which particularity as such could not exist. Despite recognizing this distance separating our conventional understanding of murder and the radically new type of crime that can 'explode the limits of the law', Arendt (OT: 379) argues for the ethical and political necessity of formulating a cosmopolitan law – a law of humanity 'guaranteed by humanity itself' – capable of satisfying the need for justice, even though this law and the justice it provides will remain imperfect precisely because the concrete experience of evil always has the potential to shatter established 'common sense' and confound our moral expectations.

We can better understand Arendt's insistence on the necessity of imperfect justice in the case of crimes against humanity when considering her rethinking of cosmopolitanism in relation to extreme evil and late modernity. Cosmopolitanism has a long history, reaching back at least to the Stoic notion of a universal human community based upon the equal worth of each human being. This core idea of classical cosmopolitanism contains the notion that each person is a 'citizen of the world' and owes allegiance, first and foremost, 'to the worldwide community of human beings' (Nussbaum 1996: 4). Classical ideas about belonging to a universal human order were taken up later by a number of Enlightenment philosophers, most notably Kant. He was convinced of the necessity of establishing a cosmopolitan order of federated republican states because war undermines the rights to freedom and equality of republican citizens. A cosmopolitan association would be, for Kant, a 'universal community … where a violation of rights in one part of the world is felt everywhere' (Kant 1991: 107–8).

Catherine Lu (2000) has written convincingly of three core ways in which cosmopolitanism has been faulted by its various critics. The first is to be found in how the cosmopolitan vision of human unity might be put to ideological use through violent or coercive means. This perspective of cosmopolitanism as 'imperialism' raises the danger that a doctrine of universal human harmony can 'too easily play into the hands of the powerful', who will feel justified in imposing their grand aims upon others (*ibid.*: 252). On this view, cosmopolitanism amounts to little more than absolutism. The second reason that cosmopolitanism has been treated sceptically by critics is that its presumed impartiality towards others might actually mask either indifference or hostility towards plurality and the particularities of diverse societies and cultures. Critiques of cosmopolitanism as 'rationalism' argue that the abstract category of 'humanity' presupposes belief in a universal conception of immutable reason that is thought to trump 'the passions of moral commitment' and 'parochial communities, bounded by kin, culture and state' (*ibid.*: 248). The third line of critique targets the utopian and naive assumptions of cosmopolitanism, such as the inevitability of moral progress, human perfectibility, and the harmonization of interests. This form of cosmopolitanism as 'idealism' has been targeted frequently by political realists and has served as 'the defining divide in twentieth-century international relations' (*ibid.*: 246).

While acknowledging that 'some historical conceptions of cosmopolitanism have indeed been guilty' of these defects, Lu's analysis also suggests that 'a realist view of the human condition can lead us toward rather than away from embracing cosmopolitanism' (*ibid.*: 247). Arendt is, I believe, an important example of the effort to embrace some fundamentally cosmopolitan ethical and political commitments, while translating these commitments through 'a realist view of the human condition'. Cosmopolitanism need not be imperialist, rationalist or idealist, provided it pays sufficient attention to force and violence, cruelty and suffering, and the interactions between plural human beings. Arendt's wider thinking on the human condition and the need to protect the human status was informed precisely by her awareness of the ways in which racism, imperialism, militarism, and the calculative rationality of bureaucratic domination are intimately intertwined with the development of modern society and politics. Arendt arrives at a critically realist cosmopolitan position because she recognizes that, in the words of Lu (2000: 256), 'the suffering of the exile, refugee, enemy and stranger' have become widely normalized within the modern world and represent the destruction of those conditions that enable all of us to become human.

While Arendt drew some inspiration from the classical and Kantian cosmopolitan traditions, she thought that what was missing from these approaches to cosmopolitanism was the modern experience of extreme political evil. For Arendt, the reality of genocide and crimes against humanity requires the amendment of cosmopolitanism in two fundamental respects: first, it must relinquish the ideal of human perfectionism and ever-progressing human history (LK: 77); and second, it must replace the certitude of moral transcendentalism with the uncertainty of political action and the vulnerability of the political itself. Arendt thus suggests a kind of modest, unsentimental cosmopolitanism that can be depicted as distinctively realist rather than idealist (see Klusmeyer 2005; Owens 2007: 145–46).

Many classical realists understood the prevalence of evil in political affairs. Hans Morgenthau, for instance, stressed 'the tragic presence of evil in all political action' (Morgenthau 1946: 203). Similarly, Michael Spirtas (1996) has argued that realist theories of international relations can be classified into two schools of thought: the tragedy tradition and the evil tradition. While the tragedy school of realism emphasizes how the anarchic structure of international politics leads to tragic although unintended consequences, the evil school underlines the egoistic, aggressive and power-hungry motives attributable to the flawed human nature intrinsic to individual actors. But Arendt was not a scholar of international relations, and she was neither concerned with explaining the 'nature' of international conflict *per se* nor guided methodologically by any formal school of thought within the discipline of international relations. Therefore the particular type of realism that may be reconstructed from her thought cannot be categorized according to the typology identified by Spirtas. Indeed, as a political theorist Arendt would take exception to the reductionistic treatment of classical realist thinkers (such as Machiavelli) by many contemporary international relations scholars. The most we can say is that Arendt's realism has an affinity with the sentiment expressed in the Morgenthau quote above, namely that the ever-present human capacity for evil action (which is not the same thing as a flawed or malevolent human nature) is itself the 'tragic presence' that haunts all politics in view of action's unpredictability and uncertainty.

Arendt's facing up to the reality that the capacity for evil is interwoven with political action is not a political realism shorn of the humanistic demands of cosmopolitanism, rather it is a cosmopolitanism tempered by the reality that organized programmes to annihilate the human status now constitute a ubiquitous possibility of political life. The primary emphasis here is that political thinking and action must respond to the facts of a changing political reality grounded in awareness of human imperfections and limitations, that power is constitutive of political action yet is inseparable from responsibility, and that scepticism is needed regarding the possibility of progress in politics, at least in a teleological sense implied by moral and political idealism (PP: 3). Arendt's work was driven by attentiveness to the reality of 'what man is capable of' (EU: 134) as a persistent threat to the 'frailty of human affairs' (HC: 188, 222). In her essay 'Concern with Politics in Recent European Thought', Arendt concludes that while for the ancient Greeks philosophy began with wonder prompted by the experience of beauty, for us the sense of wonder arises from concrete experience of the 'sheer horror of contemporary political events' (EU: 444). Given the atrocities borne of the twentieth century, it is no longer possible to make sense confidently of such events or to 'see something good in every evil'. On the contrary, 'the speechless horror at what man may do and what the world may become' constitutes the basis for 'owning up' to the manifest human capacity for extreme evil and grasping its political significance (EU: 445). Elsewhere, Arendt affirms that 'in light of present realities' Enlightenment cosmopolitan humanism looks like 'reckless optimism' (MDT: 84).

While Arendt does not flinch from drawing this conclusion, she also tells us that, in conjunction with the darkness of the twentieth century, a major historical transformation occurred. Previously, the idea of humanity was no more than an abstract concept. Now, however, humanity has become, Arendt concludes, 'an urgent reality' (MDT: 82). Humanity, in other words, no longer signifies a transcendental ideal but refers to a historically embodied norm that translates the increasingly global nature of political events. Using the work of Jaspers to reflect upon cosmopolitanism in the present, Arendt appeals to the intensification of world interconnectedness from the nineteenth century onwards in order to describe how a *cosmopolitanized* humanity has been forged by cultural, economic, social, political and legal forces on a global scale – shadowed, she notes ruefully, by a fearful symmetry of colonial conquest (see Axtmann 2006). This process has both universalized the model of the sovereign state and forced each country to become 'the immediate neighbour of every other country' (MDT: 83). Arendt's cosmopolitan realism thus begins from the historical reality that 'for the first time … all peoples on earth have a common present', but it is a common present brought into existence unintentionally, as it were, and fraught with danger.

Against cosmopolitan idealists, Arendt contends that there are no guarantees that this newly formed humanity will find itself enthused about the ideal of a worldwide civilization it is thought to embody; indeed, the ever-closer proximity to other peoples is just as likely to lead, she says, to 'political apathy, isolationist nationalism … mutual hatred and a somewhat universal irritability of everybody against everybody else' as it is to peace, mutual understanding and global justice (MDT: 83–84). Moreover, any sense of unity or solidarity shared by the peoples of the earth is, in the first instance, merely negative: because there is no common past upon which the new humanity is based, nor a common future that can be assured, what binds humanity together is the 'fear of global destruction' in the present. Right here and now, other human beings may act in ways that bring about the 'end of all human life on earth' (MDT: 83). It is no wonder, then, that Arendt's version of cosmopolitanism leads to the rather ambivalent assertion that the 'solidarity of mankind may well turn out to be an unbearable burden' (MDT: 83).

But it must be noted that this ambivalence is motivated not by indifference or resignation, but by an acute sensitivity to the dangers of prescribing a programmatic or abstractly formal solution to the political problems of the present. The tangible reality of humanity and the dangers inherent within it is not simply a bare fact – it is an urgent problem that demands new forms of political action, but with the recognition that such actions will always come up against other actions that limit and contradict them. For this reason, Arendt argues that the negative solidarity founded upon humanity's potential obliteration can be made 'meaningful in a positive sense only if it is coupled with political responsibility' (MDT: 83). In order to disrupt the destructive logic of superfluity and to have any hope of preventing the completely free reign of evil, Arendt maintains that political power must be employed to create both human rights and the juridical–political institutions required to protect such rights and achieve justice in the event of grave violations of them (see Isaac 1996; Cotter 2005). Arendt puts it thus: 'Human dignity needs a new guarantee which can be found only in a new political principle, in a new law on earth, whose validity this time must comprehend the whole of humanity while its power must remain strictly limited, rooted in and controlled by newly defined territorial entities' (OT: xxvii). This new cosmopolitan law is urgently needed because the evil of crimes against humanity has 'become a precedent for the future' and 'no people on earth … can feel reasonably sure of its continued existence' without some legal protection (EJ: 273).

Arendt's cosmopolitan realism seeks to avoid the despair of political realism, as well as the false consolation of idealism, by acknowledging simultaneously the thoroughly historical and contingent nature of 'actually existing' cosmopolitanism as well as the necessity of acting to reinforce positively the fragile solidarity of the new human reality (MDT: 93). For this reason, Arendt adopted a resolutely 'realist' perspective on human rights, defining them as the product of collective political action and negotiated political power, but nevertheless action motivated by principles of freedom and equality. As she astutely observes in *The Origins of Totalitarianism*, the idealist notion of inalienable prepolitical natural rights proved to be a useless myth to those stripped of citizenship and left unrecognized and unprotected within the international vacuum of statelessness (OT: 341 ff.). She also notes that 'a world government is indeed within the realm of possibility, but one may suspect that in reality it might differ considerably from the version promoted by idealistic-minded organizations' (OT: 379). Strategically, cosmopolitanism must be forged in line with a reconstructed state and not against the polity as such, for it is only by belonging to specific political communities that the human rights of individuals as citizens can be exercised and feasibly protected.

As I argue in Chapter 3, Arendt would find the idea of 'rootless' cosmopolitanism a dangerous analogue to the 'nowhere' zones of refugee and concentration camps, where the 'deprivation of a place in the world' is precisely what exposes the uselessness of the idea of natural rights when persons are reduced to the 'abstract nakedness' of 'bare life' (OT: 380–81).[6] Yet this also means that sovereignty must be distanced reflexively from nationality and rendered morally conditional *vis-à-vis* a robust international human rights regime; sovereignty unlimited by law is little more than an illegitimate form of violence aimed at the political equality and reciprocity embodied in the idea of human rights (EU: 131; OR: 164–78). While individuals must in some sense be 'rooted' to possess rights effectively, they should also be entitled to possess 'multiple roots' to reflect the transportability of human rights (Lu 2000: 257). Arendt's concept of the 'right to have rights' – that is, the right to belong to an organized community where one is recognized meaningfully as a distinct person within the rule of law – captures the dual aspect of her cosmopolitan realism. Only through a political 'framework of universal mutual agreements' (MDT: 93) grounded on the public and intersubjective juridification of evil can the 'right of every individual to belong to humanity' as a new cosmopolitan law be guaranteed (OT: xxvii). But it is, Arendt hastens to add, 'by no means certain whether it is possible' (OT: 378).

Cosmopolitanization, global politics and the ICC

In appealing to the reality of a historical humanity forged from the genocidal horrors of the twentieth century, Arendt pushes cosmopolitanism in a critically realist direction. With the appearance of a new type of crime that takes aim at the human status as such, universal solidarity is born. However, it is a solidarity based initially on an 'elemental shame' at the human capacity for extreme evil (EU: 131), rather than on the abstract fiction of a prepolitical 'world citizenship'. Political thought and action, including cosmopolitanism itself, must begin 'in fear and trembling' from fidelity to the dreadful experience of the 'incalculable evil that men are capable of bringing about' (EU: 132). Yet this sense of shame is still only a 'non-political' insight (EU: 131), and cosmopolitanism must be purged of all sentimentalism so that it is able to grasp that the Holocaust is both an end and a beginning: on the one hand, the end of an illusionary world history whereby 'the world spirit uses and consumes country after country, people after people, in the stages of its gradual realization' and, on the other hand, the beginning of a 'new fragile unity' of humanity that finds its historical expression in the formation of juridical–political institutions to protect human rights and hold perpetrators of extreme evil to account (MDT: 93). For Arendt, to begin means to act, to take an initiative, particularly to establish a political principle which is then set into motion (HC: 177; OR: 212–13). One new beginning to be embraced by cosmopolitan realism, then, is to speak and act in favour of the juridification of extreme evil into the legally sanctionable acts of genocide and crimes against humanity. In this way, cosmopolitan realism is grounded upon the norm of historical humanity, which then governs the formation of institutions. Even so, cosmopolitan realism recognizes that juridification has its limits. Placing acts of extreme evil within the juridical context does not in itself pre-empt the human capacity for evil.

In this section I want to tie Arendt's arguments into the sociological framework provided by Ulrich Beck, in order to argue that we should take seriously the idea that the ICC is a manifestation of the realistically cosmopolitan sensibility adopted by Arendt. Arendt argued that the novel concept of crimes against humanity was needed to give expression both to the universal scope of the evil committed and to the 'general responsibility' entailed by the emergence of humanity as a sociopolitical reality. When historical humanity is understood from the perspective of cosmopolitan realism, that is, in political terms, it has 'the very serious consequence that ... all nations share the onus of evil committed by all others ... excluding no people and assigning a monopoly of guilt to no one' (EU: 131). A new criminal law suited to the reality of crimes against humanity was needed for several reasons: to demythologize the perpetrators of extreme evil; to hold individuals personally accountable for their efforts to exterminate humanity; and also to publicize the widespread complicity that inevitably accompanies genocide and crimes against humanity (EJ: 125, 289; AJ: 410–20).

In her analysis of the Eichmann trial, Arendt supported (although not uncritically) the right of Israel to prosecute Eichmann on the basis of the legal precedents introduced by the Nuremberg trials (she also invokes, although somewhat reluctantly, the doctrine of universal jurisdiction). Nevertheless, aware of the tensions and limitations inherent in this approach – in particular, misunderstanding the nature of the crimes as being against the Jewish people *per se* rather than against the human status as embodied in the Jewish people – Arendt called for the establishment of a 'permanent international criminal court' that would represent humanity as a whole, as required both by the 1948 Genocide Convention and by the political principle of collective responsibility for the new community of humankind (EJ: 270; AJ: 416). Unfortunately, as Arendt was well aware, all proposals for an international criminal court during the post-Second World War period were rejected by the United Nations General Assembly, exposing the problematic links between power, ethics and politics in the new cosmopolitan age (Schabas 2001: 8–9). To help make sense of developments since Arendt's diagnosis of such links, especially the establishment of the ICC, I now want to turn to the work of Beck, who recently has employed his reflexive sociology to articulate a new critical theory of cosmopolitan realism.

Although Beck does not frame his arguments from the perspective of political evil, his arguments are consistent with it. He poses the necessity of a 'new critical theory with cosmopolitan intent' that surpasses the analytical limits of the nation-state, driven by the historical transformations associated with processes of 'reflexive modernization' (Beck 2003). This shift in sociopolitical reflexivity can be captured by the transition from first to second modernity. 'First modernity' refers to the rationalization and industrialization of society enabled by secular Enlightenment ideals, scientific developments and technological controls. This conventional description of progressive modernization became problematic, Beck contends, with increasing awareness that its very successes have put human life at risk. 'Second modernity' has arisen from the historical relocation of the category of risk – from nature to the (frequently unintended) consequences of human action (Beck 1992, 1999). The 'world risk society' of second modernity has become increasingly oriented around the tensions between rapidly globalizing threats to human beings and the frequently ineffectual state-based efforts to provide security from these. Because the new risks are 'deterritorialized', simultaneously local and global, they can no longer be viewed solely as national questions. The cosmopolitan vision is fundamental to understanding the new dynamic of global sociopolitical relations which coincides with the emergence of globality, that is, the 'common human awareness of the global' (Beck 2005: 14–15, 82).

According to Beck, inasmuch as the concepts of power, action, sovereignty and politics remain fixated upon the nation-state, they have become 'zombie categories': signifiers of a departed Westphalian order kept hopelessly animated through the epistemic transmission of methodological nationalism.[7] Methodological nationalism is the conventional social scientific account of international politics, which takes the 'objective' demarcation between the national and the international as the 'fundamental organizing principle of politics' (*ibid.*: 21). In this respect, argues Beck, methodological nationalism is a source of errors; it no longer accurately represents the global reality of political life. In contrast, cosmopolitan realism recognizes that the classical limits between the national and international have been erased, obscured or transformed, that the distinction between separate spheres of political action must be freed of the dogmatism of the national perspective, and that our understanding of political action must be reinscribed within a critical cosmopolitan outlook. The result is that 'the spaces of our emotional imagination have expanded in a transnational sense' (Beck 2006: 6).

The core of Beck's argument for our purposes is this: reflexive modernization arises from awareness that the primary threats to human existence come no longer from nature, but from humanity itself (Beck 1992). For Beck, the reflexive preoccupation with the simultaneously local–global dangers to humanity suggests the need for a reinvention of politics anchored in a 'new cosmopolitanism' that can place 'globality at the heart of political imagination, action and organization' (Beck 2005: 9; see also Beck 1997). To do so means that a static, idealist conception of cosmopolitanism must give way to a realist, dynamic conception of *cosmopolitanization*: the ongoing historical process whereby the norms and forms of political action are reconsidered and renegotiated, and the very definition of humanity is contested and reformulated in ways that seek to preserve the universal and the particular as mutually constitutive rather than mutually exclusive. The actually existing world remains the touchstone for political action – as realism always has advocated – yet the nature of this reality has radically altered under globalization. To be 'realistic' today entails a reflexive preoccupation with how to act in light of the mutually constitutive categories of the global and local, which in turn contributes to the cosmopolitanization of 'everyday consciousness', moral discourse and political action (Beck 2002a: 17). The process of cosmopolitaniza-tion thus offers the prospect of endowing 'each country with a common global interest' and provides the basis 'of a global community of fate', without negat-ing the particularities of local communities and their unique ways of relating to historically universal humanity (Beck 1999; Beck 2002b: 42).

Here Beck strongly echoes Arendt: to privilege a cosmopolitan outlook is a principled political decision taken in light of concrete conditions, and motivated by a commitment to create new political realities intended to protect the human status in light of local–global threats to humanity. Cosmopolitan realism speaks to the potential that diverse individuals, groups and communities now have to *become* cosmopolitan 'on the basis of their own self-interpretation, articulation, mobilization and organization' around the norm of historical humanity and the global threat of human superfluousness (Beck 2005: 15). Yet there is no guarantee that this will occur or, if it does, that it will continue to do so, as Arendt and Beck are fully aware. For both, cosmopolitanism cannot escape the unpredictability and uncertainty of normative ambivalence as long as it remains in touch with real-ity. From Beck's sociological perspective, this leads to several conclusions about the ICC that are at odds with the idealist conception of cosmopolitanism. First, the establishment of the ICC is to be regarded as the historically contingent out-come of a precarious struggle between various state and non-state actors within the power network of global politics, not as the triumph of moral perfectionism. Second, this struggle is also being played out around the collective representa-tion of historical humanity, the symbolic meaning of which serves as a materially regulative norm or rule giving rise to obligations on the part of states that have helped to redefine sovereignty in the global age. Third, because of the contingency of strategic confrontation and the constant interplay of dynamic power relations in global politics, the accomplishment of the ICC cannot be taken for granted – its existence is precarious and always susceptible to reversal.

While I think Arendt would agree with these conclusions, what is more signifi-cant from an Arendtian perspective is that the historical cosmopolitanization of humanity adds new dimensions and even greater weight to the idea of responsibil-ity today. Arendt argues that a sense of global responsibility is the key for moving from a negative prepolitical solidarity based on shame at the human capacity for evil, to a positive political solidarity founded on the institution of human rights and a corresponding body of cosmopolitan law. Rather than presupposing the originary status of cosmopolitan individuals belonging to a prepolitical world community, Arendt's cosmopolitan realism regards this status not as 'a concept, but a living, political reality' borne of the 'earthly hell' of deliberate attempts to make human beings superfluous and the resulting struggles to establish laws that protect the right to have rights (MDT: 82; EU: 383). Arendt presciently recognized in the wake of the Second World War that the power situation in which politics is conducted has been radically altered, such that there are 'no longer any powers but world powers, and no power politics but global politics' (EU: 143).

At its core, cosmopolitan solidarity is an expression of global responsibility insofar as it embodies a reflexive refusal to commit or be complicit with political evil directed against the human status (see EU: 131). Yet the reflexive component of cosmopolitan solidarity is critical, in that it proceeds from an awareness that the problem of evil cannot be reduced to a starkly simplifying Manichaean division of the world into 'good and evil', and that complicity with evil is all too easy and frequent in the global age of genocide. Consequently, an Arendtian perspective provides an important, if somewhat counterintuitive, understanding of the normative ambivalence associated with global responsibility: because the capacity for evil is a permanent feature of the human condition (as it arises from the power to act, which always retains an element of unpredictability), the most that we can do is ceaselessly resist evil acts in whatever way possible, consistent with respect for human plurality and agency. We can only eliminate the capacity for evil as such by making humanity itself superfluous, that is, by destroying the plurality that makes us human. To believe that the capacity to commit evil acts can be permanently expunged from the realm of human action would be to succumb to a metaphysical and political idealism dangerously immune to the realities of historical experience.

The ICC and the predicament of common responsibility

Given the great burden that humanity has become for itself, Arendt prudently writes of the 'predicament of common responsibility' (OT: 303). The thought that historical humanity is solely responsible for the evil it commits against itself when juxtaposed to the naively optimistic 'ideal' of humanity crystallizes the paradoxical and disturbing reality of the common sharing of responsibility. Common responsibility proves to have a Janus-like quality; the ever-present threat of either causing or suffering evil leads humanity simultaneously to unite in solidarity and to recoil in terror. The burden of common responsibility is to face up to this normative ambivalence, to act for the sake of humanity without disavowing the human capacity for evil. Common responsibility as a principle of the solidarity of historical humanity means assuming the burden of acting in order to preserve a shared world where my fate is linked to that of others; here we are responsible both for our own actions as well as for the actions of others, which we did not commit (RJ: 149). Common (or what Arendt also refers to as collective) responsibility is always political insofar as it emphasizes the social embeddedness of individuals. Common responsibility is, Arendt notes, imputable on the basis of association; since individuals are always already members of a community, they are responsible for its collective actions. Collective responsibility is 'vicarious' in that we are liable for 'things we have not done', that is, we are liable for things done in our name by institutional structures, the foreseeable outcomes of which are the result of collective action. This 'taking upon ourselves' the consequences for things we have not done individually is, Arendt insists, the political 'price we pay for the fact that we live our lives not by ourselves but among our fellow men' (RJ: 157–58).

The predicament of common responsibility thus provides a difficult yet necessary foundation for acting in response to extreme evil. It carries with it the obligation to act and speak against evil that seeks to efface the human status and, when evil acts are done, a political responsibility to ensure that perpetrators of evil acts are brought before the ICC. While political responsibility is collective, criminal guilt is individual. Perpetrators of crimes against humanity are to be judged not for the monstrousness of their character, but for the monstrousness of their deeds. As Arendt stresses, 'Guilt, unlike responsibility, always singles out; it is strictly personal. It refers to an act, not to intentions or potentialities' (RJ: 147; see Schaap 2005). Our only possible guarantee for the right to have rights is political and legal resistance to extreme evil, that is, a general willingness to assume political responsibility for the atrocities perpetrated in the world we share with others, and an unyielding commitment to punish those who violate the fragile boundary that cosmopolitan law places around human freedom. Arendt acknowledges that the only appropriate, realistic response to evil is to struggle against it: 'If you do not resist evil, the evildoers will do as they please. Though it is true that, by resisting evil, you are likely to be involved in evil, your care for the world takes precedence in politics over your care for your self' (LK: 50).

This is why Arendt contends that a realistic cosmopolitanism would consist of a 'world-wide federated political structure' bound by interconnected global, regional, state and local levels of mutually reinforcing law (MDT: 84).[8] In order for human rights to be effective, all persons must be recognized right-holders of bounded territories, yet these bounded territories are not to be thought of along the lines of the traditional sovereign nation-state. Rather, they are 'newly defined territorial entities' insofar as the legitimacy of state sovereignty is treated as conditional upon adherence to the principle of the right to have rights, 'which must comprehend the whole of humanity' (OT: xxvii). For Arendt, citizenship and full political rights should be severed from nationality so that the legal guarantee of these rights is 'open to all who happen to live' on a state's territory (EU: 207). The 'bankruptcy of the nation-state and its conception of sovereignty' or 'the claim to unchecked and unlimited power' (OV: 107–8) must be replaced by a countervailing conception of rooted cosmopolitanism, regional federations and international legal institutions that limit state sovereignty in line with the guarantee of human rights for all. In Beck's terms, such cosmopolitan states would be 'post-national' political communities that respect plurality internally and externally, and that therefore have 'internalized the cosmopolitan outlook institutionally' by ensuring correspondence between domestic law, regional law and international human rights law (Beck 2005: 92–96, 217). The ICC, I believe, represents the type of strategic juridification embraced by cosmopolitan realism.[9]

The preceding discussion of common responsibility shows that cosmopolitan realism, while grounded in the historical reality of past and present, is committed to bringing about a normatively different future. In the remainder of this chapter I want to discuss two examples of the predicament of common responsibility that the ICC must confront, in light of the normative ambivalence arising from the complicated dynamics of local–global interpenetration, the differing ways that evil and justice may be interpreted morally and politically, and the unpredictability of human action. The first example, involving the ICC's first case in northern Uganda, may seem to have more immediate practical relevance than the second, the post-Second World War promise that 'never again' should genocide and crimes against humanity be allowed to occur, yet both examples illustrate the necessity of reflecting as accurately as possible the lived realities of our pluralistic world in the realm of cosmopolitan imagination and action. For Arendt, plurality and the world are mutually constitutive: on the one hand, the fact that people ('men') and not one singular entity ('man') inhabit the world is both the ontological condition and the achievement of politics; on the other, the existence and communication of the multiplicity of perspectives arising from human plurality constitutes our sense of reality and discloses the world as a common space for our appearance before each other (HC: 7–8, 57–58). Human plurality gives rise to the world as a meaningful public realm, and protecting and preserving these many perspectives establishes the world as the fragile object of common responsibility. The predicament of common responsibility conveys the tension and ambiguity that necessarily accompanies the concurrent affirmation of the universalism of humanity and the particularism of plural others.

One especially acute example of this tension and ambiguity confronting the ICC is presented by the Court's first case. In December 2003, Ugandan President Yoweri Museveni referred the situation concerning the Lord's Resistance Army (LRA) to the ICC (ICC 2004). The LRA has been waging an insurgency against the Ugandan government in the north of the country for more than 20 years. The conflict, which stems in part from the loss of the north's military dominance within Uganda and the socioeconomic inequalities between the north and south, has been especially devastating for the Acholi people of northern Uganda. The conflict is infamous for the brutal massacres of civilians and abductions of thousands of children carried out by the LRA, and for the internal displacement of most of the northern population (Allen 2006). In July 2004, the Chief Prosecutor of the ICC, Luis Moreno-Ocampo, initiated an investigation into northern Uganda, and in July 2005 the ICC issued arrest warrants for LRA leader Joseph Kony and four of his senior commanders, charging them with numerous crimes against humanity and war crimes.[10] However, since September 2006 peace talks have occurred between the LRA leadership and the Ugandan government, leading to an uneasy ceasefire and the signing of an agreement on Accountability and Reconciliation in June 2007 (Human Rights Watch 2007a). The agreement resolves to hold consultations and develop mechanisms designed to incorporate traditional justice systems into the wider peace process.

Unfortunately, reactions to the northern Ugandan case have become extremely polarized. On the one hand, there are those such as international human rights organizations and international lawyers who insist the ICC should proceed with prosecution in order to fulfil its mandate (Branch 2007). On the other hand, there are those such as several northern Uganda civil society groups and some international humanitarian organizations working in northern Uganda who view the ICC's proceedings as a form of international law 'legalism', which pursues formalistic universal justice at the price of sacrificing meaningful local mechanisms of justice (Allen 2005; Refugee Law Project 2005). The controversy around this case has put the ICC in an awkward position. Faced with the current situation, the Court has to decide whether to proceed with the case, or whether deference to non-prosecution is a legitimate option. Under the Rome Statue, deference to non-prosecution is possible under three mechanisms. First, a temporary suspension of investigation or prosecution can be granted if the Security Council determines these will interfere with maintaining or restoring 'international peace and security' (Article 16). Second, deference can take place under the 'complementarity regime' (Article 17), if there are alternative mechanisms of accountability in place that are deemed to fulfil the requirement of 'genuine proceedings'. Finally, the Prosecutor can drop the case if he decides that this would be 'in the interest of justice' (Article 53). The Article 53 provision is perhaps the most interesting potential avenue for action, in that it suggests the prospect of overcoming the 'peace or justice' binary in favour of a more nuanced conception of political justice in which peace and (retributive or restorative) justice connect depending upon the particular needs and interests of plural social contexts.

The Rome Statute provides few answers as to how 'the interest of justice' can be best served, but this ambiguity might be regarded as a strength rather than weakness. Because the ICC is supposed to serve the justice interests of the victims of gross human rights violations and the interests of states affected by such crimes, as well as the interests of the broader international community or community of humankind, any insistence that only strict adherence to supposedly neutral legal formalism will satisfy the demands and needs of all three groups is plainly idealistic and potentially harmful. Rather than unreflexively following a formal procedure for the application of rules, the Prosecutor is actually empowered to exercise reflective judgement as to what course of action will serve the interests of justice. As McDonald and Haveman (2003: 2) point out, underlying the ambiguity of how and whether prosecutorial discretion should be exercised is 'the deeper and much more difficult question of what the Court is actually established to achieve'. This is exactly the type of question that Arendt would have us ask of the ICC and, while the matter cannot be pursued in any depth here, it should figure in the exercise of reflective judgement which Arendt considered to be crucial to political action. Reflective judgement, according to Arendt, is a kind of exemplary 'interest in disinterestedness' through which we think in the place of those with whom we share the world (LK: 73). The cooperation of imagination and reflection captures the particularity of specific evil actions, while relating this uniqueness to larger collective histories and meanings of justice and injustice. To judge well requires the formation of an 'enlarged mentality' which attains its moral orientation not from a 'higher standpoint' above the world shared with others, but from the particularity of their standpoints, their 'possible judgements' alongside one's own;

community sense is then dialogically achieved rather than simply monologically deduced (LK: 43, 67; see Curtis 1999).

With this in mind, one significant component that must be taken into account in exercising reflective judgement in this case is the local process of making evil morally and politically intelligible, and reconstructing the sensible world shared with others. For the people of northern Uganda, this process cannot be undertaken through, and translated solely into, the idiom of international criminal law. This is because the atrocities committed during the conflict are regarded by the Acholi people in terms of the concept of *kiir*, or abomination (Liu Institute for Global Issues 2005; Northern Uganda Peace Initiative 2005; Justice and Reconciliation Project 2007). *Kiir* denotes 'evil acts' that sever social relations, cause both individual and collective suffering and trauma, and violate the moral order upon which the integrity of community life depends. Two aspects of *kiir* are worth nothing. First, the effects of *kiir* do not end when the perpetrator's act has ceased – misfortune (especially sickness, infertility and death) will continue to affect the victim (if he or she survived the initial deed), as well as the victim's relatives and community, until purification ceremonies are conducted to cleanse those involved in the abomination. Such ceremonies typically require the presence of the perpetrator and, when possible, the victim(s), and focus on restoration of social relations through public admission of wrongdoing, establishing the truth about the conflict in question, the determination by elders (*atekeres*) of suitable compensation, and employing rituals designed to facilitate forgiveness and reconciliation. Formal judicial prosecution without accompanying traditional cleansing ceremonies may, at least inadvertently, contribute to the continuing effects of *kiir*, which jeopardize the wellbeing of the community as a whole.

Second, the cleansing of grave offences through traditional mechanisms not only helps to repair the broken social body, but also contributes to the empowerment of victims of *kiir*. In other words, by translating evil deeds into the moral discourse of *kiir* and its corresponding traditional practices of healing and reconciliation, the Acholi people are able to exercise 'agency in the face of disempowering circumstances' (Finnström 2003: 15). By reasserting their agency and holding perpetrators accountable according to traditional mechanisms, victims and affected communities make intelligible what has happened to them. The past no longer controls them, the present is no longer disordered, and the future becomes meaningful; in short, 'common sense' or the sensibility of a shared understanding of reality is restored. From the Acholi perspective, seeking justice need not preclude the use of formal criminal law, but neither can justice be achieved if criminal trials completely replace customary practices.

While it would be contradictory to offer any specific policy prescriptions here, it can be said that a cosmopolitan realism informed by what Roach refers to as 'political legalism' will reflexively seek out the most realistic course of action to best achieve justice in any given situation. Roach defines political legalism as 'an informed and flexible adherence to the legal rules and principles of the ICC Statute' resulting in a 'self-directed' application of the rules that 'is both dynamic and open-ended, and is intended to represent the possibilities of the constructive intersection of politics, ethics, and power' (Roach 2006: 8). The reflexivity of political legalism is especially relevant to situations in which transitional societies attempt to come to terms with a past of extreme political evil. Hence, in the case of northern Uganda, it is not realistic to insist on ICC prosecutions whatever the cost. In a transitional context, it is realistic for the Court to take into account the particular justice interests of the locals affected by events on the ground, and to acknowledge that these might differ somewhat from those of the Court. It is, however, also realistic to expect the Court to fulfil its mandate of making sure those responsible for the worst human rights violations are rendered accountable for their actions. Yet this potentially can be done through several mechanisms, including local, customary mechanisms of restorative justice. Conversely, it would be unrealistic to insist that a blanket amnesty intended as a reconciliatory measure, yet without mechanisms of any type of procedural justice involved, can fulfil the function of accountability. In sum, what is needed is a realistic appreciation of the mutual constitution of universalism and particularism in order to 'reconcile cosmopolitanism with the unique legal, historical, and cultural traditions and memories of people' (Benhabib 2005: 160).

Turning now to the second example, the categorical promise that 'never again' should genocide occur, I briefly want to address the notion that cosmopolitan realism is an attempt to connect awareness of past evils committed against the human status with a promise for a better and less horrible political future.[11] In her analysis of promising as a form of political action, Arendt notes that, by its very nature, the promise reveals the human condition of plurality: promises are always mutual, they are made between 'men' and not 'man' (OR: 175). Promises have plurality both as their condition and their end; without plurality promises could not be made, and promises are made in order to preserve the plurality of 'human worldliness' through the common bonds they entail. Further, the mutuality presupposed by promises discloses the 'syntax of power' as the performative joining together of individuals with each other, the commitment to act together to establish and found a 'stable worldly structure' or 'public body' so that succeeding generations may continue to exercise their capacity to act. It is for this reason, Arendt writes, that 'in the realm of politics' making and keeping promises 'may well be the highest human faculty' (OR: 175).

On the one hand, then, the promise 'never again' can be seen to represent a positive moment in the collective commitment to bring perpetrators of political evil to justice. Common responsibility was manifested, in part, by the performative power of making this promise to protect and defend human plurality from criminal attempts to make humanity superfluous. Indeed, the word responsibility has its roots in the Latin '*spondeo*': to bind or obligate oneself through a solemn promise, to make a sacred pledge. It is related as well to the verb '*respondeo*', meaning to answer, to reply or respond to another (Wright 1982: 161–62; Agamben 1999: 21; Derrida 2001: 49–56). The promise 'never again' is therefore a solemn pledge to the plurality of others with whom we share the world, a response that bears witness both to the human capacity for evil and to the new humanity established in the age of genocide. It also reinforces the notion that the new humanity is a political community brought into being by the act of promising itself, and sustained only by a reflexive commitment to be bound in the future by the pledge made in the past. It is a reality 'guaranteed for each' only when the continued 'presence of all' is promised (HC: 244).

On the other hand, the promise contains a negative moment as well, namely the implication that the future can be politically controlled or predicted. Arendt states that the function of promising is to cope with the 'two-fold darkness of human affairs'; the unreliability of human beings who cannot guarantee that they will be the same people tomorrow as they are today, and the impossibility of foretelling the consequences of our actions given the contingency and unpredictability of human initiative (HC: 244). The risk here is that the maxim of evil, 'everything is possible', will become harnessed to ostensibly humanitarian ends. For Arendt, spontaneity and unpredictability lie at the root of the human condition – making possible freedom and action – and the only way to constrain these absolutely is by attempting to destroy humanity itself. What must be avoided, then, is the danger of falling into the trap of thinking that the promise 'never again' is a licence to employ all possible means to secure the unhindered progression of a more 'genuine' humanity, for falling into this trap is a recipe for grave injustice. Since the future of human history cannot be made fixed and stable, the potential for evil to occur will remain a permanent fixture on our political horizon. To believe that we can literally actualize the promise '*never* again' is to succumb not only to a performative contradiction, but to the antipolitical fantasy of omnipotence, which would betray the very sense of responsibility that gave rise to the promise in the first place. For the sake of humanity in all its diversity, cosmopolitan realism requires us to accept the limits inherent in the act of promising in the public realm.

Conclusion

To promise 'never again' thus involves being bound between the obligation to prevent, suppress and punish crimes against humanity whenever possible, and the realization that the promise is caught in the unpredictability of an incalculable future of human action and plurality.[12] To sustain the promise of 'never again', we must heed both its positive and negative aspects, and embrace that it is a pledge simultaneously possible and impossible for us to fulfil. The predicament of common responsibility means precisely to live with the paradox that we must, here and now, resist evil and hold perpetrators accountable, but also admit the impossibility of guaranteeing absolutely the total elimination of evil in a future that remains open.[13] As long as human beings exist, the potential for evil action exists as well. But so, too, does the potential for cosmopolitan responsibility around the norm of historical humanity. This at least affords the possibility of justice – however limited or imperfect it must be – through 'realistically' cosmopolitan institutions such as the ICC.

2 Superfluous humanity
The evil of global poverty

In her initial confrontation with evil and the tragedies of the Holocaust, Arendt suggested that the 'abyss of Auschwitz' confronted us with something 'to which we cannot reconcile ourselves' (EU: 14). What the extermination camps epitomized was a 'monstrousness' that challenged the capacity for human explanation (AJ: 54). Yet Arendt quickly recognized that the problem of evil referred to the inadequacies of our traditional moral, legal and political categories to account for the historical reality of humanity being rendered superfluous by a genocidal state, rather than the metaphysical problem of the ineffability of a transcendent evil. As she wrote to Karl Jaspers, what constitutes the 'monstrousness' of the Nazis is not a demonic otherworldliness, but the fact that their policy of state-coordinated mass murder 'explodes the limits of the law' as it had been conceived up to that point in history (AJ: 54). It is for this reason, Arendt maintained, that 'the problem of evil will be the fundamental question of postwar intellectual life' (EU: 134). The problem as Arendt understood it is to interpret how evil actions occur under particular historical, social and political conditions without either mythologizing such actions or demonizing their agents. If that is the central problem of modern political life, then what are we to make of the fact that today, nearly half of all humankind lives on less than $2 a day; that 30,500 children under five die every day of mainly preventable causes; and that severe global poverty causes human death and suffering on a scale never previously witnessed? Why is it that the 1994 Rwandan genocide led many to evoke the concept of evil, while at the same time not similarly characterizing the many more preventable deaths caused by global poverty that same year, the death toll of which, Thomas Pogge provocatively suggests, may constitute 'the largest crime against humanity ever committed' (Pogge 2005a: 2)?

Although the horror of the Holocaust and of subsequent genocides may overshadow the human rights consequences of global poverty in the public's consciousness, the aim of this chapter is to expose this state of affairs as well as to examine some of the unfortunate humanitarian implications of this overshadowing effect. This chapter seeks to move the debate about political evil within normative international political theory into the realm of global poverty and radical inequality. In doing so, I will employ several insights contained in Arendt's political thought, although it must be emphasized that the following discussion is to be seen as inspired by Arendt, rather than one that Arendt herself might entirely agree with.

With this in mind, the chapter presents four key arguments. First, the manner in which the discourse of evil has appeared on the international agenda reflects a narrow equation with one particular type of political evil, namely with direct, physical violence, which is supposedly extraordinary, demonic, and of a type or scale that seemingly defies comprehension. Second, the international agenda thus has been dominated by an emphasis on gross violations of civil and political human rights, rather than on gross violations of socioeconomic rights. Third, this bias should be challenged on the basis that the severe and widespread wrongs arising from extreme global poverty and attendant forms of indirect, structural violence are a form of political evil as well. Fourth, the political evil of global poverty is not the result of 'demonic' intentions, but instead of the preponderance of banal thoughtlessness. This is not to suggest either that genocide and similar large-scale atrocities are not horrendous in nature, or that the majority of human rights violations are themselves banal. Rather, I contend that we have become desensitized to the banal, thoughtless, 'ordinary' *origins* of such violations, which renders them invisible insofar as these have become normalized in the global politicoeconomic order. The focus of this chapter therefore is the serious intellectual, ethical and political failing occasioned by neglecting the political evil of gross economic rights violations – arguably a larger contributor to human suffering than state-directed collective violence – even though these, too, destroy the basis of human dignity or, in Arendt's terms, 'human status'. In sum, my main argument is to critique the contemporary confrontation with political evil as unjustifiably and tragically selective.

Modernity and the problem of superfluousness

Arendt's characterization and corresponding critique of modernity is complex and multifaceted (see Benhabib 2000). In this section, I want to focus on three interrelated aspects of modernity that Arendt found particularly disturbing. First, I recapitulate briefly Arendt's analysis of capitalist expansionism initiated through European colonial imperialism. Second, I discuss the political evil of human superfluousness that Arendt suggests was first spawned by imperialism and then radicalized by totalitarianism.[1] Third, I highlight Arendt's concept of the banality of evil as a partial explanation for the administrative organization of actions that make human beings superfluous, which she believes has become a central feature of the bureaucratization of modern life. An examination of these three tragic aspects of modernity, as conceived by Arendt, will then help us to interpret the phenomenon of global poverty as a manifestation of the 'modern expulsion from humanity' suffered by superfluous human beings (OT: 384 n. 54).

Arendt's analysis of modern imperialism is presented in the second part of her ambitious *The Origins of Totalitarianism*, originally published in 1951. *The Origins of Totalitarianism* attempts to 'crystallize' the key elements of modern European history that culminated in Nazi Germany and Soviet Russia (see Tsao 2002a). While Arendt is at pains to show that totalitarianism is an unprecedented and distinctive phenomenon, she is also concerned to demonstrate that its novelty, nonetheless, is rooted in determinate historical conditions, especially those of anti-Semitism, colonial imperialism, racist ideology and bureaucratic rationality. Moreover, these familiar social conditions did not come to an end with the demise of the totalitarian regimes, but instead continue to operate within ideological and material forces that infuse world politics today.

Arendt places her account of imperialism within the context of the decline of the modern nation-state brought about by the melding of politics with capital, the displacement of representative government by administrative rule, and the consequent betrayal of the principle of equality. According to Arendt, this decline of the nation-state was precipitated by the 'political emancipation of the bourgeoisie' in the nineteenth century (OT: 167). Faced with a crisis of capital accumulation, state power was harnessed by the bourgeoisie in order to expand capitalist markets beyond the confines of national borders. This integration of economic and state power resulted in modern imperialism as monopoly expansionism coupled with military intervention, a crucial historical precursor to totalitarianism (OT: 170–71). Yet in contrast to many Marxist accounts of the imperialist adventures of the period, Arendt viewed imperialism not as 'the last stage of capitalism' but as 'the first stage in political rule of the bourgeoisie' (OT: 185). With the political ascendance of the market-oriented bourgeoisie, the state operated according to the dangerous principle of the unlimited expansion of power *and* capital. As this principle came to guide political action in its entirety, the basis of solidarity and political community – the reciprocal recognition of the other's equality within the shared space of the public realm – was undermined.

The decay of the modern nation-state thus coincided with the reduction of politics to the systemic accumulation of wealth and the reckless 'introduction of power as the only content of politics' (OT: 185). In essence, what Arendt depicts is the historical development of a new state form configured along the lines of colonial administration. As Arendt points out, the modern European nation-state was founded on the twin ideals of consent and democratization. Yet the state that took shape in the late nineteenth and early twentieth centuries eschewed popular consent and public accountability, as administrative rule required powers of independent policy formation, decision-making and 'efficient' bureaucratic rationality. In this way, the exercise of political power began to replicate the standards of commercial market competition, where the accumulation of power is pursued for its own sake. Furthermore, the new modern state was underwritten by a racist ideology that marked a strict distinction between the 'superiority' of Western civilization and 'inferiority' of 'barbarian Others' (OT: 210 ff.). While these institutional innovations initially took place on the periphery of empire, they soon rebounded into the European states themselves; as the form of the nation-state was placed under pressure by the forces of expansionism, the processes of democratic participation and consensus came to be regarded as inefficient obstacles to state power. Consequently, the dual mechanisms of apolitical bureaucratic administration and the subordination of 'inferior' groups of people became embedded within both foreign and domestic policy; in effect, external and internal colonization were two sides of the same coin.

These political developments mirrored the effects of global capital expansion. Although the expansion into colonial territories was intended to resolve the crisis of capital accumulation presented by the limits of national production and consumption, the crisis was simply deferred temporarily until the structure of capitalist society was reproduced in the colonies. No longer confronting 'localized' and 'temporary' economic crises, imperial states instead entrenched such crises across the globe, since colonial territories were no longer 'outside' the capitalist system, but firmly within it. As a result, the crisis of 'surplus' capital became inseparable from the crisis of 'surplus' people, 'the human debris that every crisis ... eliminated from producing society' (OT: 200). Because colonial imperialism was 'based on maldistribution', both domestically and globally, it created not only extreme wealth for the few, but acute marginalization for increasingly large numbers of 'superfluous men' lacking any standing within the political community (OT: 198–99). Thus a crucial point emphasized by Arendt is that global capital accumulation necessarily functions by producing (and reproducing) a systematically silenced group of superfluous people. The ideal of a never-ending process of accumulating power and wealth can be realized only by building destruction – of 'every man and every thought' that does not serve and conform to the purpose of accumulation – into that very process (OT: 193). This is because, as the bourgeoisie and the capitalist state came to realize, even the globe has limits. Continual expansion can be achieved only by destroying whatever represents those limits, whether individuals, groups or even entire countries, so as to 'begin anew' the process (OT: 196). For this reason, Arendt claims that the nihilistic (and supremely utilitarian) principle that became a cornerstone of global politics in the modern age is that 'everything is permitted' (OT: 568). Under totalitarianism, this principle is transformed into the attitude that 'everything is possible', and the production of superfluous humanity is taken to its most radical extreme.

Arendt interprets Hobbes as providing a prophetic exposition of the 'philosophy of power' accomplished in the political emancipation of the bourgeoisie and imperialist expansion. Turning to Hobbes's *Leviathan* also helps provide an answer to the question 'why did the European comity of nations allow this evil to spread' (OT: 197)? For Hobbes, of course, all individuals are motivated by 'a perpetual and restless desire of power after power' (Hobbes 1996: 58), and this presumed rapaciousness corresponds perfectly with the self-interested pursuit of comparative advantage in the competitive marketplace, and thus with the 'new body politic ... conceived for the benefit of the new bourgeois society as it emerged in the seventeenth century' (OT: 188). Politically, Hobbesian individuals demand from the state only protection of their life and property, which promotes the bourgeois belief that 'private interest' is synonymous with 'public affairs' (OT: 186). In Arendt's estimation, Hobbes's political logic capably justifies the bourgeois individual's abdication of the responsibilities of citizenship in exchange for security from the state, the protection of private property, and unfettered development of the 'free market'. As later demonstrated by imperialism – and, as I argue in Chapter 4, by contemporary neoliberalism – this meant that narrowly individual interests in the accumulation of power eclipsed the responsibilities of citizenship as the public realm became dominated by the 'private' economic interests of capitalism (OT: 194). Most importantly, Hobbes's belief in the perpetual war of all against all, inscribed within the international state of nature, justifies 'the endless process of capital and power accumulation' (OT: 209). Because each state 'naturally' pursues its own economic–political interests at the expense of others, the 'idea of humanity' and the solidarity that comes from recognition of a world shared in common are necessarily excluded as principles of action. Arendt thus contends that, according to this logic, 'nothing is more plausible' than the imperialist pursuit of power and the production of super-fluous people who have lost 'all natural connections with their fellow-men' (OT: 209). From the perspective of global power politics, the superfluous are regarded as the 'losers' of untrammelled market competition, destined to lives that are truly 'solitary, poor, nasty, brutish, and short' (Hobbes 1996: 76).

Arendt goes on to show that the political evil of imperialism paved the way for the uniquely 'radical' evil embodied in totalitarianism (OT: 592). For Arendt, what is crucial to the nature of this evil is that it emerged in connection with the 'uproot-edness and superfluousness which have been the curse of modern masses since ... the rise of imperialism' (OT: 612). In their systematic attempt to eliminate human spontaneity, individuality and plurality, totalitarian regimes were liquidating not simply individuals, but rather the very idea of humanity itself. All human beings, including the leaders of totalitarian regimes themselves, were treated as com-pletely superfluous and dispensable. As Arendt suggests, 'perhaps what is behind it all is only ... that an organized attempt was made to eradicate the concept of human being' (AJ: 69). Making humanity superfluous is the essence of extreme political evil. As discussed in Chapter 1, for Arendt the horrifying characteristic of political evil in late modernity is the fact that it can be 'committed on a gigantic scale' on the basis of the most mundane, petty and all-too-human motivations (RJ: 159). For this reason, the modern evil of making humanity superfluous is not only political in nature, it has also become increasingly banal.

Arendt's concern with political evil as an ever-present threat to the 'frailty of human affairs' is perhaps the most fundamental problematic with which she grappled throughout her writings (HC: 188, 222). As Phillip Hansen suggests, we can read Arendt's *Eichmann in Jerusalem* (1963) as a sequel to *The Origins of Totalitarianism*, insofar as the former work exposes how making human beings superfluous can become *normalized* within modern bureaucratic social and politi-cal orders (Hansen 1993: 131). While Arendt argues in *The Origins of Totalitari-anism* that evil may rise to the level of the radically extreme, she found appeals to the pathological motives of the exceptionally wicked individual to be wholly inadequate to explain evil as a sociopolitical phenomenon. Perpetrators of politi-cal evil do not transcend the human realm, and cannot be conveniently relegated to the 'monstrous', 'extraordinary' or 'demonic'. As in the paradigmatic case of Adolf Eichmann, this is because they often consider themselves as nothing more than instruments for managing and implementing a bureaucratic programme to 'clean up' human waste from the world (EJ: 218–19). Arendt proposed the notion of the banality of evil in order to explain how 'perfectly normal men' are capable of facilitating and accepting the complete dehumanization of others.

In her observations of the Eichmann trial, Arendt described yet another dimension to the process of normalizing political evil initiated with imperialism and 'crystallized' within the modern bureaucratic state. Despite the nature and extent of the crimes committed by Eichmann, what was most striking to Arendt was that while his actions clearly were horrifying, his motivations seemed quite ordinary. This dissonance demanded a reconceptualization of the traditional association between agency and evil: evil is not to be attributed to fixed, intrinsically corrupt properties of human nature, but must be understood in terms of the concrete social, political and ethical actions of human beings, even if the motivations for these actions often are mundane (see JP: 245). For instance, while Arendt did not question Eichmann's normality, inasmuch as he was not an exception to the rule under the Nazi regime, she did not think this was simply the superficial mask of an otherwise demonic person, since the same allegation would then have to be attributed to the overwhelming majority of the German people.[2] Rather than assuming the existence of deeply held evil motivations beneath the appearance of normality, Arendt argued that such motives did not exist:

> Eichmann was not Iago and not Macbeth, and nothing would have been farther from his mind than to determine with Richard III 'to prove a villain'. Except for an extraordinary diligence in looking out for his personal advancement, he had no motives at all. … He *merely*, to put the matter colloquially, *never realized what he was doing.*
>
> (EJ: 287)

This brings us to a fundamental insight of Arendt's concept of the banality of evil. For Arendt, it was 'sheer thoughtlessness' that made Eichmann 'perfectly incapable of telling right from wrong' in the sense that he chose not to exercise the capacity to think about and judge his actions in light of the ends of the social system within which he functioned as an agent (EJ: 287). Indeed, Arendt's point is that Eichmann's normality 'was much more terrifying than all the atrocities put together. For it implied that this new type of criminal … commits his crimes under circumstances that make it well-nigh impossible for him to know or feel that he is doing wrong' (EJ: 76).[3] Even in the absence of monstrous motives, political evil can arise when individuals 'thoughtlessly' adapt themselves to a system that makes human beings superfluous. While the fact that thoughtlessness and its apparent normality can lead to more destructive consequences than diabolical wickedness is a dismal conclusion, it plainly conveys the normative ambivalence captured by the phrase 'banality of evil'. I will return below to this 'strange interdependence of thoughtlessness and evil' (EJ: 288).

Global poverty and superfluous humanity

The crucial feature of extreme evil in Arendt's analysis is that it makes humanity superfluous. Extreme political evil takes aim at the human status in its relentless drive to deprive individuals *qua* human beings from having a place in the world. To be superfluous is to cease to belong to humanity, that is, to belong to a commonly shared world in which we recognize each other as free and equal members of the public realm. The phenomenon of the banality of evil identified by Arendt refers to a specifically modern condition which makes politically evil deeds possible, namely the normal, matter-of-fact motives associated with an overriding personal ambition pursued within the context of a bureaucratized social system. Such motivations are not demonic, yet they nevertheless serve as a kind of preparation for, and acceptance of, the occurrence of cruel deeds actualized within concrete modes of politicoeconomic organization. I will develop these claims in the following section. Here I want to expand on Arendt's insights and concentrate further on the matter of what constitutes political evil itself. In particular, I want to argue that there are two general forms that political evil takes in the modern age. First, as argued in Chapter 1, political evil is manifested in overt forms of direct violence such as genocide, ethnic cleansing and mass political murder. Second, political evil is manifested in indirect or structural forms of violence, including the pervasive degradation of the human status associated with global poverty and radical inequality. Yet concern with political evil in the post-Second World War period has been dominated by overt forms of direct violence, culminating in the seemingly exclusive focus on (non-state) terrorist violence since the attacks of September 11 (Bernstein 2005). Consequently, I contend that global poverty has been unjustly neglected as a form of political evil, and the failure to recognize it as such constitutes one of the most pressing problems in global politics today.[4]

To begin, we must examine the relationship between the two broad forms of political evil identified above. Although Arendt's main concern was to identify and condemn overt forms of political evil, she nonetheless cleared the way to recognizing that political evil can find expression in various types of mass suffering. This is particularly true in the era of dehumanizing bureaucratization, as violence is increasingly facilitated by 'banal' causes and motivations. In an instructive passage, Arendt alludes to the way that the characteristics of totalitarianism parallel the conditions of modern society:

> The totalitarian attempt to make men superfluous *reflects the experience of modern masses of their superfluity on an overcrowded earth*. The world of the dying, in which men are taught they are superfluous through a way of life in which punishment is meted out without connection with crime, in which exploitation is practiced without profit, and where work is performed without product, is a place where senselessness is daily produced anew.
>
> (OT: 589; emphasis added)

Whatever form they take, politically evil acts involve 'offenses against human dignity so widespread, persistent, and organized that normal moral assessment seems inappropriate' (Nino 1996: vii). Thus the common ground of both forms of political evil is the systematic destruction of people's humanity *by means of rendering them superfluous*. It is my contention that the perpetuation of global poverty constitutes a structural process of superfluity and that it is a political evil in the Arendtian sense.

The appalling effects of global poverty have become crucially intertwined with contemporary economic globalization, and should be seen against this background. I am not attempting to demonstrate here that global poverty is the only possible causal effect of globalization. My point in what follows is to focus attention on the superfluity or dehumanization of large segments of humanity, which is manifested as one component of the globalization of capitalism. The negative effect of neoliberalism on the political itself is another component of economic globalization, which I examine in Chapter 4. For now, whatever else might be said about the potential benefits of economic globalization – for clearly it has generated great wealth for some – it is also politically imperative to diagnose the worst offences of global capitalism as being none other than making numerous human beings superfluous. With this in mind, we must consider that globalization has been accompanied by growing inequality – both between nations, in terms of the gap between the rich and the poor world, and within nations, as the rich get richer and the poor poorer.

At present, around 1.2 billion human beings live on less than $1 a day, and another 1.5 billion people live on less than $2 a day. Further, around 850 million people are chronically malnourished, although 80 per cent of the malnourished in the developing world live in countries with food surpluses, and 1.3 billion people lack access to clean water (UNDP 2005: 24). The global distribution of income reveals an extraordinarily high degree of structural inequality. In 1998, the per capita GDP of OECD countries stood at $20,357, compared with Latin America's $6510, Eastern Europe's $6200, $4140 for the Arab states, $2112 for South Asia and $1607 for sub-Saharan Africa (Kennedy 2002: 7–9). The richest 1 per cent of the world receive as much income as the poorest 57 per cent, and the wealthiest three people in the world have assets greater than the combined GNP of the 48 least developed countries and their 600 million people. In 1960, the income of the richest 20 per cent of the world was 30 times that of the poorest 20 per cent; by 1997 it was 74 times as great. Meanwhile, the ratio of income of the world's richest 10 per cent against the poorest 10 per cent has grown from 51:1 in 1970 to 127:1 in 1997.[5] The richest 20 per cent of the world's population hold 75 per cent of the world's income, while the poorest 40 per cent hold just 5 per cent. Nine out of every ten of the citizens of affluent countries are among the world's richest 20 per cent, and 'the gap between the average citizen in the richest and in the poorest countries is wide and getting wider' (UNDP 2005: 36–37).

In addition, the UN estimates that income, life expectancy and literacy declined in 21 countries during the 1990s, this being a particularly dismal decade for sub-Saharan Africa and Latin America (UNDP 2005: 21–23). Roughly one-third of all human deaths, some 50,000 daily, are due to poverty-related causes, and of these more than 10 million annually are children under five: '98% of children who die each year live in poor countries' (UNDP 2005: 24). 100 million children live on the streets; half a million women die during pregnancy or in childbirth every year; 1 million a year die of malaria and 2 million of tuberculosis (WHO 2004); and more than 40 million people are infected with HIV/AIDS, nearly two-thirds of whom live in sub-Saharan Africa (UNAIDS/WHO 2005). Despite such widespread yet preventable misery, total external debt for the world's poorest countries in 2003 stood at a shocking \$2.43 trillion (World Bank 2004), virtually preventing any chance of addressing many of these issues. The nations of sub-Saharan Africa, in particular, are in a state that Arrighi describes as tragedy. In 1975 the GNP of the region stood at 16.6 per cent of world per capita GNP; by 1999 it stood at just 10.5 per cent (Arrighi 2002). In light of this radical inequality, Manuel Castells speaks of the emergence within the global economy of a new 'fourth world' (Castells 1998: 70–165). This refers to the emergence of an 'underclass' of 'millions of homeless, incarcerated, prostituted, criminalized, brutalized, stigmatized, sick, and illiterate persons', across every country, who are excluded from the benefits of globalization and marginalized in terms of political participation and social belonging (Castells 1998: 165). The UN's *Human Development Report 2005* remarks that 'more than 40% of the world's population constitute, in effect, a global underclass' (UNDP 2005: 24).

A stark example of this underclass of humanity is the swelling numbers of the world's urban poor, indicative of a shift in the locus of poverty from rural areas to urban centres. In its recent report, *State of the World's Cities 2006/7*, UNHSP (2006) estimates that nearly 17 per cent of humanity – about 1 billion people – now live in urban slums; 72 per cent of the world's slum-dwellers are in sub-Saharan Africa. Globally, the slum population is expected to grow at a rate of 27 million people per year over the next 15 years. Despite their proximity to services, durable housing and government institutions, the UN report concludes that the urban poor are almost wholly excluded from access to them, and thus suffer from a systemic 'urban penalty'. The 'multidimensional nature of poverty experienced by the urban poor' includes environmental degradation, discrimination, violence, chronic malnutrition, disease, a high premature mortality rate, and recurrent dispossession. Yet, notwithstanding their rapidly growing numbers, the urban poor remain 'hidden' and the slums in which they live are 'largely ignored' (*ibid.*).[6]

There are other aspects of the horrendous effects of poverty in relation to neoliberal economic globalization that need further exploration. Consider, for instance, the prevalence of what Kevin Bales (2004) calls 'new slavery' around the world today. Arendt, particularly in the chapter entitled 'Race and bureaucracy' in *The Origins of Totalitarianism*, compellingly exposed the ways that racism, violence and exploitation accompanied European expansionism into Africa, Asia, Australia and the Americas. Under these conditions, the institution of classical or 'old' slavery thrived as an integral part of the local institutional dynamic of virtually every European and settler society. Orlando Patterson points out in *Slavery and Social Death* that in the past, enslavement was the result of capture in war, kidnapping, tribute and tax payment or debt, punishment for crimes, abandonment or sale of children, or selling of self (Patterson 1982: 105). Whatever the method of enslavement, the basis of classical forms of slavery was an assertion of legal ownership, the establishment of a long-term relationship between the slave and slaveowner, and the characterization of slaves as a form of capital investment

(Bales 2005: 114). Old forms of slavery began to decline through the efforts of the abolition campaign in Europe and North America in the eighteenth and nineteenth centuries, ultimately leading to the international legal proscription of slavery with the adoption of the Slavery, Servitude, Forced Labour and Similar Institutions and Practices Convention of 1926. The 1926 Slavery Convention was followed by the Supplementary Convention on the Abolition of Slavery, the Slave Trade, and Institutions and Practices Similar to Slavery of 1956. 'Today', writes Bales, 'slavery is illegal everywhere, and there is no more *legal* ownership of human beings' (Bales 2004: 5).

Consequently, slavery is generally thought to be an evil that belongs in the past (Bales 2005: 24).[7] Paradoxically, however, international efforts to outlaw slavery have, in part at least, contributed to the conversion of 'old' slavery into a ubiquitous underground system of human bondage and trafficking, built on permeable borders and the growth of a world economy that is conducive to the exploitation of cheap and disposable labour. For that reason, slave*holding* has replaced slave*owning*. Bales estimates that currently there are at least 27 million slaves worldwide, although it is likely that the actual number of slaves is considerably higher (Bales 2004: 8–9). The International Labour Organization (ILO), for instance, estimated that in 2004 there were 218 million children in forced labour worldwide (ILO 2006: xi) There are several glaring differences between the nature of 'old' and 'new' slavery. First, the financial cost of a slave today is cheaper than it has ever been (Bales 2005: 9). This is due, to some extent, to post-1945 population increases, most notably in developing states in Africa, South America and Southeast Asia. This abundance of people made vulnerable by economic inequality makes the cost of an individual low, attaching a 'disposable' quality to their services and rendering them unworthy of long-term investment (Bales 2004: 15–16). Open-ended debt bondage, for instance, has become a common form of modern slavery, especially in India. Given the large population and scarcity of land in India, 'the resulting pressure on agricultural wages pushes free laborers toward bondage' in exchange for a relatively small loan (about $12–23) (Bales 2004: 16). Yet because it is the slaveholder who decides when the debt is repaid, it 'may carry over into a second and third generation', and the children of the bonded labourer may be seized and sold against the debt (Bales 2004: 17). Further, while a bonded labourer in India can be obtained at low cost, he or she will return a profit of more than 50 per cent in a single year. Compare this scenario with the case of slaves in the American South prior to 1860. Then, the price of an African slave was on average $1000–1800, equal to approximately $40,000–80,000 today, but these slaves generated only 5 per cent profit per year (Bales 2004: 17). These figures reveal why contemporary bonded slaves are not lifelong 'investments'. Perversely, since the burden of legal ownership no longer exists, and slaves can be 'disposed of' or let go at any convenient time (such as when they become ill or injured), it becomes far easier to avoid legal efforts to stop slavery.

While the racist classification of human beings into those possessing 'superior' and 'inferior' status played a significant role in old forms of slavery, the most common criterion for being a slave today is simply a person's degree of vulnerability in the face of economic disparity (although this is often linked to racial, ethnic or religious discrimination). An example of widespread vulnerability spawning modern slavery is the population of Burma. With a military government that is wrought by corruption, repression, and mismanagement of resources and economic policies, many Burmese citizens subsist in a continual state of poverty and are constantly exposed to the threat of being enslaved by the military for purposes of forced labour (Bales 2004: 247; US Department of State 2008: 79). As a result, 'tens of thousands of men, women, and children have been used as laborers or bearers in military campaigns against ethnic groups or on construction projects' such as the natural gas pipeline built for the US oil company Unocal and the French oil company Total (Bales 2004: 21). In addition to being exploited by their own government, Burmese men, women and children are sourced and trafficked to neighbouring countries, including China, Bangladesh, Malaysia, South Korea and Thailand, to serve as domestic servants, child soldiers and sex slaves (Bales 2004: 34 ff.; US Department of State 2008: 78–79).

Indeed, human trafficking is perhaps the most crucial aspect of the contemporary slave trade, as it is numerically the most common form of modern-day slavery (Craig et al. 2007: 25). Human trafficking (as well as smuggling of people) illustrates the permeability of borders and the effects of globalization that have reshaped slavery in its modern form. In addition, it illustrates how the prohibition of legal slavery has altered the nature of the institution from being an open and traceable social practice to becoming a secretive and complex practice that is extremely difficult to quantify. The US State Department conservatively estimates that approximately 800,000 people are trafficked across international borders each year, and that 80 per cent of those trafficked transnationally are women and girls; millions more are trafficked into forced labour and debt bondage within national borders (US Department of State 2008: 7). It is estimated, as well, that worldwide trafficking is worth at least $32 billion annually. This lucrative business is distributed between varying forms of coercive exploitation. The ILO estimates that of all trafficking, 43 per cent is devoted to sexual exploitation, 32 per cent to labour exploitation, and 25 per cent to both labour and sexual exploitation (Craig et al. 2007: 20). Those trafficked across borders are typically subject to sexual abuse, entrapment via locked 'safe houses', electrical fences and physical violence, and confiscation of their legal documents – with the latter leaving them particularly vulnerable to *de facto* statelessness once they leave their home state. The problem of statelessness will be explored in greater depth in the following chapter. In sum, slavery is no longer a standing investment in and of itself; rather it is merely a means to enhance global economic progress. Governments and private businesses alike utilize slavery as a means to generate wealth by exploiting those unable to contribute to the economic game in a 'legitimate' manner. The contemporary global economy has advanced in such a way that gross human exploitation has become an integral part of its functioning through a surplus of people who are vulnerable and marginalized enough to be superfluous.

Zygmunt Bauman discusses the problem of global poverty in terms that help to illuminate how Arendt's characterization of political evil as making human beings superfluous may be applicable here. For Bauman, poverty takes on an intense significance today in a globalizing world. We have moved, he argues, from a social order in which people were engaged primarily as workers, and where the non-working population existed as a reserve army of labour, to a society where people are engaged within social orders primarily as consumers (Bauman 1998: 27). Unemployment and insecurity become permanent for hordes of the 'redundant'. The main figure of the poor today, then, is as 'flawed consumer'. In Bauman's view, the poor today are regarded as having no function, and they tend to be blamed for their condition. Their plight is no longer viewed as a collective social problem; rather, it is linked with criminality in that the poor are regarded as a 'nuisance and worry'. The only role left to the poor is invisibility, to behave as if they do not exist.

Much like Arendt, Bauman argues that modernity is characterized by instrumental rationality and a drive towards bureaucracy and technological order, with a resulting emptying out of moral responsibility. The era of neoliberal globalization, Bauman contends, exposes how the project of modernity – or more accurately, of compulsive modernization – necessarily produces 'human waste' (Bauman 2004: 5). Here, three historical strands of modernization converge: order-building, economic progress and capitalist globalization. For Bauman, the modernization process is defined by the drive to design, engineer and administer society, most fundamentally in terms of the 'freedom' to consume. The corollary of this process is that whatever cannot be assimilated into the model of modernization (or 'development') as consumption must be treated as unfit, undesirable, redundant, useless and disposable. Immigrants, refugees and the impoverished are simply superfluous populations who, if they cannot be directly eliminated in the 'post-totalitarian' era, at least can be made to disappear from our consciousness. In Bauman's words, we 'dispose of leftovers in the most radical and effective way: we make them invisible by not looking and unthinkable by not thinking. They worry us only when the routine elementary defences are broken and the precautions fail' (*ibid.*: 27). The wasted lives of human refuse are stripped of dignity, driven to the farthest margins of society, and eradicated from public space while hidden in plain sight. In this way, the global poor have no part to play in a common world of human interaction. Although they are not exterminated in the gas chambers and ovens of death camps, they are nevertheless condemned to live and die in the most degrading conditions of the human waste dumps that are beyond sight of those who 'count'.

Bauman's argument, couched in language that evokes the parallels drawn by Arendt between totalitarian systems and the basic conditions of modern capitalist society, lends support to the central claim of this chapter: that global poverty 'erases' the global poor, excludes them from recognition as fellow human beings, and denies them standing as equals within a shared public world. Simply put, global poverty makes a vast portion of humanity superfluous. The global poor have become, to borrow Arendt's phrase for those deprived of their human rights, 'the scum of the earth' (OT: 341), because of who they are (or where they are born) rather than what they have done. As Dana Villa asserts, in today's world 'untold millions will have to suffer the crushing fate of being no use to the world economy' (Villa 1999: 12). Along these lines, Thomas Pogge has proposed that extreme global poverty may constitute 'the largest crime against humanity ever committed, the death toll of which exceeds, every week, that of the recent tsunami and, every three years, that of World War II, the concentration camps and gulags included' (Pogge 2005a: 2).

Pogge maintains that abject global poverty offers evidence of what he refers to as 'radical inequality'. Pogge (2002: 198) defines radical inequality in terms of the following five conditions:

1. Those worse-off are very badly off in absolute terms.
2. They are also very badly off in relative terms – very much worse off than many others.
3. The inequality is impervious: it is difficult or impossible for the worse-off substantially to improve their lot; and most of the better-off never experience life at the bottom for even a few months and have no vivid idea of what it is like to live in that way.
4. The inequality is pervasive: it concerns not merely some aspects of life, such as the climate or access to natural beauty or high culture, but most aspects or all.
5. The inequality is avoidable: the better-off can improve the circumstances of the worse-off without becoming badly off themselves.

Pogge condemns not only the extreme (both absolutely and relatively), pervasive and persistent characteristics of global poverty that make it unjust, but most importantly that it is *avoidable*. As Pogge notes, if global poverty were simply a matter of 'bad luck', of the uncontrollable consequences of natural events and simple chance, then while it might be unfortunate, it would not necessarily be unjust. Contrary to this, he counters that while it 'is bad luck to be born into a family that is too poor to feed one ... the fact that a quarter of all children are born into such families is not bad luck but *bad organization*' (Pogge 1998: 531 n. 12; emphasis added). Advancing what he calls an 'institutional' understanding of human rights, Pogge argues that the grave injustice of global poverty arises from the fact that it is produced by shared global institutions with which, under conditions of economic globalization, we all are engaged in some form. In other words, within the global political and economic order, we are all connected to extremely powerful institutions such as the International Monetary Fund, the World Bank and the World Trade Organization, which determine and mediate our relationships to one another to a significant degree insofar as they govern markets, trade and foreign affairs. Because these institutions, and the governments through which they operate, constitute a highly integrated whole that designs and coordinates policies, decisions and actors for the purpose of producing specific consequences, the outcomes of this scheme must be ascribed to identifiable social structures and agents.[8]

Hence Pogge contends that radical inequality is an extreme injustice, in that it foreseeably and avoidably results in the severe impoverishment of billions of human beings. Global poverty is not due simply to unavoidable extrasocial factors (although such factors, like natural disasters, may exacerbate the conditions of poverty), but most fundamentally to institutional design, decisions and actions. What is crucial to note here is that feasible alternative decisions and actions can be taken; alternative institutional schemes can be implemented that do not produce pervasive, persistent and radical inequality. Pogge, for instance, proposes a Global Resource Dividend, which taxes the extraction of resources for the benefit of developing countries. He calculates that it would take only 1.2 per cent of the high-income economies, or about $312 billion annually, to eliminate the aggregate shortfall of those living on less than $1 per day from the $2 threshold (Pogge 2002: 196–215). That such alternatives are not adopted means that the worse-off are knowingly being starved and impoverished, as the foreseeable and avoidable conditions of extreme poverty are imposed upon them and they are coercively excluded from the benefits of economic globalization.

To put this all another way, the foreseeable and avoidable infliction of the ongoing harm of global poverty is an extreme political evil, in the sense that it arises from a coordinated institutional scheme, the effects of which make huge numbers of human beings superfluous. While it may not be the explicit *intention* of political leaders, and heads of multinational corporations and transnational financial institutions such as the World Bank and IMF, to make a large portion of humanity superfluous, the fact that such a systemic outcome is knowingly perpetuated allows us to judge as radically unjust the institutional design and policies of the current global politicoeconomic order. For this reason, global poverty cannot be regarded as a 'non-moral' form of evil, that is, as a terrible event 'that is not caused by human agency' or that results from 'unchosen' human action (Kekes 1990: 47). Given the case put forward by Pogge and others, this is a conclusion that has become difficult if not impossible to sustain. Rather, as George Kateb has argued, 'deliberate impoverishment or neglect or correctable misery' may be properly regarded as a moral and political evil (Kateb 1992: 201).

In contrast to the argument put forward here, it has been suggested recently that extreme poverty is an 'unintended "structural" evil' and thus is non-moral because it is in some sense 'unavoidable' (Rengger and Jeffery 2005: 5–6). However, this claim overlooks that it is precisely the structural nature of global poverty today that makes it possible to trace back to specific institutional contexts the agents and policies responsible for creating or continuing radical inequality. And insofar as these structural conditions can be identified as the products of human agency, they may also be avoided through deliberate systemic change. Change may be difficult, of course, since structural violence becomes normalized in institutional conditions that produce or reinforce social, economic and political disparities. In most cases, the institutions that contain elements of structural violence are longstanding, giving these forms of violence an appearance of normality and even acceptability. As such, they are 'symptoms of deeper pathologies of power and are linked intimately to the social conditions that so often determine who will suffer abuse and who will be shielded from harm' (Farmer 2003: 7). Those on the disadvantaged side of structural inequalities often are rendered voiceless as their suffering and concerns go unheard, and they remain invisible within a stratified social order.[9] In effect, gross social inequalities inhibit the establishment of, in Arendt's terms, a common world where each person is able to see this world 'from the other person's standpoint' (LK: 74).

In this respect, Arendt's work is useful because her conception of the banality of evil draws attention to the central role played by organizational structures, institutions and policies. While Arendt's analysis of the ordinary motivations exhibited by individual perpetrators of political evil has been widely recognized, insufficient consideration has been given to the fact that her analysis of modern society exposes structural factors that impede the ability of normal citizens to identify cruel policies and institutional schemes as destructive of the human status. Arendt was highly attuned to the structural conditions that enable large numbers of people to support and implement extremely unjust policies. This follows from her insight that blaming the phenomenon of political evil on a few deviant and pathological individuals obscures the fact that so many people, to varying degrees of complicity, are required for such evil to occur at a structural level. The 'hallmark' of political evil, Arendt remarks, is a 'structural element in the realm of human affairs' (HC: 241).[10] If we cannot account for the scope of political evil simply on the basis of a few deviant actors, then we must look to structural conditions that 'normalize' actions which, while harming or killing others on a large scale, are nevertheless preventable. As Hanna Pitkin observes, 'even these structural conditions are continually reproduced only by human activity. They are not inherent inevitabilities. The joint-stock, limited-liability corporation, for example, is a human creation, sustained only by what we are continually doing' (Pitkin 1998: 26).

Thoughtlessness and complicity with political evil

The failure to prevent poverty 'caused by an unjust coercive institutional order' (Pogge 2002: 24) can be clarified, at least in part, by appealing to Arendt's notion of 'thoughtlessness' and the constellation of concepts that surround her idea of the banality of evil: imagination, judgement, understanding and responsibility. Although he does not address the matter himself, Pogge's work also points us in this direction by noting that the understanding that radical inequality is a foreseeable and avoidable consequence of the global economic order is not always explicit. Similarly, Arendt comments that the 'sad truth of the matter is that most evil is done by people who never made up their minds to be or to do either evil or good' (LMT: 180). Indeed, one of the conditions that sustain the perpetuation of radical inequality is that the affluent 'have no vivid idea' of what it means to live with such enduring and appalling misery (Pogge 2002: 198). Unable to imagine themselves in such a situation, the affluent then find it 'unthinkable' that they 'are actively responsible' for the catastrophe of global poverty (Pogge 2005a: 1).

In Arendt's view, the banality of evil is made possible by a profound lack of thought and judgement. It was, for instance, Eichmann's 'inability ever to look at anything from the other fellow's point of view' (EJ: 48) and his 'lack of imagination' (EJ: 287) which enabled him to act as he did. By 'thoughtlessness', or an absence of thinking, Arendt means a lack of critical judgement (LK: 43–44). Most importantly, Arendt is concerned about the ability to judge particulars by employing imagination and, following Kant, 'common sense' (*sensus communis*, the sense of a human community) as a way to understand our belonging to a world shared with others as equals. Elaborating upon Kant's analysis of aesthetic judgement in his *Critique of Judgement*, Arendt suggests that moral and political judgement requires the ability both to imaginatively bring others into one's own position and to place oneself into their circumstances, so as to compare one's judgement with the possible judgement of others (see Parekh 2008: 80–90). Arendt refers to this capacity variously as the 'enlargement of the mind', 'enlarged mentality' and 'enlarged thought', the capacity to think representatively or from the standpoint of everyone else. As Arendt puts it:

> Political thought is representative. I form an opinion by considering a given issue from different viewpoints, by making present to my mind the standpoints of those who are absent; that is, I represent them. ... The more people's standpoints I have present in my mind while I am pondering a given issue, and the better I can imagine how I would feel and think if I were in their place, the stronger will be my capacity for representative thinking and the more valid my final conclusions, my opinion. ... The very process of opinion formation is determined by those in whose places somebody thinks and uses his own mind, and the only condition for this exertion of the imagination is disinterestedness, the liberation from one's own private interests.
>
> (BPF: 241–42)

The 'maxim of the enlarged mentality' (LK: 71) – thinking and communicating from the other person's standpoint – underwrites the 'general viewpoint or standpoint' of cosmopolitanism (LK: 58). The enlarged mentality is a conscious commitment to engaging with as many of the plurality of viewpoints making up the world as possible (see LMT: 19); thus the *sensus communis* is performative rather than primordial. When an enlarged thought strives for representativeness and impartiality, it fosters a 'general standpoint' by critically reconstructing the particular standpoints of diverse individuals and bringing these to bear upon its own judgements. In this way, according to Arendt, by recognizing relevant differences and treating other individuals as equals, it is possible to arrive at a conception of common humanity (a human community) in which the other's perspective as a human being is taken into account. Properly understood, *thinking* involves the imaginative representation to oneself of the conditions which other individuals 'are subject to' and reflective consideration of their standpoint (LK: 64–65). The commitment to enlarged thought is morally and politically significant in that it fosters the 'ability to think without rules', to cultivate judgement and conscience capable of 'thinking through' the purposes and consequences of our actions from different perspectives, without proceeding in automatic fashion through obedience to pre-existing social conventions (RJ: 18–27).[11] The enlarged thought amounts to a form of political responsibility offered in the name of cosmopolitanism, according to which the ability to think in terms larger than oneself becomes the principle of both judgements and actions taken from the standpoint of 'a world citizen and, therefore, also a *Weltbetrachter*, a world spectator' (LK: 76; see also EJ: 22).

As Arendt explains, the ability to take into consideration the perspectives of others is normatively crucial, in that it allows us to liberate ourselves from the 'subjective private conditions and ... idiosyncracies which naturally determine the outlook of each individual in his privacy' (BPF: 220). It was the abdication of judgement and the failure to imagine the world of the other as a fellow human being that Arendt found typified in Eichmann. The only 'remarkable' character-istic that could be discerned in his behaviour was a lack of reflection: Eichmann simply resorted to stock phrases, stereotypes, routine procedures and standard-ized codes of conduct, in order that he might regard himself as a mere 'cog' in a machine that he was otherwise 'helpless' to control or affect. He simply did what any other 'normal' actor in his situation would do, for the same reasons. He failed to exercise independent thinking and judging, and to make reasoned decisions that included the standpoint of other persons. This lack of imaginative reflection, Arendt tells us, was not the result of forgetfulness or stupidity; rather, 'thought-lessness' served to shield him from reality. It allowed him to fashion an image of himself as a good, 'law-abiding citizen' performing his duties, and it relieved him of the need to 'fall back on his "conscience"' (EJ: 135–37, 293). For Arendt, thoughtlessness is, in the end, an escape from personal and political responsibility in a cosmopolitan world of plurality.

Returning to the problem that the better-off find it 'unthinkable' that they may be responsible for the misery of global poverty, it may be said that in not having a vivid idea of what it is like to live as the worse-off do, the better-off do not lack an empirical basis for forming such an idea (hardly a convincing explanation, given the amount of information widely available), but rather they neglect to exercise their enlarged imagination and judgement at the moral–political level. In other words, the better-off fail to consider reflectively the standpoint of the worse-off, and to identify with the worse-off as living human beings like themselves. Thus the absence of any imaginative identification with the global poor contributes to their dehumanization and to the normalization of extreme poverty as a form of structural violence. On this view, because the better-off live 'structurally separate lives', it makes it easier for them not to treat the worse-off as fellow human beings (Pitkin 1998: 106).

Drawing out the implications of this argument, it is possible to identify at least five ways in which 'thoughtlessness' is pertinent today with regard to the con-tinuation of global poverty. First, the post-Second World War discourse on gross violations of the dignity of human beings has focused narrowly on the traditional conception of radical evil. Contrary to what Arendt came to realize, the tendency has been to assume that cruel deeds are necessarily the outward expression of demonic personalities that lie hidden beneath them. The insistence that all radical evil has its roots in malevolent intentions buttresses the belief that only 'mon-sters', not ordinary men and women, are capable of facilitating the systematic destruction of the human status. Exceptionally 'demonic' figures such as Hitler,

Stalin, Idi Amin, Pol Pot, Osama bin Laden and Saddam Hussein are vilified not simply for their deeds, but more so for their irredeemably corrupt and depraved personalities. Such 'evildoers', as George W. Bush describes them, are portrayed as almost single-handedly responsible for all that is wrong in the world. Yet the more inhuman these figures become, the easier it is to distance ourselves from any association with them and thus to ignore that their crimes would not have been possible were it not for the complicity of thousands of ordinary people.

Second, the traditional conception is flawed in that one particular type of extreme evil has been reified into political evil as such. In other words, there has been a reductive focus on political evil, as manifested *exclusively* in overt violence such as genocide and ethnic cleansing. This can be seen most clearly in the international human rights system that emerged following the horrors of the Second World War. Although the foundational text of this system, the 1948 Universal Declaration of Human Rights (UDHR), advanced a holistic vision of human rights norms encompassing civil and political as well as economic, social and cultural rights, this holism was soon fractured. Under the treaty system built upon the International Covenant on Civil and Political Rights (ICCPR) and the International Covenant on Economic, Social, and Cultural Rights (ICESCR) of 1966, an unfortunate rights hierarchy was introduced. While socioeconomic rights bear the same formal legal status as civil–political rights, the obligations attached to the former are virtually non-existent in comparison with the latter (Ignatieff 2000: 19 ff.). For instance, although Article 2.2 of the ICCPR stipulates that state parties will take 'the necessary steps' to realize all of the rights contained in the Covenant, Article 2.1 of the ICESCR declares that each state party will take 'a view to achieving progressively' the rights in the Covenant according to 'the maximum of its available resources'.

On the one hand, for most states the provision and protection of socioeconomic rights remains nothing more than a rhetorical ploy, an illusory promise never to be fulfilled. On the other hand, ensuring civil–political rights has become the *sine qua non* of modern world politics, especially with the 'triumph' of neoliberal governance. The result has been a considerable bias in favour of civil–political rights at the international level, which has relegated talk of socioeconomic rights to the consumerist model of 'development'. All too often, 'human rights are confined to political and personal rights ... they do not include economic rights to subsistence, education, health care, housing and employment'; thus, 'if immiseration follows from the normal workings of the market system ... no human rights violations are involved' (Herman 2002: viii). Not only does the privileging of civil–political rights actually erode respect for human rights as a whole, it obscures awareness both that human rights are contextualized by structural conditions, and that violations of socioeconomic rights cause far more death and suffering than do violations of civil and political rights. As Pogge argues:

> Socioeconomic human rights, such as that 'to a standard of living adequate for the health and well-being of oneself and one's family, including food, clothing, housing, and medical care' (UDHR Art. 25) are currently, and by

far, the most frequently violated human rights. Their widespread violation also plays a decisive role in explaining the global deficit in civil and political human rights which demand democracy, due process, and the rule of law: Very poor people – often physically and mentally stunted due to malnutrition in infancy, illiterate due to lack of schooling, and much preoccupied with their family's survival – can cause little harm or benefit to the politicians and officials who rule them. Such rulers therefore have far less incentive to attend to the interests of the poor compared with the interests of agents more capable of reciprocation, including foreign governments, companies, and tourists.

(Pogge 2005b: 718)

Third, the dominant traditional version of radical evil, combined with the bias that civil–political rights violations are the source of human degradation proper, lends itself to a simplistic Manichaean perspective of the world. On this view, evil has a 'real existence' in the world, independent of human actions, and is opposed to the power of 'the good' in a cosmic battle. Adherence to such a stark dichotomy that cleanly separates the side of the good from the side of the bad has been most recently and prominently expressed in George W. Bush's speeches, such as when he declared at West Point in 2002 that 'We are in a conflict between good and evil, and America will call evil by its name' (Singer 2004: 1).[12] Several negative implications follow from this view. For instance, it disconnects evil and human agency; it is thought that while the acts perpetrated by individual agents may be the immediate cause of evil, the ultimate source of evil is theological and transcends the human will. In addition, it contributes to the characterization of the 'other' as necessarily or inherently wicked; in effect, those who are allegedly opposed to the side of the good must be viewed as carriers of pure evil and thus as 'risks' to be contained or, preferably, eradicated. Related to this, once the identities of the 'evil ones' have been fixed, any action may justifiably be taken against them and, moreover, any harm visited upon them not only is deserved, but is something they bring upon themselves – after all, the waste bin is the 'natural prospect' and 'ultimate destination of the excluded' (Bauman 2004: 131). The end result is dogmatic demonization of the 'other', simultaneously blaming them for the harms they suffer, and relieving those who are 'good' from having to examine their own causal and moral role in the harm caused. The absolutist Manichaean framework once again undermines the possibility of achieving an enlarged cosmopolitan thought where different standpoints are placed into a critical dialogue with one another. Ultimately, this constitutes nothing more than 'an escape from reality into a cosmic fight in which man has only to join the forces of light to be saved from the forces of darkness' (EU: 135).

Fourth, we can also draw a connection to the nature of ideology, as conceived by Arendt and reflected in neoliberal economic globalization today. For Arendt, one of the most troubling features of totalitarian ideology – of the left and right – is the surrender of independent thought to some overarching scheme of historical or natural necessity. Here, flesh-and-blood human beings vanish under the weight of 'an inevitable logical conclusion', and the deaths of millions mean little when compared with 'some superior, superhuman sanction' from which a doctrine 'derives its absolute, not-to-be-questioned force' (EU: 203–4). Ideological beliefs tend to ossify into commonly accepted opinions and standards, into conventional categories that are elevated to supreme wisdom and which compromise the ability to think, to explain, to understand, and to judge from the perspective of an enlarged mentality. Arendt suggests that this feature of ideological thinking has become endemic to modern capitalist and bureaucratic society.

While capitalism is an ideology predicated on the 'law' of incessant expansion, justifying 'the limitless pursuit of power after power that could roam and lay waste the whole globe' (OT: 161), bureaucracy is the 'rule of Nobody' (EJ: 289) where anonymity reigns, standardized roles are performed by interchangeable 'consumers', and responsibility becomes increasingly difficult to assume, much less to attribute to others. Such conditions provide fertile ground for banal motivations to grow. As with Eichmann, whose 'memory functioned only in respect to things that had a direct bearing upon his career' (EJ: 62), the principles of neoliberalism have become for many the ascendant 'matter-of-course conclusion' (EU: 204) of a doctrine that excuses the excesses of the wealthy states and validates the thoughtless careerism of their citizens. Like Eichmann, most of the better-off today do not have a fanatical attachment to neoliberalism or a pathological desire to 'do evil'; they simply have no other motives than the relentless pursuit of career success. The operation of the global economic order follows its own supposedly 'inexorable laws, compelling us' in turn along a path for which no-one takes responsibility (OV: 86). Consequently, the better-off have no vivid idea of what it means to live in the circumstances of severe poverty inasmuch as they shield themselves from the reality that how they 'do business' foreseeably shortens and worsens the lives of affected populations; they thereby thoughtlessly reproduce radical inequality. Although their motivations are 'normal', they nevertheless contribute to reproducing a system that asymmetrically values the lives of millions.

Finally, there are good reasons to conclude that 'most of the vast human rights deficits persisting in today's world can be traced back to institutional factors – to the national institutional arrangements in many so-called developing countries, for which their political and economic elites bear primary responsibility, as well as to present global institutional arrangements, for which the governments and citizens of the affluent countries bear primary responsibility' (Pogge 2005b: 721). In emphasizing the politicoeconomic structures that normalize immiseration and economic inequality, it is necessary to come to grips with the responsibility borne both by powerful governments and elites, and by citizens of the affluent countries. On this point, Pogge echoes a central concern of Arendt's, namely the 'total moral collapse' indicated by the personal acceptance of political evil and made possible by the abdication of critical judgement (RJ: 24). Although Arendt objected strongly to the idea of collective guilt – since 'where all are guilty, no one is' – she also recognized the danger of the bureaucratic 'cog-in-the-machine' excuse, which deflects attribution of responsibility. Yet, as she states with regard to Eichmann, 'if the defendant happens to be a functionary, he stands accused precisely because even a functionary is still a human being, and it is in this capacity that he stands

trial' (RJ: 30). The question to be posed to those who take refuge in thoughtless irresponsibility is: 'And why, if you please, did you become a cog or continue to be a cog under such circumstances?' (RJ: 31). The real matter is not that of apolitical cowardice, greed or envy – the customary vices of the traditional view of evil – but of slavish cooperation with a particularly demeaning institutional scheme, which is an intensely political problem.

In the essay 'Collective Responsibility' (1968), Arendt explains the distinction between collective guilt and collective responsibility: 'Guilt, unlike responsibility, always singles out; it is strictly personal. It refers to an act, not to intentions or potentialities' (RJ: 147). The notion of collective guilt is problematic for two reasons. First, it imputes blame irrespective of the actions (or inactions) of the individual members of a group: guilt for wrongs, in other words, can arise only from the particular actions of individuals. Second, it eliminates the necessity of judging particular acts, policies and institutions that produce identifiable harms. For Arendt, the abstract generality of the notion of collective guilt reinforces thoughtlessness and an unwillingness to judge, and therefore is manifestly unpolitical.

Collective responsibility, on the contrary, is always political insofar as it emphasizes the social embeddedness of individuals. To make sense of the notion of collective responsibility, Arendt points out that 'I must be held responsible for something I have not done, and the reason for my responsibility must be my membership in a group (a collective), which no voluntary act of mine can dissolve' (RJ: 149). Collective or political responsibility is, Arendt insists, imputable on the basis of association: since individuals are always already members of a human community, they are responsible for its collective actions. Collective responsibility is 'vicarious' in that we are liable for 'things we have not done', that is, we are liable for those things that are done in our name by institutional structures, the outcomes of which are the result of collective action. This 'taking upon ourselves the consequences' for things we have not done individually is, Arendt insists, 'the price we pay for the fact that we live our lives not by ourselves but among our fellow men' (RJ: 157–58).

Arendt's account of collective responsibility underscores the ways that personal and political responsibility link up because individuals share a world in common with others, and brings together her observations on political evil in *The Origins of Totalitarianism* and *Eichmann in Jerusalem*. *The Origins of Totalitarianism* approached the problem of political evil primarily from the perspective of the pathology of modern institutional structures – from governments, to international organizations, to the capitalist system of production – which have progressively globalized policies and modes of action that have resulted in large-scale human superfluity. Yet Arendt also observed that the ideology and bureaucracy of modern politicoeconomic structures degrades the ability of individuals to think and judge, not only about the rightness or wrongness of systemic elements themselves, but also about their individual adherence to the rules and norms of these structures. Hence Arendt's notion of the banality of evil was meant to convey the ways that individuals relieve themselves of both the personal responsibility to think and judge, and the political responsibility to recognize that collective wrongs can be actualized only through our continuing to perform the institutionalized functions that lead to such outcomes. 'Normal' individuals thus can be responsible for the political evil resulting from the social structures to which we belong, even though they may not 'personally' intend such outcomes.

By failing to assume personal and political responsibility for their substantial contributions to severe poverty, both the citizens and the governments of the affluent countries (predominantly those whose comparative advantage derives from the imperial legacy) enter into complicity with the political evil of human superfluousness. Arendt's diagnosis of the ways in which superfluous human beings are produced led her to the conclusion that such political evil could not be confined solely to Nazi and Soviet totalitarianism, but that it has become an 'international modern phenomenon' (JP: 233). Similarly, Kevin Bales contends that with economic globalization comes the 'globalization of complicity': 'Today the individual's complicity in perceived evil may be connected to trans-national perpetrators' no longer restricted to the nation-state (Bales 2004: 64). While most of us do not design the policies and institutions that entrench radical inequality ever deeper into the 'wasted lives' of the global poor, our continuing acquiescence to the *status quo* 'without much thought about the origins of our affluence' nevertheless provides the banal foundation for massive misery and deprivation (Pogge 2002: 26). If we are to begin to counteract this widespread political irresponsibility, we must find the courage to think about and judge our actions, and those of the institutional arrangements to which we belong, from the local to the global; to draw connections between our individual choices and actions and their necessarily political impact upon the world; and to condemn those modes of politico-economic organization that radically degrade others and alienate them from the 'world common to all people' (MDT: 16).[13]

Conclusion

Arendt's critique of modernity is centred on the emergence of various forms of human superfluousness, as found not only in direct violence but also, I have suggested, in the 'normalized' structural conditions of global capitalism and the 'human debris' resulting from extreme poverty across the world. The modern state, animated by the accumulation of power and capital as *raison d'état*, was 'constructed in such a way that it can devour the globe simply by following its own inherent law' (OT: 194). A decisive way in which the global poor are made superfluous is through the negation of their socioeconomic human rights, and consequently their systematic exclusion from the common public world. Whatever else it produces, the global market economy also engenders extreme poverty in the midst of its wealth, and this managed inequality functions as the coercive imposition of extreme suffering on a 'useless', disposable population. This catastrophe confronts us squarely with the problem of 'rightlessness'. To be rightless means to have lost one's place in the shared public world, to be divested of political and legal standing, and to be denied recognition of one's humanity (OT: 372–76). Rightlessness amounts to dispossession of the ability to function as a moral and political agent. For Arendt, rightlessness is inextricably tied to 'worldlessness', which is the political and economic exclusion of human beings reduced to 'disposable, dispensable creatures' (Isaac 1996: 67; see also Parekh 2004). The condition of 'worldlessness' brings to our attention the fragility of the human status and how deprivation of what Arendt referred to as the 'right to have rights' underlies the annihilation of human dignity (OT: 376; see Benhabib 2004: 49–69).

As a symptom of contemporary society, human superfluousness has become manifested in the extreme poverty that spreads across the globe. The global situation today has created 'a new class of human beings who have lost even the elementary human usefulness for society as a whole of which slaves and serfs were never deprived' (EU: 195). In this way, the extreme suffering of the global poor – 'those whom an accident of birth condemned to death' – has become 'the basic experience and the basic misery of our times' (EU: 198, 200). Hence an unacknowledged political evil of the current global order is, I have argued, the systemic yet avoidable violation of the basic socioeconomic rights of many millions of people. By portraying political evil only in terms of gross violations of civil and political rights, those who are most powerful politically and economically deflect accusations that they perpetuate atrocities in the form of structural violence, and deny responsibility for the wrongs of severe poverty. Because the confrontation with political evil today is unjustifiably selective, much that is truly evil in the world passes by largely unnoticed, taken for granted as ineradicable features of our moral and political landscape. Focusing only on the most brutal and shocking forms of direct violence allows one of the most massive atrocities of our age – the global 'war on the poor' – to be relegated to the background (Farmer 2003) and met with unimaginative thoughtlessness. As Arendt insisted, however, we must strive to understand the 'nature of political phenomena which determine the whole innermost structure of entire eras ... as signs of the danger of general trends that concern and eventually may threaten all societies' (EU: 360). The danger of superfluity constitutes such a 'general trend' that cannot be restricted solely to the phenomenon of totalitarianism. As a 'symptom' of contemporary society, superfluity has become manifested in the extreme poverty that spreads like a 'fungus' across the globe.

The post-Second World War discourse on political evil has had a paradoxical result. Although this discourse drew valuable attention to the horrors of genocide and mass violence, it also established an unduly narrow conception of political evil as being exhausted by overt forms of direct violence. The persistence of this bias into the age of global terror has meant that, rather than coming to terms with the various forms that human superfluousness may take, and with the structural conditions of modern society that make assaults on the human status possible, we have avoided a true reckoning with the catastrophes of our age.

3 Citizens of nowhere
The evil of statelessness

Arendt became a stateless person in 1933. Following the burning of the Reichstag on 27 February, the German Parliament approved a state of emergency decree or 'Enabling Act' recognizing Hitler's sovereign power to suspend *habeas corpus* and other civil liberties and to pass laws by decree.[1] In the months following the Reichstag fire, Arendt became politically active, conducting research in the Prussian State Library for her friend Kurt Blumenfeld, a leader in the Zionist movement, in order to document anti-Semitic statements made by German civil society groups, business associations and professional societies. Arendt was then arrested and interrogated for eight days by the police in Berlin in connection with this work (EU: 5–6). Soon after her release, Arendt fled Germany without travel documents, escaping first to Prague, then Geneva, and finally to Paris, where she lived as an 'undocumented' (*sans-papiers*) refugee for the next seven years (Young-Bruehl 2004: 105–7). In May 1940, the Vichy government designated numerous stateless persons and refugees in France (primarily German Jews) as 'enemy aliens' and ordered them into internment camps. Arendt was separated from her husband, Heinrich Blücher, and sent to the Gurs internment camp in south-west France. Arendt managed to escape from the camp in July and make her way to a safe house, where she was fortuitously reunited with Blücher, who had also managed to escape from the camp outside Paris where he had been sent. After living as fugitives for several months, Arendt and Blücher obtained emergency visas to the United States. They then had to make their way to Lisbon, where they waited for three months before securing passage to New York, arriving in the United States in May 1941 (Young-Bruehl 2004: 152–59). Ten years later, Arendt became a naturalized US citizen.

For 18 years, Arendt lived the perilous and uncertain existence of a stateless person. In her 1943 essay 'We Refugees', Arendt reflects upon her experience as a stateless person and the degradation that ensues from being variously and arbitrarily reduced from a human being to nothing more than either a 'prospective citizen' at best or an 'enemy alien' at worst (JW: 266). The special significance of statelessness for Arendt consists in the absence of a distinct place in the world, the loss of home, occupation, language, family and rights induced by the deprivation of legal and political status (JW: 264). Arendt's experience was more than personal, however, in that it exemplified a much larger pattern of political catastrophe in the twentieth century, and was symptomatic 'of underlying structures which today have come into the open' (EU: 74). The phenomenon of mass statelessness starkly revealed 'what had been hidden throughout the history of national sovereignty', namely the destructive contradiction between universal human rights and the sovereign power of the modern state (OT: 354). Contemporary history shows that the construction of the international system upon the sovereign power to exclude has created a tangible hell 'as real as houses and stones and trees', one that leads to the formation of superfluous human beings 'put in concentration camps by their foes and in internment camps by their friends' (JW: 265).

The political realities painfully experienced by Arendt and her fellow refugees have not disappeared, but have instead become the order of the day. The Office of the United Nations High Commissioner for Refugees (UNHCR) estimates that at the end of 2006 there were 9.9 million refugees, 5.8 million stateless persons, 12.8 million internally displaced persons, and 4.4 million asylum-seekers and other 'persons of concern', producing a total of 32.9 million displaced persons globally (UNHCR 2007b). These figures are conservative, however, because they include only those persons of concern specifically receiving protection and assistance from the UNHCR. Other stateless peoples include, for instance, the 4.3 million Palestinian refugees dispersed across the Middle East, who fall under the mandate of the United Nations Relief and Works Agency instead of the UNHCR. Thus the actual numbers of displaced persons globally are likely to be considerably higher. Recent research suggests that there are at least 11 million stateless persons around the world (UNHCR 2007b). While stateless persons can be found not only in the 'anonymous' flows of refugees and internally displaced persons, as well as in 'recognizable' groups such as the Roma, Kurds and Biharis, unlike refugees, they do not have legal or effective citizenship in relation to any state. Without legal or effective citizenship, stateless persons in essence have no rights. According to the UNHCR, the deprivation of rights that accompanies statelessness often leaves stateless persons 'in a Kafkaesque legal vacuum' that reduces them to 'non-persons, legal ghosts' (UNHCR 2006). What the UNHCR does not address, however, is the underlying structural condition that continually produces widespread statelessness.

This chapter explores Arendt's critique of sovereignty and her account of the structural contradiction between sovereign power and universal human rights, and suggests that the arguments put forth by Arendt are quite useful in attempting to understand and theorize the continuing legal and political exclusion of the stateless. The most important aspect of Arendt's critique, I contend, is that it highlights how statelessness is not an aberrant or accidental phenomenon occurring despite the best efforts of states to prevent it, but a 'normalized' systemic condition produced by an international order predicated upon the power to exclude as the essence of statist politics. In ceasing to belong to any rights-guaranteeing community whatsoever, the stateless person stands in stark contrast to the citizen located in the public sphere. Whereas the latter become fully human in a common world shared with others, the former are alienated from this world and lose their relevance to others; they are, paradoxically, stripped of something fundamental to their humanity exactly when they are 'nothing but human beings'

(JW: 273). Statelessness is, I contend, another instance of the political evil of rendering millions of innocent people superfluous. I first address Arendt's analysis of the defects and contradictions of the modern conception of human rights so as to develop her focus on statelessness as the increasingly global predicament of rightlessness. I then turn to her critique of sovereignty in order to argue that Arendt grasped the biopolitical nature of sovereign power as the 'right to exclude', and identified immanent linkages between colonial racism, modern imperialism and contemporary anti-refugee policies.[2] I then deploy her critique of sovereignty in order to call attention to the relationship between 'inclusive exclusion' and the efforts of powerful states globally to integrate a strategy of containment of stateless persons and refugees. I ultimately argue that this strategy reinforces a coercive system of global apartheid.

Situating Arendt on statelessness and human rights

Arendt offers a powerful critique of the modern conception of human rights that repudiates naturalist metaphysics and liberal subjectivism as the bases for a philosophy and politics of human rights. Arendt's conception of human rights dismisses any theory that considers rights to be eternal and inalienable, that is, as possessed naturally by an autonomous prepolitical subject. Arendt's critique, as an expression of her cosmopolitan realism, reveals that the failure of universal human rights was most clearly exemplified by the problem of refugees and stateless persons in the twentieth century. Even more significantly, this critique exposes the fact that the international order systematically generates statelessness as a consequence of several contradictions at the core of its normative and organizational principles. She observed that the international system has normalized the condition of displacement and political exclusion, ensuring that millions of innocent people are consigned daily to the oblivion of rightlessness. Despite the force of Arendt's critique, however, it is necessary to bear in mind that her aim is to contribute to renewal of an active commitment to realizing human dignity via human rights. In contesting the dominant approach to human rights, Arendt usefully draws attention to the ways that human rights idealism obscures and increases the vulnerability of individuals and groups to conditions of rightlessness.

Arendt's approach to the 'perplexities' of human rights identifies how a number of problematic philosophical and political assumptions became entwined throughout the development of the modern international human rights regime, leading to theoretical confusions as well as practical impotence in regard to the human rights claims of an ever-expanding group of displaced persons in the aftermath of the First World War. Arendt believed that stateless persons comprise 'the most symptomatic group in contemporary politics' (OT: 353). She highlights the abject status of those who have ceased to belong to any state thus:

> No paradox of contemporary politics is filled with more poignant irony than the discrepancy between the efforts of well-meaning idealists who stubbornly insist on regarding as 'inalienable' those human rights, which are enjoyed only

by citizens of the most prosperous and civilized countries, and the situation of the rightless themselves.

(OT: 355)

The modern conception of human rights has been philosophically advanced on universalist grounds. Natural rights theorists, for instance, proposed that some essential feature common to all persons, such as rationality, grounds certain inherent rights in human nature. While early natural rights theorists identified only a limited number of general rights (such as to life, liberty and property), what is most notable about their doctrine is that those rights are understood to exist prior to, and independently of, any given political society. As such, natural rights are conceived as inalienable, that is, they can be neither surrendered to nor conferred by government. This way of framing human rights remains influential, as evidenced by reference to the 'inherent dignity' and 'equal and inalienable rights of all members of the human family' in the Preamble to the 1948 Universal Declaration of Human Rights (UDHR). Clearly, the ethical and political views of the natural rights theorists and the tradition of political liberalism motivated, to varying degrees, the revolutionary struggles in France and America in the eighteenth century, struggles fuelled by 'self-evident' truths regarding the inalienable rights inherent in the nature of each individual (see Tuck 1993; Herbert 2002).

In *The Origins of Totalitarianism*, Arendt illuminates how the paradoxes and weaknesses of human rights revealed by events in the twentieth century were foreshadowed in the philosophies and declarations of the eighteenth century. According to Arendt, the 1789 Declaration of the Rights of Man and Citizen was able to proclaim the complete emancipation of humanity because it relied upon an abstract conception of the subject as fundamental bearer of natural rights. From that moment each individual, conceived as representative of a generalized humanity existing independently of any particular political community, was presented as the source of all legitimate law. No longer subject either to the commands of divine right or to the oppressive dictates of tradition, the rights of the autonomous individual were derived solely from humankind's inherent nature. In appealing to the notion of natural rights, the aim was to provide a secure foundation for the Rights of Man. Because these rights were defined as natural and inalienable, they belonged to each human being directly without appeal to an external authority, and required no other source for their guarantee than 'man himself'.

However, the conception of human rights as the natural and inalienable Rights of Man rests upon an insurmountable contradiction between individual sovereignty and national sovereignty. In the liberal tradition, sovereignty, which had once been deemed to belong to God, nature or monarch, was transferred to the individual as the source of all legitimate law. As is well known, Hobbes defined the fundamental natural right to life of each person as 'the liberty each man hath, to use his own power, as he will himself, for the preservation of his own nature' (Hobbes 1996: 91). According to Hobbes, each individual is sovereign in the state of nature, possessing the inalienable right to act in whatever way necessary in order to preserve his or her own life. Hobbes thus provides to political thought the notion that individual sovereignty constitutes the sole basis of human rights which, in turn, constitutes the basis for civil law. The idea that civil laws were supposed to rest upon the Rights of Man is precisely where the notion of natural rights begins to founder. For even Hobbes admitted that, given the insecurity and conflict of the state of nature, natural rights could be guaranteed only by a political system created through the mechanism of a social contract. Similarly, the French Revolution and its Declaration of the Rights of Man and Citizen made clear that the rights proclaimed as natural and inalienable required the protection of a political sovereign and the civil laws of a government and constitution.

Arendt points out that despite positing the autonomous sovereign subject as the foundation of universal rights, human rights were in fact first realized only in the particular contexts of the two national struggles of the American and French revolutions. The contradiction here is that the sovereignty of each autonomous individual had to be reconciled with that of all others in forming the body politic. Individual sovereignty, as Rousseau argued, must be superseded by collective, national sovereignty, or binding the wills of many individuals into the common interest of 'the people' (OR: 77–79), in order to preserve the equality of each person. What this meant was an essential devaluation of the importance of the inalienable rights of the individual *vis-à-vis* the national will and the collective right to self-determination. It follows that the rights set forth as resting solely upon the human being's natural life in reality presupposed not only the existence of a polity, but also the sovereignty of the general will of the people. As Arendt effectively shows, this awkward coupling of individual sovereignty as the expression of subjective inalienable rights, and national sovereignty as the expression of the collective rights of the people to self-government, underwrites the emergence of the modern nation-state. This implies that 'man had hardly appeared as a completely emancipated, completely isolated being who carried his dignity within himself without reference to some larger encompassing order, when he disappeared again into a member of a people' (OT: 369). Philosophically, then, the 'whole question of human rights ... was quickly and inextricably blended with the question of national emancipation; only the emancipated sovereignty of the people, of one's own people, seemed to be able to insure them' (OT: 370).

Arendt's critique of the modern formulation of human rights therefore turns on the inherent contradiction that arises from the demand for national sovereignty as an ultimate or 'sacred' right. This demand generated a contradiction within both the nation-state and human rights themselves. On the one hand, writes Arendt, the 'same essential rights were at once claimed as the inalienable heritage of all human beings *and* as the specific heritage of specific nations', while on the other hand, 'the same nation was at once declared to be subject to laws, which supposedly would flow from the Rights of Man, *and* sovereign, that is, bound by no universal law and acknowledging nothing superior to itself' (OT: 297). The idealization of human rights based upon the metaphysical notion of a sovereign subject elevated the abstract individual above the nation-state, while simultaneously the affirmation of national sovereignty idealized as the 'nebulous representative of a "national soul"' meant that 'human rights were protected and enforced only as national rights' (OT: 297; see also OT: 347).

The contradiction between human rights and national sovereignty had further implications for the legitimacy of the modern state. The ascendancy of national-ism transformed the state from an entity whose 'supreme function' was protec-tion of the human rights of 'all inhabitants in its territory no matter what their nationality', into one whose function was to distinguish between nationals and non-nationals and thereby to 'grant full civil and political rights only to those who belonged to the national community by right of origin and fact of birth' (OT: 296). The state, in other words, was transformed from an impartial instrument of the law committed to the equal protection and guarantee of each individual's rights, into an ideological instrument of the 'pseudomystical' nation whose 'will' and interests were committed to protecting only the members of this nation (OT: 297). With the ascendancy of nationalist sentiment over the rule of law – what Arendt refers to as the 'conquest of the state by the nation' (OT: 296) – the abstract 'national inter-est' became prioritized over the interests of singular and concrete human beings. From this point, the 'tragedy of the nation-state' (OT: 296) and, by extension, that of the international system of states, was embodied in the fact that legal protection of rights extended only to those persons recognized as 'nationals' (OT: 379). All non-nationals within a given territory were immediately subject to the potential for exclusion from the polity and its guarantee of equal rights. The 'decline' of the state thus signifies that its legal institutions no longer functioned equally for all its inhabitants, leaving non-nationals not simply on the margins of society, but outside the law itself as 'threats' to the national interest.

The association of human rights with nationality meant in practice that these rights existed solely within domestic law, and belonged only to recognized citizens of particular nation-states. The identification of citizenship with nationality rather than humanity became the precondition for the effective possession of human rights and coincided with the emphasis on mutually exclusive citizenries within the nation-state system. Thus human rights were strictly delimited to the domain of a specific state and placed under the protection of a single government. This situation divested the Rights of Man of their supposedly universal and inalienable character, exposing them as entirely contingent and social. In the new statist era, only membership within a particular nation-state could guarantee rights their legal status. However, those persons excluded from having a recognized place within a polity were compelled to live either as 'exceptions' to the general equality assured to citizens (defined as nationals) or, what became increasingly the norm, 'under conditions of absolute lawlessness' (OT: 343). The paradoxical implication of this identification between human rights and nationality is that expulsion from a state results in the loss of legal and political status and therefore all human rights. 'The Rights of Man', Arendt underscores, 'had been defined as "inalienable" because they were supposed to be independent of all governments; but it turned out that the moment human beings lacked their own government and had to fall back upon their minimum rights, no authority was left to protect them and no institution was willing to guarantee them' (OT: 370).

Arendt's critical analysis of the philosophical underpinnings of the modern conception of rights thus identifies two fundamental contradictions at the heart of this doctrine. The first is that the interests of the prepolitical sovereign subject as the bearer of individual rights conflict with the interests of the political sovereign state as the bearer of collective rights. The second is that as citizenship entitlements within the context of a particular state, human rights are conditional and exclusive, premised upon nationality rather than humanity. This critique not only exposes the conflict between universalist ideals and particularist realities that erode the integrity of the conventional formulation of human rights, but more importantly makes clear that within an international system predicated upon the supremacy of national sovereignty, human rights cannot be enforced outside the state. Arendt draws two further insights from her analysis: first, states have been empowered historically with the 'sovereign' right to determine who is entitled to nationality and thus to possession of human rights, and second, that any person not accorded full citizenship status is excluded, to some degree, from human rights. The central paradox of the notion of inalienable human rights is that while the protection of human rights within the international system is inseparably tied to state sovereignty, states are also authorized to deprive citizens of those same rights and to exclude individuals from the condition of nationality that would enable them to have human rights. In other words, states' 'sovereign right of expulsion' inevitably forces them into committing 'illegal acts' (OT: 360). By controlling admission into or expulsion from nationality or citizenship, states thereby control each individual's prospects for the effective possession and exercise of human rights.[3]

In addition to tracing the conceptual tensions that emerged when the figure of the universal sovereign subject possessing inalienable natural rights became equated with the figure of the citizen possessing civic rights dependent upon membership within a particular nation, Arendt also documented the historical events that made apparent how these contradictions now animate modern political practice. For Arendt, the incongruity between the philosophical assumptions of inalienable human rights and the politically exclusionary practices of the modern nation-state system became blindingly obvious with the problems posed by national minorities and the development of statelessness in the wake of the First World War.

With regard to the problems of national minorities, Arendt focuses on the 1919 Peace and Minority Treaties adopted during the Paris Peace Conference. The purpose of the Peace Treaties was to establish new states throughout Central and Eastern Europe and the Middle East following the dissolution of the multinational Austro-Hungarian, Ottoman and Russian empires. The major powers of Britain, the USA, France and Italy insisted on the creation of new territorial boundaries based on the principle of self-determination, reflecting the conceptual and historical integration of national and state sovereignty noted by Arendt. This meant that the institution of the state was supposed to correspond directly with a homogeneous nationality and a distinct territory; each 'people' had a sovereign right to govern themselves, thereby realizing collectively the rights of its individual members. In reality, the new successor states grouped together people from several nationalities without the benefit of a historically formed sense of national tradition. The instability of the situation was exacerbated by the fact that in each new nation-state, a single group was declared a 'state people' entrusted with government; some other groups were 'silently assumed' to be 'equal partners in the government'; while the remaining groups were labelled 'minorities' (OT: 344–45).

The creation of the successor states thus led to the extensive exclusion of national minorities from government and immediately rendered them unequal to the dominant national groups within each state. Consequently, a series of Minority Treaties were adopted by the League of Nations, with the aim of protecting national minorities within the newly created states, categorizing these groups as 'exceptions' requiring 'special regulations' compared with the majority groups (OT: 345). These special regulations were, in effect, an admission of what until then 'had been only implied in the working system of nation-states, namely, that only nationals could be citizens' and thus that nationality rather than residence was the basis for the full protection of human rights (OT: 350). However, because participation in the League of Nations' minorities system was imposed upon the successor states as the price of international recognition of their sovereignty, these new states regarded the Minority Treaties as 'an open breach of promise and discrimination' because 'their implied restriction on national sovereignty' was not applied to other states (OT: 345, 348). The victorious European powers refused to be bound by the Treaties, within both their home territories and their colonial empires, and the USA never became a member of the League of Nations. The inadequacies of the Treaties soon became clear. For their part, minority groups 'strove to secure recognition and participation in public affairs', including by means of violent national liberation movements, precisely on the very principles of national freedom and self-determination that had been denied them (OT: 346). These peoples argued, in line with the established yet contradictory conception of human rights, that a 'people without their own national government were deprived of human rights' (OT: 347).

Even more troubling from the perspective of events to come, the newly created states, now able to claim the right of sovereignty, proceeded to ignore the Treaties and deny the League of Nations entitlement to intervene into their 'internal' affairs. The governments of the successor states then proceeded to 'oppress their [minority] nationalities as efficiently as possible' (OT: 347). There were two principal facets to this oppression. First, and in line with Arendt's broader analysis of how colonial imperialism contributed to undermining the modern state as an institution of the equal and impartial rule of law, was that the denial of self-determination to all European peoples meant that more than a quarter of the European population was condemned 'ruthlessly to the status of colonial peoples' (OT: 346). This 'evil' of the introduction of 'colonial methods into European affairs' represented the association of nationalism with racism, and contributed to the widespread use of policies of exclusion on the basis of racist doctrines legitimized by the sovereign right to protect the 'national interest' (OT: 346). Second, the definition of national minorities as 'exceptions' reinforced not only the idea that those who were not members of an officially recognized people were less than equal to majority nationals, but also that they were 'an obvious risk to the security of their countries' (OT: 349).

Exploiting the sense of fear raised by these supposed threats to national existence, it was at least implicitly accepted in a number of territories that 'minorities within nation-states must sooner or later be either assimilated or liquidated' (OT: 348). Further, a third option – denationalization – came into widespread practice.

Despite the precarious status of national minorities, Arendt notes that, in principle, some of their more elementary rights, such as the right to residence or work, remained in place. As a consequence, the minorities still retained some degree of membership within a formal political body (OT: 352). The full implications of the sovereign power to exclude persons from political community soon became apparent when European governments began to denaturalize (to revoke the citizenship and rights of) large segments of their populations, leading to the creation of entire groups of people for whom 'there was no country on earth in which they enjoyed the right to residence' (OT: 352). Arendt cites several notable examples of 'mass denationalizations' during the interwar period, which frequently utilized new legislation based on earlier wartime measures, such as the French statute of 1915 that allowed for the deportation of 'naturalized citizens of enemy origin who had retained their original nationality' and the Portuguese decree of 1916 that 'automatically denaturalized all persons born of a German father' (OT: 355). Belgium passed laws in 1922 and 1934 that 'canceled naturalization of persons who had committed antinational acts during the war', while Italy (1926), Egypt (1926), France (1927) and Turkey (1928) all issued laws that allowed for the denaturalization of persons 'who were a threat to the social order' or 'who committed acts contrary to the interests' of the state. Both Austria and Germany followed earlier Russian decrees (1921) by passing laws in 1933 that allowed the state to denationalize any citizen living abroad (OT: 355). In 1936, the Greek government revoked all naturalizations of Armenian refugees carried out since 1923 (OT: 353). Although denationalization became a favoured weapon of totalitarian states, this particular prerogative of 'full sovereign power' in principle can be wielded by *any* type of state (OT: 354); further, the mass denationalizations of the 1920s and 1930s established an 'easy precedent' for the postwar period (OT: 353). Indeed, at the time of writing *The Origins of Totalitarianism*, Arendt was deeply disturbed by proposals in the United States to strip US-born nationals who were communists (or suspected of being so) of their citizenship (OT: 356). What made these measures so 'sinister' is that they could be proposed 'in all innocence' as expressions of the sacrosanct sovereign right to protect national interests (OT: 356).

The deportations and forced expulsions of unwanted minority groups, the displacement of persons *en masse* by war and revolution, and the mass denationalizations of 'undesirable' populations led to the emergence of the *apatride* as a figure symptomatic of 'a world organized into nation-states': the stateless person lacking governmental representation and protection and thus forced to live outside the pale of the law (OT: 354, 343). The explosion in stateless and refugee numbers in the mid-twentieth century effectively exposed the structural deficiencies of the international system, in particular the 'inability of European nation-states to guarantee human rights to those who had lost nationally guaranteed rights' (OT: 343). From this point on, mass statelessness, which was and continues to be treated discursively and practically as an exceptional or temporary problem, in fact became a permanent phenomenon constituted by the sovereign rights of expulsion and denationalization. This had several further negative effects upon the nation-state system and the doctrine of human rights. First, the right of asylum, associated with the longstanding practice of providing refuge, protection and sanctuary to exiles and the persecuted since ancient times (see Marfleet 2006: 97–98), collapsed because it was considered anachronistic and 'in conflict with the international rights of the state' (OT: 357). Second, the two 'remedies' of repatriation and naturalization were ineffective in the face of statelessness as a mass phenomenon. Naturalization was both restrictively offered to small numbers of individuals, and persistently susceptible to revocation by states, while repatriation proved equally problematic in that neither the country of origin (which typically caused the problem to begin with by expelling the person who thereby became stateless) nor any other state would accept stateless persons (OT: 357–61). In essence, stateless persons were consigned to zones of lawlessness subsisting within and between the juridical territories of sovereign states. This situation led to the creation of novel sites designed specifically to accommodate the increasing numbers of stateless persons and refugees globally: the internment camp. The internment camp, writes Arendt, 'has become the routine solution for the problem of domicile' and 'the only practical substitute for a nonexistent homeland' which the world has 'to offer the stateless' (OT: 355, 361).

It is important to note that Arendt's analysis of statelessness goes beyond the narrow juridical definition that distinguishes between the stateless person and the refugee. Instead, Arendt insists on the need to recognize both the *de jure* stateless, or 'a person who is not considered as a national by any State under the operation of its law' (Convention relating to the Status of Stateless Persons, Article 1; www. unhchr.ch/html/menu3/b/o_c_sp.htm), and the *de facto* stateless, such as refugees, internally displaced persons, resident aliens and immigrants threatened by denationalization or ineffective nationality, or unable to prove either their nationality or that they are legally stateless (OT: 356).[4] Arendt stresses the *qualitative condition* of statelessness as extending beyond the merely factual deprivation of national legal status, and as occurring irrespective of territorial boundaries. Indeed, the stateless are distinguished precisely by the fact that they have 'been ejected from the old trinity of state–people–territory' (OT, 358). For this reason, Arendt claims that 'the core of statelessness' – the deprivation of one's legal status and thus loss of the ability to exercise rights effectively within a political community – is 'identical with the refugee question' insofar as refugees are, for all practical purposes, unable to enjoy the rights and protections afforded by citizenship (OT: 357). Using this understanding of statelessness as her focal point, Arendt describes the condition of rightlessness suffered by stateless persons as follows: 'Once they had left their homeland they remained homeless, once they had left their state they became stateless, once they had been deprived of their human rights they were rightless, the scum of the earth' (OT: 341).

It is at this point that the philosophical and political dimensions of Arendt's critique of the traditional doctrine of human rights converge, providing the basis for her claim that the only fundamental human right is the right to have rights. For Arendt, it is clear that the loss of membership in a political community – in modern terms, the loss of nationality or citizenship – is equivalent to the loss of all human rights and dignity: it is the condition of complete rightlessness suffered by the abstract human being. This is because nationality has become the defining qualification for the individual exercise and the state protection of rights under international law. To be 'merely human' means that a person is excluded not simply from any particular state but from *all* states; such persons 'no longer belong to any community whatsoever' and therefore are thrust 'out of legality altogether' (OT: 375, 373). It is for this reason that Arendt insists that the most basic right of each individual, prior to any of the specific human rights proclaimed in various declarations, is the right to have rights, that is, the right to be legally and politically included in a community that guarantees the equal status of all persons residing there, citizens and non-citizens alike, regardless of nationality (OT: 377). Arendt's conception of human rights thus dismisses any theory that considers them to be eternal and inalienable, possessed naturally by an autonomous sovereign subject. Because such rights can be neither exercised nor protected outside a political context, they must be viewed realistically as contingent and historical. Human rights are not guaranteed by an autonomous subject's innate humanity, but by those actual others of cosmopolitanized historical humanity with whom we must necessarily share a world. The fact that we must guarantee them *for each other* as part of political life is what makes human rights both incredibly fragile and ethically and politically important. This is the point behind Arendt's remark that 'We are not born equal; we become equal as members of a group on the strength of our decision to guarantee ourselves mutually equal rights' (OT: 382).

Deprived of their rights, the stateless are 'forced to live outside the common world' and thus are 'thrown back … on their natural givenness' (OT: 383). This condition reduces the stateless to the status of physical object and is a sign of the loss of human dignity. Specifically, to suffer a total deprivation of rights means losing the political agency and legal recognition by which one rises above 'the abstract nakedness of being human and nothing but human' (OT: 377) to become a person (*persona*), an agent in the public realm where one's actions are acknowledged and valued by others. The stateless, in other words, are continually at risk of becoming irrelevant to the world in that their actions and opinions no longer matter to anyone; it is as if they cease to exist. The cruel irony of rightlessness, Arendt remarks, is that the rightless remain 'free' to think whatever they please, yet this is nothing but 'a fool's freedom, for nothing they think matters anyhow' (OT: 376). The stateless are deprived not of the right to freedom and the right to thought, but of the right to action and the right to opinion, neither of which can be exercised in isolation. In other words, stateless persons are not denied freedom in the abstract so much as places within a publicly organized realm in which their freedom to speak and act acquires meaning (OT: 383). That is why Arendt contends that the 'fundamental deprivation of human rights is manifested first and above all *in the deprivation of a place in the world which makes opinions significant and actions effective*' (OT: 376; emphasis added).

In Arendt's view, the stateless suffer a total privation of human rights because they are excluded from the relational communities within which their identities and equality can be recognized and their rights assured. It is because the stateless are isolated and expelled from political communities that they are no longer able to claim human rights. More pointedly, it is because these individuals are 'only human', that is, simply abstract entities not recognized by concrete others as having equal standing within an actual political community, that they are in fact 'rightless'. The most profound paradox of universal human rights identified by Arendt is that the general principle which holds that membership in the human species underwrites our possession of human rights, and thus that each individual carries 'his dignity within himself' (OT: 369), is wholly inadequate to guarantee that individuals retain their rights in practice. Indeed, the oft-repeated claim that human rights are, by definition, the rights that all human beings have *simply* because they are human, proves in practice to be little more than 'hopeless idealism or fumbling feeble-minded hypocrisy' (OT: 344).

This last point is crucial to understanding Arendt's conception of dignity and its relationship to the larger question of human rights. For Arendt, it is only when I am in the company of others who recognize me as their political equal that I can be said to exist in a relationship with the common world, a world shared with others. Without this public recognition I am in a very real sense politically 'impotent', because I exist in a condition of isolation arising from the fact that 'there is nobody who will act with me' (OT: 611). The capacity for political action – understood as acting with others in the public realm in pursuit of a common concern – is dependent, then, upon each individual being recognized by others as being both different, that is, unlike any other human being who has come before and who will come in the future; and equal, in the sense of having the status of agency reciprocally affirmed within a community of plural others. The isolated individual, excluded or exiled from the web of human relations, is deprived of the dignity proper to human beings because nothing that he or she does and thinks will matter to others. This situation of isolation and separation from a political community destroys what, since Aristotle, has been considered an essential characteristic of the human condition, namely the power or 'relevance' of speech and thought possessed by those recognized as having a valued place within the human community (OT: 377).[5] The basic problem with the notion of human rights that emanate solely from 'man himself' is that it relies upon an image of an abstract, universal human being who continues to remain human and in possession of dignity even in the social vacuum created by exclusion from the public realm of collective life and political agency. In Arendt's view, because human rights discourse ought to reflect the real, and not merely ideal, dignity of human beings, any theory that abstractly posits such rights independently of human plurality in community has lost sight of the proper meaning of dignity. The abstract individual, all declarations regarding the Rights of Man notwithstanding, is not the possessor of natural inalienable rights, but the epitome of rightlessness, a political nonentity.

The further point to take from Arendt's analysis of human rights is that while the loss of one's place in the world is what activates rightlessness, what makes rightlessness such an acute political harm is the virtual 'impossibility of finding a new one' (OT: 372). In the case of stateless persons, for instance, Arendt notes that their lack of legal status perversely makes their situation worse than that of ordinary criminals. While criminals at least have a body of national law that recognizes and assists them, even if ultimately they are punished on the basis of this law, the stateless have recourse only to international human rights and thus must 'live outside the jurisdiction' of national legal institutions (OT: 363). Unlike the criminal, what the stateless person faces is not merely the temporary and partial suspension of some rights as a consequence of legal punishment, but 'the deprivation of legality' as such, that is, 'of *all* rights' (OT: 374). Even for the criminal, some trace of citizenship rights remains. In short, no law effectively exists for those who no longer belong to, and are no longer legally claimed as citizens by, any community. As a result, the stateless person is confronted with a morally unjustifiable choice: either remain completely outside the pale of the law, protected by none and liable to arbitrary abuse by all, or resort to transgression of the law, since committing a criminal offence at least provides the 'opportunity to regain some kind of human equality, even if it is to be as a recognized exception to the norm' (OT: 364). Yet the latter option provides only the provisional protection of the law, and fails to resolve the underlying political evil of statelessness: that those who remain unclaimed by any community can be considered 'perfectly superfluous', their lives constantly endangered by the power of states to effectuate the condition of rightlessness (OT: 375). Because we 'have really started to live in One World' (OT: 377), in which there is seemingly no escape from the globalized system of sovereign states, the continued insistence that state sovereignty entails an unimpeachable right of exclusion is a sure recipe for mass human tragedy.

For Arendt, the lesson to be learned about the historical failure of human rights within the international system is twofold: the notion of a presocial, universal human nature is an inadequate basis for guaranteeing the possession of human rights; and while states profess respect for human rights, their actual practices will inevitably lead to violations of these rights as long as states insist on the supremacy of their sovereign right of expulsion. As Arendt notes, citing international jurist Lawrence Preuss, 'in the sphere of international law' it has always been true that 'sovereignty is nowhere more absolute than in matters of "emigration, naturalization, nationality, and expulsion"' (OT: 354). Arendt's contention that we need to devise a new guarantee for human rights requires recognition that the continued insistence that state sovereignty entails an unquestionable right of exclusion is a sure recipe for political evil. Indeed, Arendt suggests 'One is almost tempted to measure the degree of totalitarian infection by the extent to which the concerned governments use their sovereign right of denationalization' (OT: 354–55). Perhaps even more pernicious than the actual use of the right of denationalization in any specific case is the potential for all states to adopt at any time national policies that are 'always phrased to allow for getting rid of a great number of its inhabitants at any opportune moment' (OT: 355). Stateless persons are not simply found 'outside' society, but instead are a byproduct of the society of states, an 'inevitable residue', to borrow a phrase from Arendt (OT: 247), of the nation-state system which relentlessly produces superfluous human beings.

Statelessness and the sovereign biopolitics of superfluousness

Whereas Max Weber (2000) defined sovereignty as monopoly over the legitimate use of force or the means of violence, Carl Schmitt conceived of sovereignty as the ultimate decision-making power which is at the foundation of any social order. More particularly, Schmitt (1985: 5) declared that 'Sovereign is he who decides on the exception'. For Schmitt, the domain of decisionist sovereign power consists in making authoritative distinctions as to what divides one particular social order from another in terms of who, or what, is to be included as the norm and excluded as the exception. The privileged nature of sovereignty, according to Schmitt, lies in differentiating between friends and enemies, insiders and outsiders, citizens and foreigners, and, furthermore, defining sovereignty in this sense as the ultimate power over life and death: the right to include and protect the lives of some in the interest of the state necessarily entails the right to exclude and destroy the lives of others. In Schmitt's view, the decisionism of sovereign power is contingent and arbitrary; it is neither founded upon nor constrained by divine, natural or even human law, since the essence of the state's authority consists precisely in the power to suspend the law. In light of this conception of sovereignty, Schmitt asserts that 'All law is "situational law"' (*ibid.*: 13). Schmitt's characterization of the nature of sovereignty corresponds with the sovereign power of exclusion exposed by Arendt's critical analysis of human rights and the modern nation-state. Yet while Schmitt regards the sovereign power of exclusion as the essence of the political and thus as beyond reproach, Arendt considers it little more than a cynical abuse of power and a structural pathology of the nation-state system, which threatens freedom and the right to have rights.

Arendt's treatment of the human rights problem coincides with a scathing critique of sovereignty as it has developed conceptually and normatively within the framework of modern statist politics. Arendt's dissatisfaction with modern statist politics ran so deep, she insisted that 'If men wish to be free, it is precisely sovereignty they must renounce' (BPF: 165). Here I want to focus on the two interrelated facets of popular or national sovereignty and state sovereignty in Arendt's critique, and the way that modern sovereignty as a combination of these two facets has promulgated forms of customary state power that in reality are racist, oppressive and cruel. Arendt's critique of sovereign power, I will argue, is a theoretical precursor to the recent analyses of biopolitics in the state and global systems. Utilizing the discourse of biopolitics helps to shed light not only on Arendt's political thinking about human rights and sovereignty, but also on the condition of statelessness in the global arena.

Sovereignty, the foundational concept and institution of the international system, consists of two dimensions. Internal sovereignty refers to 'a supreme authority within a defined territorial realm', while external sovereignty denotes that 'the state has constitutional independence' (Holsti 2004: 113). While analytically distinct, these two dimensions have merged historically into the unified practice of modern state sovereignty. As we have seen, Arendt recognized that the theory of sovereignty emerged in the late sixteenth century, in conjunction with the central-ized nation-state, as a counter to the disintegration of the religious and monarchi-cal orders. Arendt articulates how the nation-state embodies the dual aspects of internal and external sovereignty in terms of the fusion of national sovereignty (the right of a people to self-determination) and state sovereignty (the final and absolute political authority in a political community). Arendt also makes the point that this fusion results in a paradox in the system of sovereign states: on the one hand, the principle of popular sovereignty is regarded as necessary for the real-ization of the human rights of members of a national group; on the other hand, the principle that a state is not subject to any external authority opens the way to the complete deprivation of rights within states as well as the 'lawless' spaces 'between' them. This ideological and practical contradiction between the notion of inalienable universal rights and the nation-state as an exclusive political com-munity resting upon the general will of the people led to the tragic phenomenon of mass statelessness. For Arendt, this development signalled the demise of the state *per se*, as a legal institution committed to protecting and guaranteeing equally the rights of all persons within its borders regardless of nationality, and the ascen-dance of political authority regarded as an instrument for securing the interests of a supposedly homogeneous nation against foreign 'others'. This degeneration of the state coincided with the transformation of subjects into citizens distinguished according to the exclusionary logic of national identity.[6] In this way human rights for all were quickly trumped by national rights for some.

There is another way, however, in which Arendt illuminates the dangerous effects of sovereignty. In her essay 'What is Freedom?' she claims that the mod-ern conception of sovereign power as the absolute right of exclusion has its basis in the dominant philosophical and political understanding of freedom, deriving decisively from the Platonic and Christian traditions. According to Arendt, while the ancient Greeks and Romans understood freedom as indissociable from poli-tics, the modern age, in contrast, has 'separated freedom and politics' (BPF: 150). Arendt argues that the older notion more accurately conveys the human experi-ence of the phenomenon of freedom insofar as 'freedom is primarily experienced in action' (BPF: 151). In other words, freedom appears or attains a 'worldly real-ity' only through the performance of action within 'a politically guaranteed public realm' (BPF: 149). Freedom, in Arendt's view, is inseparable from the realm of human affairs not only because it arises from human action, defined as 'the capac-ity to begin something new' (BPF: 166), but more importantly because action pre-supposes plurality, in the sense that political action is action amidst others: acting has meaning only when it *occurs with* and *in the presence of* others regarded as equals (BPF: 154–55).

The modern conception of freedom marks a turn from this intersubjective under-standing of freedom to a subjective one, from freedom as manifested in the pub-lic realm to freedom as an inherently private experience. Following a path leading from Plato through Stoicism to Christianity, Arendt traces the development of an increasingly subjectivist retreat from politics and worldly experience towards 'inwardness as a place of absolute freedom within one's own self' where one 'may escape from external coercion and *feel* free' (BPF: 146–47). Estranged from the contingent and haphazard realm of human affairs, the subjective conception of freedom proposes that 'freedom begins where politics ends' and equates freedom with the faculty of free will: the individual's rational control over his or her decisions and actions (BPF: 149). On this conception, freedom is a psychological rather than a political capacity: the will functions independently of external action and the presence of other persons, and its remit is self-mastery, a kind of absolute 'rulership of the soul over the body' (BPF: 158).

The most significant aspect of Arendt's argument is her claim that the conception of freedom as an expression of the individual will that developed in late antiquity became transposed from the philosophical to the political sphere in the early modern period. Politically, this notion 'became sovereignty, the ideal of a free will, independent from others and eventually prevailing against them' (BPF: 163). The freedom of the body politic, in other words, was conceived of as analogous to the freedom of the discrete individual. Just as freedom for the self came to mean control over one's 'inner domain' and implied a power struggle for absolute mastery over potentially insubordinate desires, emotions and intentions, so too was sovereignty theorized as a form of power, the essence of which is 'to command and be obeyed' (BPF: 159). In a manner that parallels the historical development of human rights discourse, and with equally disastrous consequences in Arendt's view, the sovereign subject and the sovereign state were linked via the capacity for willing or complete self-control. The most 'pernicious and dangerous consequence', writes Arendt, is that it leads either to the nihilistic conclusion that such self-control, and therefore freedom itself, is unattainable; or to the equally destructive insight that the freedom of 'a body politic can be purchased only at the price of the freedom, i.e., the sovereignty, of all others' (BPF: 164). Here the modern conflation of freedom and sovereignty has contributed to divorcing freedom and equality, since sovereignty requires that those who are non-sovereign must submit to the sovereign will.

Moreover, because sovereignty is conceived as domination and subordination, it distances us further from understanding the political as the realm of cooperative action involving equals. As discussed above, Arendt considers agency to be the basis of human dignity. Yet for Arendt, agency, which coincides with freedom, is not simply an inner subjective disposition, but a feature of intersubjective experience that arises through human togetherness. Action occurs only in the public sphere and in the company of equals; by speaking and acting in the presence of others, our deeds and personal identities are affirmed and the 'who' rather than merely the 'what' of agents attains a worldly reality (HC: 180–81). From the perspective of sovereignty, however, this conception of action is troublesome for two reasons. First, action is conceived by Arendt in terms of natality, as the capacity to begin something new: natality is the fact of beginning anew, and action introduces something new (LMW: 217). Thus action is inherently unstable and unpredictable. Second, even though action is beginning anew, it always occurs within an 'already existing web of human relationships, with its innumerable, conflicting wills and intentions' (HC: 184). The human condition of natality, of the birth of the new, is always conditioned by an already existing world that both precedes and surpasses every new initiative. This means that the 'very impact of an event is never wholly explicable' (BPF: 170), its ultimate consequences often impossible to foretell and its implications exceedingly difficult to limit. If left unfettered, then, the spontaneity and contingency of action would disrupt the modern project of sovereignty as the 'ideal of uncompromising self-sufficiency and mastery' (HC: 234). The 'famous sovereignty of political bodies', Arendt concludes, 'can be maintained only by instruments of violence' directed against those whose actions appear to fall outside the control of sovereign power (BPF: 164).

Finally, the discourse of sovereignty is contradictory to reality itself. This is not only because sovereignty attempts to fix and delimit the contingency and unpredictability characteristic of human existence, but also because it seeks to overcome the human condition of plurality. Sovereignty thought of as the autarchic will 'is contradictory to the very condition of plurality' and no individual or body politic 'can be sovereign because not one man, but men, inhabit the earth' (HC: 234; BPF: 164). Sovereignty's denial of plurality has two dimensions: internally, sovereignty presupposes the homogeneity of an indivisible general will, and thus the identification of national sovereignty with the sovereignty of the state; externally, sovereignty equates national independence not only with freedom from foreign rule but with the power to subordinate others, and thus with the 'claim to unchecked and unlimited power in foreign affairs' (OV: 5). In neither case is the reality of plurality – of both individuals and nations who must live connected together in the world – reflected accurately. Both dimensions reinforce the ideal of sovereignty as *legibus solutus*, that is, not bound by law, and fully realized in the power to exclude others. Yet inasmuch as the human conditions of natality, plurality and togetherness constitute 'the very texture of everything we call real' (BPF: 169), then the sovereign model of politics based upon independent self-help assumes only 'a certain limited reality' (HC: 244). In an ironic reversal of the conventional wisdom of political realism as sensibly aligned with state sovereignty, Arendt's cosmopolitan realism instead holds that 'it is not in the least superstitious, *it is even a counsel of realism*, to look for the unforeseeable and unpredictable, to be prepared for and to expect "miracles" in the political realm' (BPF: 170; emphasis added).

Arendt's ruminations on the distortion of freedom within the modern tradition brings to the fore another, biopolitical direction that sovereignty assumes in international politics. Formulating sovereignty as control and mastery was justified by numerous modern political theorists who conceived of freedom in terms of security. In this view, the foremost aim of politics – defined within the sovereignty paradigm – was 'the guaranty of security' (BPF: 149). Hobbes, for example, claimed that absolute sovereign power is established first and foremost for the purpose of ensuring security and the preservation of order within a world of anarchy. The sovereignty paradigm of anarchical conflict and power asymmetry as the natural condition of human life – and, by extension, of the international realm of sovereign states – lends itself to a heightened sense of insecurity. Yet this insecurity is understood as a threat not simply to personal freedom, but instead to 'the life process' itself, to the 'undisturbed development of the life process of society as whole' (BPF: 150). Here the aim of government is to employ sovereign power 'almost exclusively' for the purpose of 'the maintenance of life and the safeguarding of its interests' (BPF: 155). One might conclude that this emphasis on securing 'life' would complement the similarly modern commitment to abstract human or 'natural' rights. Indeed it does, but primarily insofar as it reinforces the contradictions revealed by the proliferation of stateless persons and, as with the reduction of human rights to national rights, the notion of freedom as sovereign security must always be exclusionary. The key for Arendt to understanding this particular facet of the right of exclusion is the structural linkage between sovereignty, nationalism, and the 'humanity-annihilating power of racism' (OT: 215).

In her explanation of the historical decline of the state as an institution premised on universalist principles, Arendt constructs a genealogy of racialism or 'race-thinking' and its role first in signifying, and then in supplanting the idea of nation, leading eventually to the practice of sovereignty as modern state-based racism. Arendt argues that the works of many modern political theorists, including Burke and Hobbes, functioned as precursors to race-thinking, and their accounts of rights, sovereignty and security provided a backdrop to corresponding doctrinal developments in the political sphere. Although Arendt commends the 'pragmatic soundness' (OT: 380) of Burke's critique of the notion of natural rights and his recognition that rights can be realized only within definite political communities, she nevertheless found his anticosmopolitan account wholly unacceptable. Burke's insistence on the rights of Englishmen, as opposed to the Rights of Man, was motivated by disagreement with the egalitarian sensibilities of the French Revolution. For Burke, Arendt notes, rights are conceived as an 'entailed inheritance', the purpose of which is to protect the privileges of an aristocratic class against encroachment by inferior groups of people. Burke further identified the nobility as an 'aristocratic race' whose 'innate' qualities are naturally rather than historically transmitted. By enlarging the principle of rights as inherited privileges 'to include the whole English people', Burke unfortunately tied together the notions of nation and race and affirmed the politically unequal distribution of rights between different peoples as the inevitable result of natural processes (OT: 231–32).

Similarly, Hobbes 'provided political thought with the prerequisite for all race doctrines, that is, the exclusion in principle of the idea of humanity which constitutes the sole regulating idea of international law' (OT: 208). As we saw in the previous chapter, Arendt regards Hobbes as the pre-eminent political theorist of imperialism due to his account of sovereignty as the self-interested process of power accumulation and insatiable desire for security; power is endorsed as an end in itself. The logic of this conception of the sovereign right to accumulate power endlessly, Arendt argues, leads to severing the connections between human beings, and to the ideological splintering of common humanity into 'naturally' superior and inferior races pitted against each other in an international 'state of nature'. As with extreme nationalism, racism paradoxically induces both separation – in dismissing the idea of plural human beings entering into cooperative relationships for mutual benefit – and unification – on the basis of mutually exclusive and hostile forms of identity. Consequently, the 'transformation of nations into races', driven by the logic of Hobbes's philosophy, marks, Arendt says, 'not the beginning of humanity but its end' (OT: 209).

It is precisely this antinomy between universalism and particularism, whether expressed through human rights, sovereignty or freedom, that Arendt finds constitutive of the modern nation-state. It is not that the nation-state symbolically and politically manifests *either* universality *or* particularity, rather it has been constitutively grounded on the contradiction between the two such that, at various moments, its actual policies and actions undermine an opposing set of political principles which it claims for itself. Nevertheless, historical experience since the nineteenth century has shown that the dominant tendency is for states to reify the particularistic dimension of their political form at the expense of universality. Thus while human rights and humanitarianism have become prominent legitimating discourses of modern states, drawing upon the universalist legacy of citizenship defined in terms of abstract humanity, at the same time the discourses of sovereignty and national security have served as bases for the authority of states, drawing upon the particularist legacy of membership within a discrete national entity that excludes non-citizens from its protective embrace. For Arendt, totalitarianism, genocide, mass statelessness and other worldwide catastrophes of the twentieth century should be seen not as anomalies of an otherwise benign political form, but as the potentially recurrent consequences of the systemic contradictions immanent to the international order. One of the constitutive contradictions at work here is that between race and humanity, inextricably linked by 'the maintenance of life' within sovereign politics.

Arendt's discussion of colonialism and its transformation into imperialism illustrates how this contradiction first explicitly came to light. As mentioned above, Burke did not limit his defence of aristocracy and inherited rights to domestic politics, but 'enlarged the principle of these privileges to include the whole English people, establishing them as a kind of nobility among nations' (OT: 232). It is here that we find the genesis of racism as 'the main ideological weapon' of imperialism (OT: 213). Arendt notes the strong affinity between Gobineau, whose 1853 *An Essay on the Inequality of the Human Races* provided a new 'key' to history through his racialist theories of the 'fall of civilization' caused by miscegenation, and Benjamin Disraeli, whose belief in the 'genius of race' found expression in the idea of England's 'national mission' to civilize 'inferior races' and his government's pro-imperialist foreign policy (OT: 225–41). What linked such diverse personalities were Darwinism, eugenics and other 'naturalistic doctrines' aimed at explaining life processes, and the 'natural laws' governing the health or degeneration of ideal forms of life, virtually all of which 'denied any relationship between human "races"' and 'followed the path of the old might-right doctrine' (OT: 234). Furthermore, across the various colonial territories, new forms of power shorn of the limits found in capitalist metropolises were being theorized and imposed upon 'subject races' in the wake of the 'scramble for Africa' (OT: 241).

In contrast to colonialism, European imperialism evolved functionally as a new form of exclusive rule over foreign peoples. Arendt identifies race 'as a principle of the body politic ... [and] as a substitute for the nation', and 'bureaucracy as a substitute for government' as being the two 'new devices' for imperialist political organization and rule (OT: 242). From this interrelationship between racism and bureaucracy, Arendt argues, emerged the temptation of 'administrative massacres' first as an instrument for maintaining domination over subject races and then as a means for 'establishing a circumscribed, rational political community' (OT: 243). In tracing the historical movement from imperialism to totalitarianism, Arendt stresses a corresponding movement of European encounters with and policies towards the 'radically other': from colonization and integration, to discrimination, marginalization, and finally extermination. For Arendt, this is the necessary starting point for understanding the ideology and policies of the Third Reich in particular, but the lessons she draws implicate the European nation-states more generally. For instance, Arendt portrays Lord Cromer, British Consul General in Egypt between 1883 and 1907, in ways that are strikingly similar to her later characterization of Eichmann: Cromer the 'imperial bureaucrat' seems to embody the banality of evil in his 'indifference and aloofness', his 'genuine lack of interest' in those subjected to his control, whose method of governing was 'more dangerous ... than despotism and arbitrariness' because 'oppressor and oppressed' no longer lived 'in the same world', and who voluntarily degraded himself into a 'mere function' of the 'anonymous forces' of an 'unending process of expansion' that transcended any 'obligation to man-made laws' (OT: 274–79).

Arendt thus pays special attention to what she calls 'racial imperialism', which she describes as 'the most extreme form of the suppression of minority nations by the ruling nation of a sovereign state' (Young-Bruehl 2004: 158). Racial imperialism in this way served as the expansionistic double of the domination of ethnic minorities within European nation-states, and once more as a sign of the 'perversion of the state into an instrument of the nation' (OT: 297), with the nation now at least implicitly conceived along racial lines. This shift from state (delimited by territorial boundaries) to nation (delimited by race hierarchies) further strengthened the 'identification of the citizen with the member of the nation', that is, as the member of a particular racial group (OT: 297). Persons could then be denied their human rights not only because they were not members of a specific national–political community, but also because they did not even properly belong to the 'human race'.[7] As Arendt recounts, '"Administrative massacres" were proposed by Indian bureaucrats', while governing officials in Africa 'declared that "no ethical considerations such as the rights of man will be allowed to stand in the way" of white rule' (OT: 286). Such measures were justified in the interests of life itself, defined as the 'survival of the species' in a war of 'historical necessity' between 'higher' and 'lower' breeds', the outcome of which acted 'as a kind of unique judgment on the natural qualities and human privileges of men and nations' (OT: 285, 175, 216).

The central point of Arendt's argument is that all this reveals the genesis of the imperial nation-state upon the foundation of the modern democratic nation-state, and further, that this contradictory doubling of universality and particularity remain constitutive of the current global system of states.[8] The dangerously paradoxical nature of the nation-state can be seen historically, she argues, in the dislocating effect that imperialism had upon the European states. As the nation-state system expanded outward from Europe, the notion of the integration of conquered peoples and territories into the colonizing nation-state was supplanted by the imperative to rule over foreign peoples and thus to keep them separate. Imperial rule was underwritten by the notion that the colonial nation's own system of law was 'an outgrowth of a unique national substance which was not valid beyond its own people and the boundaries of its own territory' (OT: 171). This explains the reason for the emergence of a new form of governing by administrative decree within the colonial territories, where race and bureaucracy supplanted the nation and parliament as the principles of government, and where enforced consent or tyranny replaced active consent or justice (OT: 170). Two decisive developments followed. First, the grounding of politics upon race and discrimination within the colonies was effectively transferred back into the metropolitan nation-states, debasing their democratic institutions and reinforcing the doctrine of sovereignty as the power to distinguish and exclude those who do not properly belong to the life of a nation. Second, the racism that distinguishes between nationals and non-nationals led not only to a crisis in European identity but also, with the globalization of the state form, to the production of inhabitants of territories who nevertheless are not regarded as the nationals or citizens of the states exercising jurisdictional control over these territories. As with the subjects of imperial rule, who were simultaneously included within the scope of sovereign power, yet excluded from the juridico-political status of equality, so too the category of stateless persons has been constituted by the dynamics of the state's historical development: stateless persons are simultaneously included within the system of states that covers the globe and the concomitant sovereign right to exclude that orders this system, and excluded as those who are defined as not belonging to a determinate community and its entitlements on the basis of a wholly political decision. In the case of stateless persons and refugees, the exceptional status of nation and race has become devastatingly intertwined with the exception of sovereign power.

The logic exposed by Arendt linking racism, nationality, sovereignty and rights within the modern state has been explored powerfully in the recent literature on biopower and biopolitics, most prominently in the works of Michel Foucault and Giorgio Agamben. The utility of Foucault and Agamben lies in helping to push forward the argument I want to make, that the phenomenon of mass statelessness is a form of political evil that is at the heart of modern sovereignty. Following her analysis of imperialism, Arendt examines how 'life' became further politicized in the twentieth century, particularly in the totalitarian attempts to transform the nature of human beings by reducing individuals to the merely biological fact of 'the abstract nakedness of being human and nothing but human' (OT: 377). Yet even in post-totalitarian liberal societies, Arendt contends that control over, and manipulation of, life has been promoted as the ultimate point of reference for modern politics, a development that is 'disastrous for the esteem and the dignity of politics' (HC: 314).

Foucault, likewise, vividly describes 'the entry of life into history' through which the methods of 'power and knowledge assumed responsibility for the life processes and undertook to control and modify them' as the 'threshold of modernity' (Foucault 1990: 141–43). From the eighteenth century onwards, Foucault explains, the life of the individual and the human species entered into the strategies and calculations of political power. The vitality of biological life and the purity of the nation became foundational to 'a technology of power centered on life', and modern politics became determined and guided by the 'management of life' (*ibid*.: 144, 147). This 'biopower' was articulated in a double form: on the one hand as an anatomo-politics of the body manifested through techniques of corporal discipline, and on the other as a biopolitics of the population expressed by means of regulation, distribution, containment and ordering (*ibid*.: 139). Foucault identifies the intense emphasis placed upon the notions of sexuality, race and degeneration within the biopolitical objective of optimizing the biological quality of populations. Because the emergence of biopolitics was tied historically to the constitution of the nation-state or 'body politic' and to the transformation of sovereignty in the era of European colonialism, it was at this point that 'racism in its modern ... statist form' took shape (*ibid*.: 149).

According to Foucault, while sovereignty initially symbolized the power of death as the 'right to *take* life or *let* live', with the advent of biopolitics sovereign power focused directly on life as the calculative ability 'to *foster* life or *disallow* it' (*ibid*.: 138). The primary aim of modern sovereign power is, then, to secure normality and order at the collective level of the population. In this operation, racism is inscribed as '*the* basic mechanism of power, as it is exercised in modern States' (Foucault 2003: 254; emphasis added). State racism functions in several ways, first by dividing the population (and humanity) into distinct and divergent races or subgroups, and then by placing these different races into a relationship of war – the decisive relationship of what must live and what must die – so that 'the death of the bad race, of the inferior race ... is something that will make life in general healthier' (*ibid*.: 255). The biopolitical notion of sovereign power entails the belief that the state has an absolute right to eliminate 'biological threats' in the name of the life of the species or race.[9] Consistent with Arendt's conceptions of rightlessness and superfluousness, Foucault insists that this right to eliminate others includes not only murder, but also other forms of indirect violence such as 'exposing someone to death, increasing the risk of death for some people, or, quite simply, political death, expulsion, rejection, and so on' (*ibid*.: 255).

Foucault makes the further Arendtian point that the sovereignty–biopower nexus rests upon a fundamental paradox. Citing the example of atomic weapons, Foucault observes that these simultaneously represent contemporary sovereign power's right to kill and its right to guarantee life: such weapons, the 'legitimate' use of which is assured only to sovereign power, are capable of extinguishing life itself, yet their use is premised on securing life (*ibid*.: 253–54). It is not that sovereign power and biopower, the right to take life and the right to guarantee it, are mutually exclusive, rather they are mutually constitutive of the contradictory structure of the modern state. It is just as feasible for the state to destroy particular forms of life deemed to be 'dangerous' in order to 'guarantee' or 'improve' life 'as such', as it is for it to destroy life as a whole in order 'secure' or 'defend' a particular form of life from enemies both internal and external. Making distinctions between suitable and unsuitable forms of life – whether in the guise of the mentally and physically ill, criminals, political adversaries, immigrants, refugees or foreigners generally – has become such an 'essential function' of sovereign power that racism must be seen as a 'mechanism inscribed in the workings of the modern State' (*ibid.*: 26).

Foucault's notion of biopolitics helps to explain how the historical formation of biopower – the exercise of political power for the purpose of controlling, managing and regulating populations seen as natural living matter – animates the core of sovereignty today. For Foucault, *raison d'état* and liberalism are the historical forms from which the modern state was constituted, providing the ideas of a logic or law for the preservation of the state itself, and of the subject of the state as the natural life and rights of citizens as a 'race' (Foucault 2007: 285 ff.). Yet the concern of the state is no longer territory *per se* but population, meaning that it must coordinate its functions through a security system that becomes increasingly globalized as it mediates the constantly dynamic boundary between the inside and outside. Here Foucault's analysis joins Agamben's approach to biopolitics and the latter's characterization of the state of exception. The state of exception is the legal form that itself exceeds legal status. It is the original device by which law relates to life, and through which life is consigned to sovereign power. If, as Schmitt claims, sovereign is he who decides on the application or suspension of the legal order, then sovereignty is indeed synonymous with the state of exception, of exemption from the law. For this reason, Agamben affirms that the paradox of sovereignty consists of the fact that it is 'at the same time, outside and inside the juridical order' (Agamben 1998: 15).

Building upon (and modifying) the biopolitical reflections initiated by Arendt and Foucault, Agamben argues that the biopolitical structure of sovereignty is not limited to the modern state but instead has classical origins. According to Agamben, the problem of sovereignty traditionally was reduced to the question of 'who within the political order was invested with certain powers', an approach that neglected the more significant question of 'the very threshold of the political order itself' (*ibid.*: 12). Consequently, in reorienting the question of sovereignty towards the originary structure and limits of the state form, Agamben concludes that sovereignty functions according to a logic of the exception whose privileged object is life, and is instituted by producing a body politic through which what Agamben calls 'bare life' is included by its exclusion. To make sense of this claim, Agamben appeals to the ancient Greek distinction between different forms of life: *zoē*, the biological form of unqualified life common to all living beings, and *bios*, the politically qualified form of existence proper to a human individual or group (*ibid.*: 1). The constitution of the *polis* rested upon the exclusion, banning or excommunication of simple natural life to a sphere outside, though necessarily related to, the political realm: in this way, biological life is simultaneously included and excluded, or more precisely it is included by means of its exclusion.

For Agamben, the broader implication of this classical distinction is that sovereign power is biopower from the very start, by being linked with the exception (*exceptio*), that is, with the inclusive exclusion of biological life within the political order. Western politics since antiquity has been premised upon 'abandoning' natural life outside the domain of political existence, yet in doing so it has paradoxically included the natural in the political through the relation established by the sovereign ban (*ibid.*: 28–29). The significance of Arendt's and Foucault's work, Agamben notes, is to document how the juridical and institutional order of the modern state greatly intensified the politicization of biological life by constituting itself on the basis of the 'natural' needs and interests of sovereign subjects. This intensification has become so pronounced that the 'mechanisms and calculations of State power' are inseparable from the mutually implicative distinctions drawn between biological life and political life (*ibid.*: 3). In other words, the sovereign power of exception or inclusive exclusion – the power to decide what is to be relegated to bare life as distinct from political life – has become the rule of statist politics, the 'nucleus of sovereign power' (*ibid.*: 6). The implication of this normalization of the sovereign decision over inclusive exclusion is that each and every citizen is always potentially susceptible to being relegated to bare life, to the mode of mere physical existence that comes from being placed outside the political community yet always within the scope of sovereign biopolitics, such as through the denationalization measures described by Arendt. Bare life, the result of the insertion of *zoē* into the structures of the state, is always at the unstable threshold of the natural and the political, capable of being reinscribed in one category or the other depending upon the sovereign biopolitical decision. The dangerous paradox here is that the exception can be justified as an 'emergency measure' intended to protect the norm; yet insofar as the exception has gradually become the rule, the distinction between killing life and protecting life, between violence and justice, becomes increasingly ambiguous, if not indistinct (*ibid.*: 30–32).

Agamben argues that the modern understanding of politics as sovereign power over bare life can be expressed in the figure of *homo sacer*. *Homo sacer*, a category that Agamben draws from Roman law, refers to the life 'that cannot be sacrificed and yet may be killed' (*ibid.*: 82). This formulation reveals the contradictory features of 'sacred man' inasmuch as the Latin word *sacer* has the double meaning of 'sacred and damned': *homo sacer* referred to a human being who could not be ritually sacrificed, but who could be killed without commission of the criminal act of homicide (*ibid.*: 78). The bare life of the *homo sacer* is precisely expendable, superfluous life, which exemplifies the power over life and death that sovereignty arrogates to itself through the state of exception. Excepted from both divine law and human law, and excluded from the political community the *homo sacer* 'is reduced to a bare life stripped of every right by virtue of the fact that anyone can kill him without committing homicide; he can save himself only in perpetual flight or a foreign land. And yet he is in a continuous relationship with the power that banished him precisely insofar as he is at every instant exposed to an unconditioned threat of death' (*ibid.*: 183). Sovereignty thus refers to the activity of distinguishing between life that deserves to be lived and has juridico-political rights, and life that does not and is deprived of any juridical rights; because bare life is merely 'physical' its elimination does not constitute a crime.

Bare life, then, refers to the Arendtian condition of rightlessness associated with such 'exceptional' phenomena as stateless persons and refugees, who are exposed to the vagaries of a veritable state of nature paradoxically constituted within the realm of the political. Agamben follows Arendt's lead and argues that sovereign biopolitical power inclusively excludes bare life in zones of exception, such as the concentration and refugee internment camps.[10] These are spaces where sovereign power reigns, but where the normal rules and laws are suspended – bureaucratic administration and arbitrary decisions constitute the only rule. Although relegating the exception to the outside of the political community, this outside is captured within the ambit of sovereign power and its biopolitical organization. In effect, exceptional zones are not simply external to territorial borders, but cut across and through the state system as a whole. In other words, the function of zoning – of identifying less-than-human superfluous forms of life and consigning them to zones of exclusion where the deprivation of rights is the 'norm' – has assumed a global dimension (Agamben 1998: 38). As Arendt notes (OT: 376–77), once the statist organization of sovereign power became global, there were no longer any places or persons on earth external to that order.

Agamben suggests, after Arendt and Foucault, that the defining feature of modern politics is that the state of exception – the power of inclusive exclusion – has increasingly become the paradigm of contemporary life in current state practices within the global system. The state of exception generates, on the one hand, the suspension of law and human rights and, on the other, the expansion of bare, naked or superfluous life. What we find in global politics today is the perilous conjunction of, and conflict between, 'life' and sovereign power. On the whole, the perplexities of human rights in a sovereign state system that so troubled Arendt remain: 'The sacredness of life, which is invoked today as an absolutely fundamental right in opposition to sovereign power, in fact originally expresses precisely both life's subjection to a power over death and life's irreparable exposure in the relation of abandonment' (*ibid.*: 83). Despite the proliferation of declarations of rights – or perhaps precisely because of their conflation of *zoē* and *bios* in the notion of natural rights – modern sovereign power operates through forms of social violence that systematically exclude or destroy those deemed to be dangerous, extraneous, or simply devoid of value to the 'life' of a political community. Here the apparatus of national interest and security directed towards the stateless, refugees and immigrants constitutes a zone of exception where superfluous lives are captured within the juridical order through the sovereign suspension of the law. What is important to recognize, Agamben reminds us, is that 'misery and exclusion are not only economic or social concepts, but eminently political categories' (*ibid.*: 179).

Given the biopolitical and global modality of sovereign power, phenomena such as statelessness (and, as argued in the previous chapters, genocide and global poverty) are not simply 'naturally' occurring events external to the political realm. Rather, the globalized state system necessarily creates these phenomena within itself as the result of eminently violent political decisions.[11] If this is the case, if the designation, control and elimination of forms of existence that do not deserve to live the fully 'human' life is inextricably linked to sovereign power, then it will be possible to read the phenomenon of mass statelessness in a new, Arendtian way: as nothing less than a contemporary political evil.

From exclusion to containment: statelessness as global apartheid

Efforts have been made to address the problems identified by Arendt, but because these efforts remain configured by the imperatives of sovereign power, success in this direction has been limited at best. Considered in the context of the preceding discussion, it is clearly not coincidental that the contemporary international human rights regime continues to enshrine a set of universal human rights in conjunction with the power of sovereignty, while attempting to fashion specific protection regimes around the vulnerabilities and identities of particular groups, such as with the various refugee and statelessness treaties. The result is, to a large degree, a reinscription of the contradictions that have haunted human rights declarations throughout the age of the modern nation-state.

The 1948 UDHR, for example, contains several articles introduced because of the rise of the incidence of statelessness following the First and Second World Wars. Article 15 declares that '[e]veryone has the right to a nationality' and that '[n]o one shall be arbitrarily deprived of his nationality nor denied the right to change his nationality'. Further, Article 13 states that '[e]veryone has the right to leave any country, including his own, and to return to his country', while Article 14 asserts that '[e]veryone has the right to seek and enjoy in other countries asylum from persecution'. There are, however, several difficulties with these claims. First, because sovereign states have the self-authorized right to determine the conditions and criteria for the acquisition as well as termination of citizenship, they are supposed to remedy the problems of statelessness and denationalization of which they are the very source. Second, even the proscription of denationalization is conditional upon the sovereign determination of what constitutes an 'arbitrary' deprivation of rights, the standards of which can always be lowered in light of national security interests. Third, while the UDHR allows for a right of exit from a given state, it does not recognize a corresponding right of entry into another, which not only makes the asserted right of exit of dubious worth, but virtually guarantees the condition of statelessness for persons forcibly displaced from, or denationalized by, their country of origin. Finally, these rights are formulated in such a way as to reinforce the notion that nationality is a prerequisite to holding human rights, and thus that those without effective or legal nationality are necessarily rightless. This implication is at odds with Article 2 of the UDHR, which requires states to recognize the rights of all persons 'without distinction of any kind', including of 'national or social origin' or 'other status' (this non-discrimination clause is repeated in the 1966 International Covenants on Civil and Political Rights, and on Economic, Social and Cultural Rights).

Further international efforts directed towards refugees and statelessness occurred in the 1950s and 1960s. The Convention Relating to the Status of Refugees (Geneva

Convention) was adopted in 1951, and established a narrow definition of a refugee as a person who is outside his or her country of nationality or 'habitual residence' and is 'unable' or 'unwilling' to return to it solely because of a 'well-founded fear of being persecuted' for designated political reasons. Unfortunately, the Refugee Convention was drafted to address selectively the dilemma of refugees in Europe prior to 1 January 1951 (see Article 1, section B), and especially those fleeing the totalitarian regimes of the Eastern Bloc. It was not originally intended to embrace refugees in general, those displaced for 'non-political' reasons such as internal or international conflict, environmental disasters or economic deprivation, and there-fore it did not specifically address the situation of stateless persons (Marfleet 2006: 11, 146–47). Furthermore, the Convention does not articulate a formal right to asy-lum that states are obligated to fulfil; rather, a refugee is, in the first instance, merely an asylum *seeker* whose official (that is, 'legal') refugee status is decided by the potential host country upon its determination as to whether that person's fear of per-secution is indeed 'well-founded'.[12] In principle, states that receive refugees com-mit to protection of their basic rights and to the principle of *non-refoulement* (not to forcibly repatriate them to a country where they may be persecuted), although states may exempt themselves from adhering to this principle 'on grounds of national security or public order' (Articles 32 and 33).

In 1954 the Convention Relating to the Status of Stateless Persons was adopted, followed in 1961 by the Convention on the Reduction of Statelessness. The 1954 Convention was prompted by recognition that many stateless persons were not afforded protection by the Refugee Convention. Yet Article 1 of the 1954 Con-vention provides a purely legal definition of a stateless person as 'a person who is not considered as a national by any State under the operation of its law'. Thus the Convention's definition defines only the condition of *de jure* statelessness, apparently because the drafters of the Convention mistakenly believed that all *de facto* stateless persons were refugees (Batchelor 1995: 92). *De facto* stateless persons need not leave their country of nationality or habitual residence (such as when state succession occurs), and even if they do traverse an international border they may be unable to demonstrate either that they have been legally deprived of nationality (indeed, they may be unable to document their nationality at all), or that they have a well founded fear of persecution; if this should happen, neither the Refugee Convention nor the 1954 and 1961 Conventions may apply to them, further entrenching their statelessness (Weissbrodt and Collins 2006: 252).

While the 1954 Convention is devoted primarily to the status and protection of stateless persons, the 1961 Convention focuses on reducing statelessness by, for instance, encouraging signatory states to normalize the status of non-citizens in their territory by extending rights to them normally reserved for citizens, to elimi-nate domestic laws that may create stateless persons (such as *jus sanguinis* nation-ality laws which grant citizenship through paternal descent alone, or dependent nationality laws which link the nationality of a married woman to her spouse), to issue identity documents, and to facilitate naturalization as far as possible. Of course, neither the 1954 nor the 1961 treaty positively obligates contracting states to implement naturalizing remedies (Weissbrodt and Collins 2006: 272), and in any case, as we have seen, naturalization is always shadowed by the potential threat of denaturalization at politically opportune moments. These weaknesses are further exacerbated by the fact that the 1954 and 1961 Conventions have few state parties – just 63 and 35, respectively (as of October 2008) – and no associated treaty bodies have been established by the United Nations to monitor either of them.[13]

The inability of the human rights regime to 'solve' the burgeoning problem of stateless persons underscores Arendt's point that statelessness is fundamentally a problem not of *geographical* space, but of *political* space: the political condition that produces and characterizes stateless persons and refugees is the deprivation of human rights (Benhabib 2002; Nyers 2006: 17). The obvious remedial solution to statelessness is for states to grant nationality to all stateless persons, yet the power to grant nationality remains a sovereign prerogative immune to human rights ideals. Here the demarcations between who is, and who is not, included within the public space of a community are not territorial *per se*, but rather are ideologically, racially, economically and politically determined. Consequently, the phenomenon of statelessness is hardly accidental or aberrant. There are many ways in which forced displacement, dislocation, immigration, and other varieties of global border-crossing intersect, and numerous historical trends in how stateless persons, asylum-seekers and immigrants have been treated. A comprehensive analysis of these trends and modalities is beyond the aim of this chapter.[14] What I want to highlight instead is a single recent trend in the treatment of stateless persons and refugees that arguably signals the ascension rather than decline of the sovereign power of exclusion exposed by Arendt. This trend is, in the words of Jacob Stevens, a global 'strategy of containment' (Stevens 2006: 65).

The strategy of containment has been devised and enforced through numerous national and international mechanisms since the 1970s, when Western states began to conceive of the work of the UNHCR above all in terms of 'intervention in crisis zones of the Third World' rather than 'resettlement' of European refugees. These 'new' refugees were regarded as 'problem people', a collective source of anxiety and potential instability due to their 'irregularity' (Marfleet 2006: 150–51). The response has consisted not only of tightening border controls and immigration policies, but also of rationalizing the function of the UNHCR and other refugee organizations as 'emergency' or crisis relief. Thus, rather than focusing on granting asylum to refugees and stateless persons, integrating them legally into communities that will enable them to assert their rights, the new strategic turn is towards containment and mass repatriation without the restoration of rights. This approach is achieved primarily by means of vast networks of internment camps, 'safe havens', emergency centres, holding stations and detention facilities (Marfleet 2006: 151; Stevens 2006: 65–67). Here the logic of the internment camp identified by Arendt and Agamben, and the biopolitics of population management identified by Foucault, merge into new spaces of superfluousness. In these camps, zones, or spaces of superfluousness, undesirables who have been deemed to belong nowhere are condemned to inclusive exclusion. Dispossessed of their human rights and political agency, the stateless are simultaneously integrated within the decision-making authority of sovereign power and segregated from the normalized territory of potential host states.

These spaces of superfluousness are extraterritorial in that they may be situated either within or without the territorial borders of a sovereign state, yet in either case they are exempted from the jurisdiction of the 'normal' order of law. Perhaps the most well known recent example of such a space is the camp at Guantánamo Bay established by the US government as a centrepiece of its 'War on Terror'. Since early 2002, the USA has interned several hundred suspected Taliban fighters and al-Qaida members at several camps at the Guantánamo Bay base, on the basis of a 'state of emergency' military order which enables the executive branch to detain non-US citizens anywhere in the world and imprison them indefinitely within an extraterritorial space where US and international law are suspended.[15] Yet more far-reaching examples of the strategy of containment abound. The Australian government's two-track policy of preventive interception and detention is notable here. This policy was crafted in the aftermath of the 2001 *Tampa* 'crisis', in which more than 400 Afghan refugees in a sinking fishing boat were rescued by a Norwegian cargo ship that then attempted to offload them at Christmas Island. After the *Tampa* was denied permission to enter Australia's territorial waters, Special Forces boarded the ship and the refugees were transported by warship to the island of Nauru, where the Australian government established an offshore detention centre in which to hold and process asylum-seekers away from the territory of the Australian state (Howard 2003).

Following this incident the Australian government led by John Howard formally inaugurated the so-called 'Pacific Solution'. This policy, which remained in place between 2001 and 2008, was designed to intercept and prevent boats carrying asylum-seekers from entering Australian territorial waters, and divert asylum-seekers to detention camps established on several South Pacific island nations (Oxfam Australia 2002). One of the first components of this new policy was passage of the Migration Amendment (Excision from Migration Zone) Act.[16] This act excised a number of external territories (including Christmas Island) from Australia's migration zone, which meant that asylum-seekers ('unauthorized arrivals') arriving in these territories had no right to apply for a visa, had no recourse to Australian courts, and could be transported to offshore detention facilities. A cornerstone of the 'Pacific Solution' was the policy of mandatory detention. According to this policy, all 'unauthorized arrivals' on Australian territory were compulsorily imprisoned within one of the detention facilities established throughout Australia and the Pacific islands. Asylum-seekers could be detained indefinitely, the facilities were exempted from judicial review, and children, including infants, were detained, although often separated from close family members.

The Howard government also introduced a new type of visa, the 'Temporary Protection Visa' (TPV), to replace the Permanent Protection Visa (PPV) previously given to asylum-seekers, on the grounds that the PPVs 'were far more generous than required by Australia's international obligations'. TPVs – which were abolished in August 2008 by the new government led by Kevin Rudd – allowed visa-holders to remain in Australia for up to three years; during this period they could be deported at any time by the Australian government, and when the visa expired they had to reapply for a further TPV, which again provided the government with the opportunity to revoke their refugee status and deport them if they were 'no longer in need of Australia's protection'. In August 2003, the TPV policy was made retroactive to supersede all PPVs granted prior to that date (Phillips 2004). For seven years 'temporary protection' was the only status granted to *all* refugees in Australia, including those who had already been through a full asylum determination in light of the 1951 Refugee Convention (see Human Rights Watch 2006).

Several recent decisions by the High Court of Australia further strengthened the sovereign power of containment and exception. In *Behrooz v. Secretary, Department of Immigration and Multicultural and Indigenous Affairs* (August 2004), the High Court held that the conditions of immigration detention are irrelevant to the question of whether the detention is lawful, and thus that even inhumane conditions of detention cannot excuse escape from administrative detention centres. In *Al-Kateb v. Godwin* (August 2004), the High Court supported the government's argument that the 1958 Migration Act authorizes indefinite detention of unlawful non-citizens ('aliens'), including those whose asylum application had failed. In other words, a stateless person can be held in an immigration detention indefinitely, including for life, even if he or she wishes to leave Australia.[17] Finally, in *Re Woolley; Ex parte Applicants M276/2003* (October 2004), the High Court held that the *Al-Kateb* decision applies to all aliens, whether adults or children, therefore 'there is no constitutional limitation on the immigration detention of children' (Australian Government 2007). According to then Prime Minister John Howard, such sovereign authority is justified inasmuch as 'It is in the national interest that we have the power ... to prevent, *beyond any argument*, people infringing on the sovereignty of this country' (Kelly 2001; emphasis added). Although the 'Pacific Solution' has been abandoned by the Rudd government, the crucial lesson of this case – that the fate of stateless persons remains subject to the calculations of sovereign power – attests to the permanent potential for superfluousness.

A similar system of containment and exclusion has been assembled across Europe and the UK. With regard to 'irregular' migration, the European Union has increasingly focused on extraterritorial policing, incarceration and deportation of asylum-seekers, and hundreds of detention centres have been established in European Union states (Marfleet 2006: 4, 55). The resulting system of containment and exclusion has been referred to as 'Fortress Europe' (Geddes 2000). In 2003, for instance, the United Kingdom proposed 'a radically new approach to delivering the reduction of asylum seeker numbers' based on two types of 'zones of protection': 'regional protection zones' located outside Europe, which would address asylum claims arising from regional conflicts or natural disasters; and 'transit processing centres' located along the borders of the European Union, which would process asylum claims without asylum-seekers travelling to the countries in which they want to seek asylum.[18] As with Australia's 'Pacific Solution', this proposal has a dual effect: first, it incapacitates the ability of asylum-seekers to apply for refugee status since EU states are obligated to investigate asylum claims only when an application is lodged on the territory of a member state; second, it creates a mechanism for lowering the standards for repatriation and facilitates mass deportation by maintaining 'transit' camps outside European borders. According to one report, what is most disturbing about the recent EU asylum directives is their 'abandonment of the principle of *non-refoulement*' and their 'declared and expressed intention to return people from EU states without examining their claim to asylum' (Schuster 2005: 38).

The strategy to keep potential seekers of asylum at a distance has had extremely adverse consequences for asylum-seekers from Africa, for instance. The Spanish exclaves of Ceuta and Melilla in Northern Africa, and the Canary Islands off the north-west coast of Africa, have become key destinations for refugees seeking to reach European territory and apply for asylum. In response, NATO has installed six-metre-high barbed-wire border fences around Ceuta and Melilla, which are patrolled by Spanish and Moroccan security forces. In September 2005, at least 14 African asylum-seekers were shot dead and hundreds wounded by security forces while attempting to scale the fences and seek refuge. Thousands more are arrested each month and deported to Morocco, where they are imprisoned under inhumane conditions. As an alternative, thousands of asylum-seekers attempt to reach the Canaries or to cross the Mediterranean in small wooden or inflatable boats. Traffickers commonly chain the hands and feet of people on the boats to prevent excess movement, which means they are completely helpless if the boats capsize (Milborn 2007). The Red Cross has estimated that between November 2005 and February 2006, at least 1200 people died *en route* to the Canary Islands, and the International Centre on Migration Policy Development estimates that at least 10,000 Africans have died in the past decade trying to reach the European Union via sea routes (ICMPD 2004: 8; Wynter 2006). As if these consequences were insufficient, the Spanish government has installed a system of radar and night-vision cameras across the Mediterranean, forming a 350-mile 'electronic wall' to detect and interdict the vessels of asylum-seekers from Africa and prevent them from setting foot on European soil (Marfleet 2006: 254). Contrary to the stated aim of 'protection' zones, the increased militarization of European border control has increased the desperation, vulnerability and degradation of refugees.[19] This has led to a sharp increase in the number of people dying as they try to enter EU states, as well as the systematic rejection of the human rights of asylum-seekers.[20]

As Matthew Gibney explains, 'While variations remain across countries, in the last decade those seeking refuge have increasingly faced the prospect of detention, denial of the right to work, limitations or exclusions from welfare benefits, diminishing rights to appeal negative decisions, and, ultimately, deportation'. For that reason, Gibney adds, 'woe betide those who arrive in Western states claiming to be a refugee' (Gibney 2006: 141). Recent policies and practices towards the displaced strategically (re)define refugees and stateless persons solely through an exclusionary process which places them outside the community of 'privileged' rights-holders yet within the exceptional realm of sovereign power, constituting them as superfluous human beings in a state of permanent limbo – despite the fact that each of the countries mentioned above are signatories to all the major international human rights treaties proclaiming the 'inherent dignity' and 'inalienable rights' of all persons. The strategy of inclusive exclusion serves ultimately to buttress states' denial of responsibility to those outside their borders.

This strategy may also be viewed as an attempt to exploit racist and xenophobic tendencies in order to shape perceptions about stateless persons and refugees as undesirable 'others' seeking to squander the resources of the state and exploit the good will of the nation, thereby corrupting the health and welfare of the nation-state. Precisely because of that, as Foucault suggested, sovereign power can claim that society and the population must be defended against the 'biological enemies' that threaten it. In this way the asylum process serves predominantly a police rather than a humanitarian function. This position further enhances the notion that state frontiers are a 'natural' boundary separating an essentialist and pre-given 'us' from 'them', whereby sovereignty is premised upon the classification, regulation, restriction and exclusion of refugees as threatening 'interlopers' and 'problems'. But the paradoxical manner of this exclusion, as Arendt recognized, entails insertion within the interior of sovereign power.

From this perspective the nexus of sovereign power and statelessness can be aptly characterized as a virulent system of global apartheid which establishes a permanent underclass of superfluous human beings. One of the core functions of sovereign power – the creation and coercive enforcement of national identity boundaries – now takes place within a global context where frontiers are dynamically 'managed' in extraterritorial spaces and through deterritorialized forms of rule. Even as the nation-state has been reconfigured in the global age it nevertheless operates so as to draw new lines of demarcation for maintaining segregation between 'insiders' and alien 'outsiders', thereby perpetuating inequality of rights and social, economic, and political status. According to Anthony Richmond (1994: 206–17), the current treatment of stateless persons, refugees, and immigrants predominantly from poorer countries closely resembles the former apartheid system of South Africa because it systemically discriminates on the basis of birthplace, race, or ethnicity; differentially assigns rights (or denies them altogether) according to the naturalization of identity; employs state authority to militarize borders; forcibly expels people to zones and camps ('homelands') of containment and detention; and justifies coercive exclusion of 'others' in the name of security for a relatively homogeneous population.[21]

Étienne Balibar similarly argues that global apartheid has arrived with the transformation of the international system into a global order which nevertheless retains the nation-state as its core political and administrative unit. Following Arendt's lead, Balibar diagnoses the paradoxes that arise as state power becomes increasingly relayed through global networks. Most fundamentally he suggests: 'At the moment at which humankind becomes economically and, to some extent, culturally "united", it is violently divided "biopolitically"' (Balibar 2004: 130). For Balibar, the recent processes of European unification reveal contradictions between the universalist ideal of human rights and the practice of (European) citizenship as both a model of cosmopolitan inclusion and a mechanism of exclusion applied to immigrants, refugees, and stateless persons. The main problem is that inclusion remains structurally tied to national identity. On the one hand, the birth of the European Union brought with it the new category of 'European citizens' and the promise of the transnationalization of rights. On the other hand, while the 1991 Maastricht Treaty introduced the legal notion of a common European citizenship, according to the terms of the 1997 Treaty of Amsterdam this citizenship is reserved only to those persons who already possess the nationality of a member state. In this way the EU has further entrenched the differentiation of the entire population of Europe into citizens, or the 'European people' proper, and aliens, a class which paradoxically includes 'the immigrant population permanently residing in Europe' (Balibar 2004: 122). In basing the possession of European citizenship rights upon prior national belonging – while institutionally retaining each state's right to deter-mine its sovereign control of nationality criteria at the same time as 'harmonizing' Europe-wide refugee and asylum policies – the EU has constructed a new form of identity and citizenship that preserves rather than overcomes its colonial past.

Parallel to the historical example of apartheid, contemporary Europe includes within its borders tens of thousands of 'insiders officially considered outsiders', viewed biopolitically as a 'minority' population whose family compositions, ways of life and so forth must be controlled (or moulded) to protect the 'qual-ity' of the existing dominant national community. The intersection of immigra-tion policy with family politics in conjunction with the creation of European citizenship illustrates the 'contradictory and evolutionary pattern of "European citizenship-*cum*-apartheid" as a global-local problem (Balibar 2004: 124). For Balibar this institutionalized segregation of the European population not only establishes a permanent underclass in European states and cities but more broadly symbolizes how the globalized world is steadily divided into 'life zones and death zones' within cities, states, and regions across the globe (Balibar 2004: 126). Whether in Europe or elsewhere in the globalized world, whole classes of people – including refugees, asylum-seekers, and migrant workers – become *de facto* if not *de jure* stateless persons as the mutating borders of exclusion continually deprive individuals and communities of the ability to effectively exercise their civil, politi-cal, social, and economic rights. The destructive tendency of global apartheid to segregate certain groups of people into 'death zones' where human rights have been withdrawn is, Balibar contends, a process which reproduces 'populations that are not likely to be productively used or exploited but are always already *superfluous*, and therefore can be only eliminated either through "political" or "natural" means' (Balibar 2004: 128). As a superfluous population, stateless persons are 'neither assimilated and integrated nor immediately eliminated' but forced to remain in institutionalized 'limbo' spaces which serve as the preparatory conditions of possibility for their eventual elimination (Balibar 2005: 31–34).

The containment, detention, and segregation of stateless persons and refugees as practices of global apartheid calls for recognition of a political principle con-tained in Arendt's work which is necessarily correlative to the right to have rights: freedom of movement. What is most at stake politically for Arendt with regard to statelessness is that the deprivation of rights which accompanies this condition amounts to the destruction of the agency and dignity of the human person. To be made stateless is to be denied the capacity to act and speak in a polity where others regard one as an equal, and where one's actions and speech can assume a meaningful political presence. One can be the bearer of human rights only when one belongs to, and is claimed by a political community which recognizes one's reciprocal claim upon it. Inasmuch as the stateless are deprived of a political way of life they are deprived 'not of the right to freedom, but of the right to action; not of the right to think whatever they please, but of the right to opinion' (OT: 376). This emphasis on agency points towards what I suggest is a vital connection between the right to have rights and freedom of movement. According to Arendt freedom of movement 'is historically the oldest and also the most elementary' of all human liberties (MDT: 9). In the first instance this is because being able 'to depart for where we will is the prototypical gesture of being free', just as 'limitation of freedom of movement has from time immemorial been the precondition for enslavement' (MDT: 9). But there is a further sense in which freedom of movement is essential to the right to have rights. Arendt stresses that freedom of movement 'is also *the indispensable condition* for action' (MDT: 9; emphasis added). Further, because 'both action and thought occur in the form of movement', it is clear that freedom of movement 'underlies both' (MDT: 9).

Hence, as 'the indispensable condition for action', the right to have rights cannot be said to be properly guaranteed and exercised without a corresponding guarantee of freedom of movement.[22] It is for this reason that restrictions on freedom of movement serve as one of the unmistakable mechanisms for the production of rightlessness, most egregiously in the case of stateless persons and refugees. Similarly, forced displacement, *refoulement*, rendition, and any repatriation that is not legitimately voluntary – that is, made under conditions where the person 'making that choice is currently in possession of his or her civil rights' (Stevens 2006: 67) – perpetuate the condition of rightlessness through deprivation of the freedom of movement. All of this can be viewed in light of Arendt's critique of sovereignty. For Arendt, it will be recalled, sovereignty represents a mistaken conception of freedom precisely because sovereignty seeks to fix and delimit movement as the form of contingency and spontaneity characteristic of action and speech. Yet action, she says, 'always establishes relationships and therefore has an inherent tendency to force open all limitations and cut across all boundaries' (HC: 190). Conceived as 'uncompromising self-sufficiency and mastership' (HC: 234), sovereignty responds to the contingency of political action by asserting the absolute dominance of the sovereign will over the realm of human affairs and thus over the freedom of movement of the plurality of individuals and groups inhabiting the earth. Consequently, sovereign power requires a condition of inequality for its very functioning: it must place limits upon freedom of movement and resort to mechanisms of exclusion if it is to assert its supremacy over people and territory. The sovereignty of the modern nation-state is thus placed on a politically disastrous collision course with freedom of movement and the right to have rights.

Freedom of movement assumes its place alongside the right to have rights because it is a condition needed for the creation of the common world within which we may appear to one another as equals.[23] In reality there is, of course, a plurality of public spheres which are bounded in the sense of demarcating the dimensions of the realm of collective political action as distinct from those of private life. But under Arendt's remarkably cosmopolitan conception of freedom as non-sovereignty the boundaries that mark and preserve the space of political action are, to borrow from Benhabib's argument for immigration rights, 'porous': they are open rather than closed, inclusive rather than exclusive, rights-enhancing rather than rights-denying (Benhabib 2004: 93, 221). Indeed, the very 'worldliness' of the public realm depends upon the reception of and encounter with others in all their plurality. Arendt sees this space as having an integral part to play in the humanization of a world 'common to *all* people' (MDT: 16; emphasis added). In her discussion of *humanitas* or humaneness, Arendt explains that humanity is not a naturally occurring fact but a precarious political reality which must be brought into being and constantly renewed through our speech and action in encounters with others. It is in actively humanizing the world that 'we learn to be human' (MDT: 25).

Humanitas is disclosed principally 'in a readiness to share the world with other men' (MDT: 25). The manifestation of *humanitas* takes the interconnected forms of civic friendship and hospitality. Civic friendship, Arendt explains, is a kind of political togetherness in which we relate ourselves to others in such a way as to preserve our plurality and distinctiveness. Through relationships of civic friendship we both acknowledge the opinions and actions of others as meaningful but also question and contest ceaselessly the grounds of their opinions and the meaning of their actions through 'incessant and continual discourse' (MDT: 30). This form of political friendship actively establishes a realistic sense of solidarity with others in order to renew and reaffirm plurality, in contrast to a sentimental (and passive) fraternity of 'brotherliness' that obliterates 'all distinctions' (MDT: 30).[24] Hospitality is an 'openness to others' which serves as a precondition for the humanization of the world (MDT: 15).[25] This is because welcoming and encountering others – including foreigners, 'strangers', exiles, refugees, and the stateless – exhibits a sense of responsibility to (cosmopolitan) reality. *Humanitas* has 'not lost the solid ground of reality', Arendt writes, as long as it remains faithful to the 'infinite plurality' of human beings and their 'most elementary' freedom to move about the earth (MDT: 23, 31). In contrast, the sovereign ban on plurality and free movement will always result in 'a loss of humanness along with the forsaking of reality' (MDT: 23). Arendt describes the broad political significance of freedom of movement as follows:

> This freedom of movement, then – whether as the freedom to depart and begin something new and unheard-of or as the freedom to interact in speech with many others and experience the diversity that the world always is in its totality – most certainly was and is ... the substance and meaning of all things political. In this sense, politics and freedom are identical, and wherever this kind of freedom does not exist, there is no political space in the true sense
>
> (PP: 129)

The struggle to control people's movement, their unpredictable impulse to freedom, is an attempt to render them politically impotent and deny them the capacity to break 'into the world as an "infinite improbability"', to create their 'own worldly space' where they 'can come out of hiding'. And yet, Arendt stresses, 'it is precisely this infinitely improbable which actually constitutes the very texture of everything we call real' (BPF: 169). While discriminatory barriers to the movement of refugee and stateless populations might well dramatically reduce the number of people who will seek to enter a particular sovereign space, they do so at the human cost of both imposing an unrealistic view of the world (treating mobility and plurality as aberrant, alien, and threatening) and contributing further to the violent conditions which generate forced migration and refugee flight. Thus, to follow Arendt's advice, any doctrine 'that in principle barred the possibility of friendship between two human beings' and thus the opportunity for free passage and asylum globally must be rejected (MDT: 29). This way of framing the inhumanity of the sovereign power to exclude and contain enables us to understand the specific political evil of statelessness as nothing less than the categorical unwillingness to share the world with others, an unwillingness so extreme it risks destruction of our very sense of reality.

Conclusion

The importance of Arendt for political thinking today is in continuing the critique of the contradictory reliance upon the categories of inherent, inalienable, or natural rights within a global system of sovereign states. The right to have rights is the right to membership in a political community, and its meaning and value can only derive from each person actually experiencing the political form of life proper to human beings. By thinking of human rights in metaphysical terms – as something we possess independently of membership in a political community – we fail to fully grasp the crisis of human rights exemplified by stateless persons, a crisis that has grown more rather than less acute since the time of Arendt's intervention.

Arendt's attempt to come to grips with the degradation that results from this abject loss of one's place in the common world provoked her critique of sovereignty as the ultimate arbiter and delimiter of movement. I have sought to show in this chapter that the exclusionary logic of the globalized sovereign state continues to define in advance the existence of a class of human beings who do not belong, because they lack the illusive national, racial, ethnic, or religious identity that supposedly undergirds it. Such people are violently thrown back upon their 'merely human' status. What the conventional approach to the problem of stateless persons misses, then, is the perverse symbiosis that exists between sovereignty and statelessness: statelessness *is* only insofar as the sovereign power of exclusion overdetermines the world we share with a plurality of others. Arendt's account of rightlessness complicates the usual story. Statelessness is not simply a superstructural humanitarian problem but a recurring form of global apartheid constituted by the state and sovereign power.

Arendt's analysis of human rights, sovereignty, and statelessness relocates the focus of attention back to the political and the necessity of membership. Every stateless person is a rightless nonmember as the result of a state's action, or inaction as the case may be. When a state is faced with a stateless person, when it encounters his or her human aspiration to exercise freedom of movement, it is faced with a clear political choice: to include or to exclude this person. Insofar as the decision is exclusion, then a state is complicit in the perpetuation of rightlessness and the misery of those who are made into the type of superfluous human beings put into internment camps by their 'friends.' In ceasing to belong to any rights-guaranteeing community whatsoever, the stateless person stands in stark contrast to the citizen included in the public sphere. Whereas the latter become fully human in a common world shared with others, the former are alienated from this world and lose their relevance to others; they are, paradoxically, stripped of something fundamental to their human dignity exactly when they are 'nothing but human beings' (JW: 272).

To guarantee the right to have rights we must begin to sever citizenship from nationality and rearticulate the state as an institution of legality rather than sovereignty. In constructing the state as an 'open society', Arendt argues, 'the state knows only citizens no matter of what nationality; its legal order is open to all who happen to live on its territory' (EU: 208). The primary function of the state as protector of equality in law and rights for all of those who happen to live there is, she adds, 'not at all affected through the number of nationalities' present (EU: 210). To do anything less is to maintain the undeserved but avoidable political evil of turning the stateless into outlaws, excluded citizens of nowhere condemned to 'civil death and political silencing' (Benhabib 2004: 215).

4 Effacing the political

The evil of neoliberal globalization

Globalization, with its contradictory and powerful processes, has become the indispensable frame for reflecting on both our historical present and the future that we may invent from it. Cast in the widest of terms, globalization is equally inclusive of changing modes of governance, new forms of cultural hybridization, and subjective experiences of spatial deterritorialization and temporal compression. More pointedly, globalization refers to the system of contemporary neoliberal global market conditions, in its contrast with the declining fortunes of social democratic economic regulations and social policies. Yet if globalization remains the horizon within which we must think the present and future, it is nevertheless a phenomenon that does not go completely unchallenged. The dominant economic forces of neoliberalism are confronted regularly by passionate and sometimes militant activists associated with global civil society and the alternative globalization movement. As though attempting to counter this challenge, however, neoliberal globalization is progressively entrenching itself by defining the very ends and means of politics today. All politics is now global – but in which sense of 'the global', and what is meant by 'the political'? In the present chapter I seek to show that Arendt's work helps to illuminate how, even as globalization shapes the horizon of current political thought and action, it does so at the risk of drawing that horizon ever tighter; it is less certain that the concept of 'globalization' continues to express transformative potentials rather than functioning as a token of the very effacement of the political. Globalization has become not only the political foundation of the present, but also the suspect guardian of the future of the political itself. In this chapter I argue that neoliberal economic globalization is a form of political evil. Whereas the examples of political evil examined in the previous chapters take aim at specific, concrete persons, neoliberal economic globalization takes aim at the political realm.

I began in Chapter 1 by presenting a reading of Arendt's cosmopolitan sensibilities, and put forward the argument that this reading implies that the process of translating horrifying atrocities into politically intelligible and legally sanctionable crimes provides a new juridical idiom for resisting evil actions. In the second and third chapters, I spelt out how some of the severe and widespread wrongs arising from, and normalized within, the global political–economic order – namely extreme global poverty and statelessness – are forms of political evil in an Arendtian sense, insofar as these atrocities make vast segments of humanity superfluous. In this final chapter, I want to return to a discussion of the global political–economic order by looking into the ideational bases and interests of neoliberal globalization. This will allow me to show in more detail how the ideological ascendancy of neoliberalism and its 'social Darwinist reconfiguration of priorities, policies and outcomes' within the entirety of public affairs (Gill 2005: 56) functions not only to make millions of human beings superfluous, but also to cause the political realm itself to atrophy accordingly. I will turn first to Arendt, and in particular to Arendt's attempt to introduce the definition of 'the political' as the foremost dimension of free collective action constitutive of the human condition, which is to be distinguished from the dimensions of biological and social necessity. I will go on to consider the conceptual and historical origins of the neoliberal order that increasingly has been penetrating every region of the globe. Finally, after exploring Arendt's account of modern ideological thinking, I will argue that neoliberal globalization as ideology and practice represents the relentless global extension of 'the social' that Arendt viewed as virtually fatal to human freedom in modernity. The main contemporary effect of the social in the guise of neoliberal globalization is to 'naturalize' all political–economic relations and thereby normalize the appearance of private interests in the public realm. The political evil of neoliberalism is to depoliticize human affairs as such, to render the worldly spaces between people apolitical and devoid of care. In short, because politics for neoliberalism amounts to little more than acting against others within a metahistorical frame of socioeconomic inevitability, rather than properly taking place among political equals who act with each other for the sake of a common world, neoliberal globalization threatens to make the political itself superfluous.

The political and the social

In 1958, Arendt published *The Human Condition*, the book that sets out most fully her particular understanding of the political and its distinctive meaning and importance within human experience. In this dense work, Arendt attempts to 'think what we are doing' from 'the vantage point of our newest experiences and our most recent fears' (HC: 5). One of these experiences was the advent of space exploration, in light of which the cosmopolitan principle that the ever-shrinking earth is the shared home of all human beings assumed a tangible, and in some respects profoundly disturbing, reality for our troubled times. Many commentators have taken *The Human Condition* to be Arendt's 'nostalgic' turn back to the Greeks, a romantic evocation of a heroically glorious past (see Euben 2000; Tsao 2002b). But these interpretations, I think, fail to grasp the character of Arendt's work as a whole, and consequently the place of this particular text within it. As Mary Dietz rightly points out, *The Human Condition* is actually a 'profound response to the trauma inflicted upon humanity' by the Holocaust and the extreme forms of political evil that shattered the twentieth century (Dietz 2000: 90). It is an attempt to comprehend the reality of a late-modern world threatened by the prospect of the extermination of humanity and, in response, to convey the existential significance of political freedom as a condition of what it means to be a human person. Arendt therefore is especially concerned in *The Human Condition* with the fate of human affairs in the modern world, that is, the realm of political existence, the contours of which have been defined not only by the spectre of genocidal states, but also by the 'first atomic explosions' and our 'ability to destroy all organic life on earth' (HC: 6, 3). Each of these world-defining events defies traditional standards of morality, law and politics, and poses fundamental challenges to thinking and political action in a globalizing age.

Yet physical destruction is not the only, and perhaps not even the most pernicious, threat to the world of human affairs. The realm of the political itself may in fact be devastated to such a degree that, while biological life continues, the conditions for a distinctively human life are gradually extinguished. The danger that casts a particularly long shadow over modernity, Arendt tells us in 'Introduction *into* Politics', is that 'politics may vanish entirely from the world' (PP: 96). With this in mind, *The Human Condition* should be understood as a kind of rebuke and subversion of all those modern forms of evil that jeopardize the possibility of acting together politically. On this basis, Arendt attempts to shed light on those elements of human activity that make the political uniquely distinct from what Arendt calls 'the social'. The primary difference between the political and the social is that whereas the former arises from and is sustained by a mode of free political activity made possible only by human plurality, the latter emerges from and is perpetuated through the intractable belief in inevitability and homogeneity secreted into public affairs on the back of 'laws' of nature and historical necessity. My approach to Arendt's understanding of the political thus takes seriously, as Jerome Kohn writes, that she 'discovered the meaning and importance of the political by witnessing its negation in the multiform linkages of evil that were manifest in her lifetime' (Kohn 2000: 114).

In reconsidering the human condition in the midst of modernity's threats to the political, Arendt argues for a hierarchy of three modes of fundamental human activity through which existence is manifest: as biological life-forms, as labouring beings, and as political actors (HC: 7–9). The activities of labour, work and action collectively compose what Arendt refers to as the *vita activa*.[1] Within this triad, labouring is necessary for maintaining the life of the individual and the biological survival of the species, and is realized in the activity of *animal laborans* – human beings as an animal species. Because labour is governed by the dictates of physiological life, and occurs strictly through the physical relationship of the human body with nature, it is characterized by solitude – the absence of others. In comparison, work is the activity through which humans produce an artificial world of durable objects that supplement our natural environment. Here the activity of *homo faber* – human beings as inventive and practical workers – supplants that of *animal laborans*. Work introduces both a basic social condition, through the interpersonal exchange of technical knowledge and products, and the fabrication of tangible 'worldliness' itself. The products of work guarantee the permanence and stability without which the human world would not possible, and it is this durability of use objects which gives the world its 'objectivity' or relative independence from those who produce and use them (HC: 137).

While consumer goods and use objects provide a material stability to the human world by generating a permanence that exceeds the technical activities of work, and perhaps even the lives of those individuals who produced them, such objects are themselves inadequate to fully humanize the world. 'In order to be what the world is always meant to be, a home for men during their life on earth', writes Arendt, 'the human artifice must be a place *fit for action and speech*, for activities … of an entirely different nature from the manifold activities of fabrication by which the world itself and all things in it are produced' (HC: 173–74; emphasis added). Neither labour nor work is oriented towards creating and sustaining the relationships among unique individuals that make human existence meaningful. Arendt argues that only action freely undertaken with others is capable of generating the 'fabric of human relationships and affairs' by which the world becomes distinctively humanized (HC: 183). This is because humans act and interact with each other directly, 'without the intermediary of things or matter' (HC: 7), only within a political realm. Action is an incomparable feature of the human condition in that it depends exclusively on the continued presence of other humans and thus 'corresponds to the human condition of plurality' (HC: 7). Human plurality, the basic condition through which action and speech are possible, has the dual character of equality and distinction: 'If men were not equal, they could neither understand each other and those who came before them nor plan for the future and foresee the needs of those who will come after them. If men were not distinct … they would need neither speech nor action to make themselves understood' (HC: 175–76).

Given these differentiations, Arendt assigns the activities of labour and work to the private realm, while action is exclusive to the public realm, or the realm of the political. While the private realm is the domain of biological necessity, the public realm is the domain of human freedom. This is because to act 'means to take an initiative to begin' something new 'which cannot be expected from whatever may have happened before' (HC: 178). In Arendt's terms, action is the 'actualization of the human condition of natality', of bringing something or someone uniquely new into the world (HC: 178). For this reason, action is never equivalent to the repetitive, laborious effort of providing for biological survival or to the practical, efficient work of fabricating objects for use in the material world of durable things. Action and speech are the ways in which human beings appear to each other and disclose 'who they are', simultaneously creating and revealing their 'unique personal identities' (HC: 179). Action, in its most general sense, is an expressive activity mediated through language and the plurality of opinions, and accomplished through public dialogue, debate, persuasion and dissuasion rather than technical expertise, force or violence (HC: 26). That means that the becoming and disclosure of the unique human person requires a 'space of appearance' as the precondition for action within a formally constituted public realm (HC: 199).

As Arendt's analysis of the political proceeds, she traces the genesis of the private and public realms in the classical world. For the Greeks, the private realm was the realm of the household (*oikia*), the family, and whatever essentially was one's own rather than shared with others (HC: 24). It was based on biological relationships of kinship and tribe, and was characterized by a form of absolute rule where heads of households (the Roman *paterfamilias*) exercised despotic power over wives, children and slaves. People lived together because they were subordinated to necessity in terms of biological needs (food, shelter, security against common enemies). Necessity motivated all activity within the household: the *paterfamilias* provided nourishment and security in the face of threats internal (slave revolts) and external (other rulers who wanted to destroy a particular home and family); women were subject to heads of household and the 'urgency of life' through childbearing; and slaves provided domestic labour for maintenance of family life (HC: 30–31). The private realm was a zone of pure inequality: to be *paterfamilias* meant to rule; to be another member of the household meant to be ruled. The head of the household was not bound by any law or form of justice. Assuring the maintenance of domestic order, he exercised a total power over life and death. The private realm thus represents the deprivation of the most important of human capabilities, the capacity to initiate joint action independently of 'the unending chain of means and ends' (HC: 154). Such a reading suggests that an individual becomes human, politically speaking, only when equality and agency are introduced into a domain beyond the private realm of natural necessity.

In contrast to the private realm of the household, the public realm of action is the common world shared in the presence of others, yet separated from the dictates of biological necessity and physical survival. Arendt explains that the public realm was first embodied in the political life of the *polis*, and relied upon the use of speech and persuasion through the arts of politics and rhetoric. In Aristotle's famous formulation, the public realm was the domain of political life (*bios politikos*) exercised through action (*praxis*) and speech (*lexis*) (HC: 25). The citizens practiced the political way of life by participating in the public affairs of the *polis*. Crucially, liberating oneself from the necessities of the private realm was the condition for access to the public realm (HC: 30–31). Only one who had mastered the affairs of the household and family would have the ability to participate in the realm of freedom and equality without coercion. Those in the public realm were equals, in the sense that one neither ruled over one's peers nor was ruled by them (*isonomia* or 'no-rule'), and all were free to express their opinions. Here, the power of speech replaced the force and violence utilized in the private realm. The free and equal citizens of the *polis* were opposed to relationships of domination and ownership within the public realm. Consequently the 'good life', which Aristotle identified with political action, signified the liberation of the human being from the spheres of *animal laborans* and *homo faber*, and thus an opening up of a human mode of existence that 'was no longer bound to the biological life process' (HC: 37). In other words, political life in the *polis* was meant to recognize and affirm a political actor's autonomy and equality and to counter the 'unfreedoms', in Amartya Sen's (1999) phrase, imposed by biological life.

Arendt emphasizes that there is a mutual link between action and being together within the public realm. Although first formulated by Aristotle's notion of man as a 'political animal', this relationship was subsequently mistranslated into the notion that man is a 'social animal'. For Aristotle, man is *zōon politikon*, while for Thomas Aquinas man is *animal socialis* (HC: 23). This substitution of the political by the social reflects a subtle but nonetheless decisive difference between the Greek and Roman interpretation of 'togetherness' in the public realm. For the Romans, the Latin word *societas* expressed the undeniably crucial fact that 'man cannot live outside the company of men', and thus that human beings are by nature social (HC: 24). Yet the Greeks viewed the fact of dependence as a natural condition that the human species shared with other forms of animal life; it was not a *human* condition *per se*. Thus there is a substantial difference between the Greek *polis* as a space for the affirmation of the political life of citizens who view one another as free and equal precisely because they organize themselves through action that is not merely a response to natural necessity, and the Roman conception of society as the pre-existing natural association within which people ally themselves for specifically useful or necessary purposes. It is precisely through politics that citizens could escape from the dictates of natural association and biological life. Perhaps more importantly, however, Arendt points out that mistakenly equating the political with the social – or more accurately, reducing the political to the social – leads to the reinsertion of inequality as an 'inherent' feature of (sovereign) politics. Thomas Aquinas, for instance, equates the power and function of the head of household to that of the ruler. According to this analogy, the ruler stands to the ruled as the *paterfamilias* stands to family and slaves. The Greeks rejected the transposition of 'natural' inequality into the political domain, however, and regarded speaking and acting together as the antithesis of 'absolute, uncontested rule' (HC: 28).

According to Arendt, the emergence of 'the social', and of the modern conception of society as the locus of social activity and interests, was precipitated by the gradual blurring of boundaries between the private and the political (HC: 38).[2] Indeed, Arendt argues that the social is a kind of hybrid phenomenon that introduced the satisfaction of immediate biological needs and the manufacture of material objects into the public sphere (HC: 35). While Arendt acknowledges that the erosion of the distinction between a private and a public sphere of life is of ancient origin, she suggests that 'the emergence of the social realm, which is neither private nor public, strictly speaking, is a relatively new phenomenon whose origin coincided with the emergence of the modern age and which found its political form in the nation-state' (HC: 28).[3] In the modern age, the concerns of natural necessity have gradually displaced the freedom of joint political action within the public realm, and have subjected the political to the dominance of the social. A fundamental factor that contributed to the promotion of the social was the subordination of the public sphere to the private interests of individuals. The means by which this long historical process occurred were varied, ranging from the development of private artistic activities (poetry, music, the novel) to the normalization of behaviour through disciplines and the conformism of social groups (the general will, bureaucracy, behaviouralism, scientism, economics and the 'invisible hand', statistics, mass society, class interests, the public interest). Arendt argues that the phenomenon of social conformism and the 'leveling demands of the social' (HC: 39) is characteristic of modernity from the eighteenth century onwards. Social conformism has led, on the one hand, to the political becoming simply a container for domestic and therefore generalizable interests and, on the other hand, to social relationships shrouding the plurality of political thought and action because of the desire for uniform or conventional standards of behaviour. Indeed, with the rise of the social, Arendt notes, 'behavior has replaced action as the foremost mode of human relationships' (HC: 41).

Arendt contends that the confusion between the political and the social culminates in modernity's understanding of society, or the social realm, and its corresponding conception of politics as a mode of governing the private realm. Put simply, society is 'the form in which the fact of mutual dependence for the sake of life and nothing else assumes public significance' (HC: 46). With modernity, the nation-state comes to function instrumentally as administrator of everyday 'domestic' affairs through the 'national' or 'social' economy, and politics is configured as a type of 'collective housekeeping' (HC: 28–29). The political economy of the nation-state thereby assumed effective control over state power. Arendt contends that this development contradicts the classical notion of the political, insofar as the economic was by definition 'non-political' (HC: 29). Historically, the prepolitical private sphere of the family and household was progressively transformed into a 'collective interest' managed and controlled by the power monopoly of the sovereign state. As a result, the private and public realms have been collapsed together.[4] This position came to define modern political economy, most notoriously in the view of the Marxian tradition that politics is a function of social life, and therefore that speech and action are merely superstructural adornments dependent upon an economic base. Yet Arendt points out that Marx developed his position directly out of the 'communistic fiction' that there is 'one interest of society', first introduced by classical liberal thinkers (HC: 43–44). The social, in other words, is a kind of common denominator for both communism and capitalism in the modern age. Classical liberals also argued for the centrality of the economic base of society, which they viewed as harmonizing individual interests through the collective (although unintentional) mechanism of the 'invisible hand' of the market. Hence both Marxian and liberal economism express modernist faith in social conformism, albeit on the strength of altogether different premises; both claim the status of 'science' on the basis of their shared notion that 'socialized man' follows predictable patterns of behaviour and 'uniform motivation' (HC: 42). Economics, previously linked to the household, became the guide for modern politics in the service of normalizing 'social', that is, economic behaviour. Moreover, as we will see, the modernist view that the political is merely epiphenomenal of economic activity continues to define contemporary capitalist ideology in its dominant neoliberal guise.

With the triumph of economism over the landscape of modern politics – the contemporary ideological contours of which are discussed in the following sections – the social realm transformed all 'communities into societies of laborers and jobholders' (HC: 46). In mass society, the *animal laborans* acquired the status of employee, and all socially productive work ('livelihood') aims only at sustaining the lives of workers and their families by means of the production and consumption of 'goods'. In this way, the social promotion of labour and the labour process have led to the public space of politics becoming primarily a mechanism for the affirmation of biological survival. This development epitomizes Arendt's claim that 'through society it is the life process itself which in one form or another has been channeled into the public realm' (HC: 45). By this Arendt means that the constraints or necessities of organic life have turned into the fundamental social and thus 'political' issue of modernity. The promotion of labouring activity into the heart of modern public affairs liberated the work of biological survival (which is not to be confused with the emancipation of the working class) and incorporated it into social policy and political administration. In Arendt's perspective, this public organization of the life process points toward an impending catastrophe:

> The social realm, where the life process has established its own public domain, has let loose an unnatural growth, so to speak, of the natural; and it is against this growth, nor merely against society but against a constantly growing social realm, that the private and the intimate, on the one hand, and the political (in the narrower sense of the word), on the other, have proved incapable of defending themselves.
>
> (HC: 47)

Arendt explains that the term 'public' refers to two separate but related phenomena. First, it points to the idea of accessibility, in the sense that all speech and action which appears in the public realm can be discussed, debated, and judged by everyone. Through communicatively disclosing our thoughts and experiences and 'being seen and heard by others', we move from the sheltered realm of private subjectivity to the open space of public intersubjectivity (HC: 50). The need to guarantee 'the widest possible publicity' is crucial to the phenomenon of the political because the latter depends upon the essential condition of the 'presence of others who see what we see and hear what we hear' (HC: 50). This co-presencing, or 'being among men' (*inter homines esse*) in such a way that we acknowledge and affirm one another's appearance in a public space 'constitutes reality' as such (HC: 50). Reality is not given as a brute fact, but is created and sustained through the sharing of a world built up between a plurality of persons. The less accessibility we have to a public political realm, the less our opinions and actions are capable of being discussed, contested and judged by others, then the less assured will be our sense of reality.

Second, then, the term 'public' signifies 'the world itself, in so far as it is common to all of us and distinguished from our privately owned place in it' (HC: 52). The world assumes its status as a 'common meeting ground of all' (HC: 57) because it is both an historical object of human artifice and an intersubjectively constituted reality shared by individuals who speak and act together as equals within the realm of human affairs. The publicity of the world lies in its relational quality; as an 'in-between' the world simultaneously 'relates and separates men', that is, it gathers them together on the basis of their plurality yet prevents them 'falling over each other' (HC: 52). This means that the world manifests itself in innumerably different ways, according to the perspectives that people have with respect to this world, but simultaneously there is also a single world presented to all persons despite their different perspectives, inasmuch as the world is common to all because of its public nature (HC: 57).

For Arendt, the common world 'is what we enter when we are born and what we leave behind when we die. ... It is what we have in common not only with those who live with us, but also with those who were here before and with those who will come after us' (HC: 55). By definition, a public realm cannot belong to a single generation, it must constitute a bridge between past and future, between who and what has been, and who and what will come to be. In order to survive beyond one generation and serve as the meeting place of those who will appear to one another in past, present and future, a common world must appear in public: 'It is the publicity of the public realm which can absorb and make shine through the centuries whatever men may want to save from the natural ruin of time' (HC: 55). Again, we see that the public realm is not a natural phenomenon, but rather is a product of human action that stands out from nature and endures only through the deliberate and persistent efforts of political actors to care for the world shared between them. Arendt's emphasis on the 'artificial' nature of political life and the public realm mirrors her rejection of the concept of human nature and any attempt to base politics upon the allegedly fixed qualities of a human essence (HC: 10–11). In contrast, the move of reducing the political to the social invariably entails an appeal to human nature and corresponding innate predispositions or natural laws, the necessities of which are supposed to guarantee the appropriateness of the social order independently of shared political dialogue and action. The political retains a special meaning and autonomy for Arendt because it manifests our *humanitas* or human dignity, made visible when we are released from the strictures of necessity and freed to build a common world where political discourse and interaction can flourish.

Accordingly, Arendt argues that the expression of care for or love of the world – *amor mundi* – is an unmistakable sign of agents' commitment to the idea of political freedom.[5] The existence of the public realm allows for the emergence of freedom. Without freedom, political life as such would have no meaning: 'The *raison d'être* of politics is freedom, and its field of experience is action' (BPF: 146). Yet the public realm continues to exist only if freedom is exercised responsibly – that is, for the sake of the world itself and the plurality of human beings who appear within it. As she provocatively writes:

> Strictly speaking, politics is not so much about human beings as it is about the world that comes into being between them and endures beyond them. ... To put it another way, the more peoples there are in the world who stand in some particular relationship with one another, the more world there is to form between them, and the larger and richer that world will be.
>
> (PP: 175–76)

This responsibility, in turn, presupposes equality of political status, insofar as action can occur only on the basis of a commitment on the part of all agents in the public realm to recognize and respect one another as equally entitled to participation in a world shared with others. Freedom, for Arendt, is always to be understood politically as the freedom of equals; this is conveyed in the Greek notion of *isonomia*. The constitution of freedom as a political reality is the essence of political life, but this essence can be kept alive only by ensuring equal access to the public realm. Such is the role of the right to have rights discussed in the previous chapter. Here, too, Arendt emphasizes that equality is not a natural attribute, but is a political quality acquired through access to the public realm and guaranteed only by political institutions (HC: 215). The words and deeds of political actors assume significance only because others – regarded as peers or equals – are present to hear, see and judge in a public space devoted specifically to this activity. When this political reality takes shape, a world has formed; and when it vanishes, so too does the world.

The significance of Arendt's argument can be made clearer by emphasizing the point that there are two types of 'in-between' within a common world. The action by which a person reveals 'who' and not merely 'what' he or she is in the public realm, Arendt says, 'retains a curious intangibility' (HC: 181). This intangibility permeates all human affairs where persons speak and act together directly, rather than relating only through the intermediary of use objects or economic activity. While economic production and exchange introduce a tangible physical world of things between people, which can bind them together on the basis of their 'objective' interests, direct interaction and dialogue between people manifest the transience and spontaneity of joint political action itself, as well as the distinctness and uniqueness of acting and speaking agents. Thus the 'physical, worldly in-between' that arises through productive activities possesses a tangibility that cannot be found in the realm of human affairs and the 'altogether different in-between' of action (HC: 182–83). This does not mean that the ephemeral in-between of human interaction – which Arendt calls 'the "web" of human relationships' – is any less real than the physical in-between of material things. It does mean, however, that the public realm, as a common world that consists of web of human relationships, is fragile and can be irreparably harmed in ways to which physical objects are impervious (see BPF: 60; Taminiaux 2000: 167–68).

This emphasis on the fragility of human action and the unique world of human affairs helps to explain why the 'enlargement of the private' in the modern era 'does not constitute a public realm' (HC: 52). The sheer fact of expanding or multiplying private interests across the whole of the social field means only that the generic image of the consumer, as the mass expression of a supposedly single natural interest in consuming physical objects inherent in the human species, has displaced the delicate reality of distinct political actors 'acting and speaking directly *to* one another' (HC: 183). The continued entrenchment of the social indicates that people no longer relate to one another through a common world that exists above and beyond their private interests, but do so through the perpetual exchange of mass commodities, which are the public embodiment of their indistinguishable private needs. The homogeneity and anonymity of 'social man' foster an apolitical 'worldlessness' at the expense of the fundamentally public experiences of worldliness. Hence the simplest and most effective route to 'public' status in the consumer age is through celebrity, which itself is merely a commodity to be used and consumed. Celebrity, or what Arendt calls 'public admiration', and 'monetary reward' are therefore 'of the same nature and can become substitutes for each other' (HC: 56). Yet, as with all consumables, public admiration suffers from the transience of worldlessness, in contrast to the durability of a common world which can 'survive the coming and going of the generations' (HC: 55).

In Arendtian terms, modernity can be defined by its nearly obsessive accentuation of the social and concomitant depoliticization of the public realm. The public realm has in effect become little more than a social instrument for the protection of private wealth and possessions. Since wealth is intended solely to be used and consumed, its entry into the public realm 'began to undermine the durability of the world' (HC: 68). Yet the corruption of the common world and the public political realm was perhaps less conspicuous than one might imagine. This is because the imperative of capital is to accumulate more capital, generating an interminable process which conveys a sense of permanence nearly equal to that provided by the 'stable structure' of a commonly shared world (HC: 69). Nevertheless, the nature of the permanence of capital accumulation differs significantly from that of sustaining a common public world, inasmuch as capital remains inherently private. Whereas the public realm is shared by all, capital is possessed solely by its owner. Coupled with the Hobbesian notion of government as formed for the protection of individuals' negative liberties – that is, for protection of the social sphere in which the competitive struggle for private wealth can take place without undue interference – the modern public realm became a place 'where the only thing people have in common is their private interests' (HC: 69). While Marx is well known for identifying the ways in which the modern state always acts to protect private economic interests, Arendt goes further than this by pointing out that this development 'introduced the utter extinction' of the classical difference between the private and public realms, the substitution of private preoccupations for public concerns, and the valorization of the social at the expense of the political. The end result has been the effacement of the political through the global spread of exclusively social interests, and economic and technological logics across the public realm. The rise of the social therefore involves the development of a complex global economy and a corresponding suffocation of political freedom under the reign of socioeconomic 'inevitabilities'.

Neoliberal economic globalization

Since the end of the Cold War, neoliberalism has been consolidated as the dominant ideology of our time, one that embodies the essential features of economic globalization. Globalization refers most basically to the process of growing interconnection, interdependence and reciprocal influence between different individuals, groups, countries and regions (see Bauman 1999; Held and McGrew 1999; Schirato and Webb 2006). With the collapse of the Soviet Union and the crisis of 'really existing socialism', capitalism was disseminated and consolidated around the globe, bringing with it an increase in trade and financial flows, the development of technology and communications, and greater social and economic interdependence between states. Yet in addition to this process of integration, globalization has provoked a resurgence in nationalism and localism; cooperation across borders has been uneven, conditional and limited; and power, national interests and security have occupied a prominent place in the foreign policy of many states (see el-Ojeili and Hayden 2006: ch. 3–4). This discrepancy between the integrative and destructive dimensions of globalization might seem to be a simple contradiction, an exception to the otherwise consistent rule of neoliberalism. However, this discrepancy is more accurately a characteristic of the very logic of neoliberalism, one that necessitates the destruction of all other visions of the world in order to construct or integrate its maximal or totalizing conception of world order.

The relationship between neoliberalism and contemporary globalization is intrinsic, in the sense that economic globalization in the post-Second World War era has been shaped and increasingly determined as a distinct social project by dominant forces seeking to spread their hegemonic power on a planetary scale. In working towards the goal of a fully globalized capitalist economy, neoliberalism nevertheless manages to cloak the social origins and ideological aims of this movement. Rather, neoliberalism presents economic globalization as the expression of the 'natural' inner workings of the free-market system. From this perspective, economic globalization (of the kind that just happens to be portrayed in neoliberal theory) is an inevitable and inescapable reality, to which the only reasonable response is to adapt – or die. This emphasis on the 'necessary' character of neoliberal globalization can 'produce a fatalistic, even abject, acceptance of the idea that there was and is, as Margaret Thatcher kept insisting, "no alternative"' to the global spread of the capitalist economic system (Harvey 2005: 40). As we shall see, the fatalism spawned by the TINA ('there is no alternative') claim is one of the most profound contradictions of neoliberal rhetoric, although it functions as a positive mechanism for the reinforcement of neoliberal dominance.[6] In this respect, neoliberalism must be seen as the foundation of the edifice of contemporary economic globalization; free-market economy-centred global integration and neoliberalization go hand-in-hand.

The phenomenon of economic globalization synthesizes a number of elements and processes, only a few of which can be presented here very schematically. In essence, an increasingly globalized capitalism is constituted by converging tendencies towards the integration of all societies into a 'world ordered according to market principles' (Smith 2008: 6). This means that neoliberal globalization presupposes, as a first and most fundamental process, a growing economic integration between countries and a greater interrelation between markets. This economic integration has required an antecedent change in economic strategies for states entering the neoliberal fold. For instance, policies of import substitution, whereby national industries are fostered by subsidies or tariff protections and thus remain relatively 'closed', had to be replaced by policies of vigorous export trade – both of raw materials essential to development and of high-tech consumer goods – as well as the opening of internal markets to foreign capital investment.

In order to carry out the changes in economic strategy required by 'trade liberalization', countries must reduce or eliminate tariffs to open their borders to cheap import products while also producing and exporting goods at competitive prices (see Gilpin 2001; Brakman *et al.* 2006).

The opening up of markets to global exchange further suggests the removal of all barriers to the free mobility of capital between sectors, regions and countries. It has become a normal process for capital movement to be unimpeded globally, as it searches out ever more attractive conditions for investment, higher interest rates, greater guarantees against losses, and more reliable rates of return. As a result, states compete with each other to attract capital, compelling them to provide optimum conditions for finance capital and to relax laws on foreign investment and ownership. With the liberalization of financial transactions, the flow of money has become faster and easier than the movement of goods (Burton and Nesiba 2004). This enhanced mobility is made possible, in part, by the revolution in information technology, which has also contributed to the spread of a new paradigm of production based on computerization. This process has paralleled the introduction of the methods of capitalist organization of work into virtually all social activities, particularly through the automation of services (Castells 1998). The deployment of 'capital intensive manufacturing', such as with computer-controlled machine tools and automated, 'just-in-time, just-in-case', flexible production, is equally important. The goal has been dramatically to increase the productivity of labour, both in direct production processes (whether in the factory or the office) and in the stages of connecting direct production with markets (whether the supply of inputs or sales to consumers of goods and services) (Munck 2002). It has become imperative for companies to incorporate new technologies in order to enter into and maintain their position within the most profitable markets. The advances in automation, computing and information technology have been one of the key drivers of economic globalization in other, related ways: enabling the exchange of information between remote locations; mobilizing capital from one country to another in search of higher interest rates; facilitating the production and exchange of goods between distant factories; and spreading new techniques and procedures at high speed (Sennett 2006: 42–46).

A further consequence of these advances in information technology and processes of integrating worldwide production has been the simultaneous standardization of modern consumption and the demand for consumer goods (Sennett 2006: ch. 3). Because these goods tend to be the same in all the major markets of the world, and the demand for them is no longer segmented into national markets *per se*, it is possible to speak of the universalization of both consumers and products. The purchasing power of certain social groups converges on a global scale, reinforced by the homogeneity of advertising messages transmitted by the mass media and by the ubiquitous networks of virtual communication (email, instant messaging, texting, mobile phones) that facilitate and encourage the formation of globally shared consumer identities. Advocates of neoliberal globalization, such as Kenichi Ohmae, interpret this formation of 'borderless' consumer identities alongside the emergence of a single global market as a positive sign that 'consumer needs' now function as the axis around which all social activity is articulated (Ohmae 1999). In the global economy, consumers are portrayed as possessing power in terms of being able to influence the economic process via the free flow of information; consumers thus represent the 'new sovereignty' of neoliberal globalization. Further, the new role of consumers modifies the fundamental equation of economic performance. Within a neoliberal world order, the economic process is 'liberated' from political considerations, and corporations are able to deliver their goods to consumers at the lowest prices, no matter where in the world they are produced (Ohmae 1995).

In short, following the collapse of Soviet-style communism, contemporary globalization emerged when neoliberal expansion occurred between different countries and the capitalist economic system required the removal of barriers to trade and capital flows. Globalization thus marks the beginning of an era in which a single economic system – neoliberal capitalism – prevails in the world. But beyond examining the devastating economic impact of the process of neoliberal globalization, as analysed in Chapter 2, we must also question its fundamental political implications. What is at stake with regard to the political itself if neoliberalism manages to accomplish what no other ideology has managed to do before – to make itself the only viable political project and philosophical world view on the planet? To begin to address this question, it is necessary to look in greater detail at the underlying conceptual and normative assumptions of neoliberalism, and to establish its specific ideological character.

What are the basic ideas guiding the vision of neoliberal globalization? The most obvious tenets, implicit in the preceding brief survey of the phenomenon of globalized capitalism, are the free competition of market forces, the reduction of government regulation, efficiency and productivity, technological development, individual choice, and the primacy of economic growth (see Steger 2005: 8–9). National economies are to be integrated on the basis of the 'laws' of the market, free competition, and supply and demand. This process requires a focus on individual efficiency and productivity across diverse fields: employees must be flexible, adaptable and proactive; entrepreneurs must be both efficient and risk-seeking in order to survive in the face of domestic and foreign competition; administrators and politicians must be successful in the management of public affairs in order to ensure the successful integration of their businesses and countries into the world economy and to boost the competitiveness and efficiency of government activities and private services alike. Enhanced efficiency and productivity depend upon the reduction of state intervention in favour of the extension of the private sector. The neoliberal state should be minimal or *laissez-faire*, employing the rule of law and its monopoly of the means of violence to enforce strong individual property rights and contracts, and to ensure the free interplay of businesses and corporations in the economic and social arena (Harvey 2005: 64–65). Yet this minimalism is of a peculiar kind, since states must also manage the integration of their countries into the world economy, conclude trade agreements with other states, fix exchange rates, interest rates and tax policies, and coordinate the privatization of assets and services. In the neoliberal perspective, the function of the state is to monitor, protect, support and encourage the opening of markets to global exchange and the movement of capital, without 'interfering' with capital itself (Tormey 2004: 34).

The intellectual origins of neoliberalism can be traced back to the theoretical developments of classical French and English liberalism of the seventeenth and eighteenth centuries, although the theoretical structure of neoliberalism differs from classical liberalism in several respects (Turner 2008: 22). Adam Smith, for instance, provided a crucial impetus towards the abstract analysis of society as a whole, based on the explanation of the existence and functioning of the capitalist market. In *The Wealth of Nations* (1776), Smith argued that the competitive market society is consistent with the natural order of things. For Smith, the social process is subject to natural laws that exceed merely voluntary design or institutional structures. The science of economics is nothing more than the application of the constant and universal principles of the natural order in the functioning of market societies. When not subjected to intrusive governmental restraints and interference, the natural efficiency of free-market mechanisms will achieve a self-regulating system providing for a sustainable equilibrium between supply and demand and the most efficient allocation of resources. This naturalization of the market economy was mirrored by the image of human beings as naturally self-interested, competitive and acquisitive. Classical liberalism's conception of the natural freedom of *homo economicus* is that it consists of the individual pursuit of self-interest within the market system, without restrictive governmental regulations. Not only will this self-regulating system encourage entrepreneurialism, productivity and efficiency, but it will enhance individual freedom of choice and the satisfaction of individual needs. In this way, the free market's 'invisible hand' will translate the individual pursuit of self-interest into the virtuous, though not necessarily intended outcome of the optimal well-being of society (defined as the maximization of the total utility of the sum of individuals acting for themselves). As a 'natural' circuit composed of individual interests harmoniously interacting via competition and exchange, the free-market system of society is represented as superior to and determinative of the realm of politics. The result of free-market competition, Smith proclaimed, is a 'natural system of perfect liberty and justice' (Smith 1976: 651).[7]

Developing out of the legacy of this branch of classical liberalism, neoliberalism became a genuinely distinct paradigm on the initiative of the Austrian economist Friedrich von Hayek when, along with Ludwig von Mises, Milton Friedman, Karl Popper, Walter Lippmann and other economists, philosophers and politicians, he formed the Mont Pelerin Society in 1947. At the founding meeting of the society, Hayek suggested that its task should be 'purging traditional liberal theory of certain accidental accretions which have become attached to it in the course of time' (Hayek 1967: 149). These 'accidental accretions' were identified primarily with the 'arbitrary extensions of power' associated with the rise of the welfare state, and the concomitant 'decline of belief in private property and the competitive market'. The Society's members believe that the 'central values of civilization are in danger' by social democratic and quasi-collectivist tendencies to restrict the individualism of 'natural' freedom manifested in the free-market system.[8] Over the past 60 years, a comprehensive neoliberal theory encompassing epistemology and science, anthropology, sociology, economics, law and politics has been articulated under the auspices of the Mont Pelerin Society.

The neoliberal movement initiated by the Mont Pelerin Society soon expanded its scope and influence through numerous think-tanks, such as the Institute of Economic Affairs in London and the Heritage Foundation and Cato Institute in Washington, and academic institutions, particularly at the University of Chicago, where both Hayek and Friedman taught (Harvey 2005: 22). By the late 1970s, neoliberalism had become the reigning economic orthodoxy, displacing Keynesianism and its justification for state intervention in the economic domain. Embraced by both Margaret Thatcher and Ronald Reagan, neoliberal ideals of macroeconomic discipline, economic development through free-market competition, and openness of the world market, evolved into a set of definitive policies guiding institutions such as the World Trade Organization, the World Bank and the International Monetary Fund. The so-called 'Washington Consensus' of the leading banks, economic organizations and Western governments consolidated around the implementation of strong monetary austerity programmes, reduction of taxes, decline in social spending, wages and union power, deregulation of markets, privatization of state enterprises, and increased international competition (Steger 2003: 52–55). From the corridors of power in Washington and London issued the new rules of the neoliberal global economy, to be imposed and enforced throughout the 'developing' world by means of 'structural adjustment'. Without any hint of contradiction, the advocates of neoliberal minimalism and 'invisible hand' self-regulation – what Hayek (1952) referred to as the 'spontaneous order' of a harmonious yet 'unplanned' and decentralized market – have constructed a Leviathan of economic globalization actively shaped and managed through the 'hidden fist' of political, military and economic dominance. With surprising candour, neoliberal enthusiast Thomas Friedman openly admitted to the manipulative character of the 'golden straightjacket' crafted by Washington Consensus-led globalization:

> The Golden Straightjacket was made in America and Great Britain. The Electronic Herd is led by American Wall Street Bulls. The most powerful agent pressuring other countries to open their markets for free trade and free investments is Uncle Sam, and America's global armed forces keep these markets and sea lanes open for this era of globalization, just as the British navy did for the era of globalization in the nineteenth century.
>
> (Friedman 1999: 381)

Neoliberalism can be regarded as the most dominant ideological metanarrative of our global age, not only because it has been disseminated globally through the discourse of economic and political elites in many societies, but because it is the primary body of thought guiding international economic institutions in their attempt to reconstruct all societies along neoliberal lines. As conceived by the Mont Pelerin Society, this project of global social reconstruction rests upon 'the reassertion of valid ideals',[9] that is, upon a comprehensive form of intellectual, social and economic thought that functions as the logical determination of all socioeconomic activity. As such, the neoliberal metanarrative attempts to answer all major questions about the nature of human beings, freedom, the meaning of life, and social institutions. Neoliberalism purports to be the single true interpretation of human and social reality, the principles of which possess a timeless validity inaccessible to alternative traditions of thought.

Neoliberals have constructed their theory in much the same way as did Hobbes and Locke, basing their conception of society upon a coordinated theory of knowledge, science and 'human nature'. The theoretical structure of neoliberalism thus consists of a set of high-level, internally consistent abstractions. Following Macpherson (1962), the most basic of these is the principle that man is a 'possessive individualist'. The relation of ownership, of one's 'lives, liberties and estates', is the main connection to others and to the world. Lockean property rights are of the utmost importance, and the principal human activity is economic (Locke 1989). The most essential human functions – exchange, consumption, accumulation and ownership – take place in, or are mediated by, the market. Human beings are rationally self-interested by nature, and their conduct ought ideally to be guided by cost–benefit calculations (the utilitarian ethic being inherent to the free-market system). Similarly, neoliberalism also conceives of the human being as monadic, fundamentally separate from others and possessing a substantive existence independent of society. Indeed, as Margaret Thatcher famously declared, society consists only of 'individual men and women' who 'look to themselves first' (Thatcher 1987). Collective entities, such as classes, nations and humanity itself, are merely illusory categories that displace proper attention from the individual as such.

Another key theoretical tenet of neoliberalism is that reason is subjective and instrumental. Reason's singular purpose is to employ considerations of utility for the purpose of individual choice regarding the satisfaction of preferences and the optimization of market transactions; reason expresses the 'sovereign' decisions of the subject as consumer. In this vein, Ludwig von Mises argued that the power of capital really lies in the hands of the seemingly omnipotent consumer as social sovereign:

> Neither the entrepreneurs nor the farmers nor the capitalists determine what has to be produced. The consumers do that. If a businessman does not strictly obey the orders of the public as they are conveyed to him by the structure of market prices, he suffers losses, he goes bankrupt, and is thus removed from his eminent position at the helm. ... The consumers patronize those shops in which they can buy what they want at the cheapest price. Their buying and their abstention from buying decide who should own and run the plants and the farms. ... They determine precisely what should be produced, in what quality, and in what quantities.
>
> (von Mises 1949: 269–70)

According to Milton Friedman's formulation of subjective rationality, human beings are not only rational maximizers, they are simultaneously subjects of desires which are administered by calculative reason. In other words, the market mechanism is not only external, but also functions within subjectivity, on the basis of which the subject calculates how best to maximize or trade-off time for work, leisure, and the relative weighting of wishes. Couples, for instance, can (or should) analyse children as types of consumer goods and capital in order to decide rationally whether or not to have them (see Friedman 1962). Instrumental or economic calculation thus becomes the principle of intelligibility for all human phenomena. It also implies human homogeneity by making every single human being the bearer of the same mode of rationally self-interested consciousness, the key motivator for all social activity.

Further, neoliberalism endorses the notion that human beings are naturally unequal, and therefore that no ethical, legal or political equality can justifiably compensate for innate inequalities. Since an individual's social status reflects the inherent strengths and weaknesses of his or her essential being, it is natural for people to be differentiated in the social hierarchy. Natural inequalities 'explain' the presence and persistence of socioeconomic and political inequalities, and the latter are given a legitimizing moral basis by the former. In this vein, Hayek argues that a natural hierarchy exists that divides the majority of people – those motivated by atavistic impulses and a lack of self-discipline with regard to the application of rational calculation – from a small elite who possess self-control and comprehend clearly the 'abstract laws which govern social life' (Hayek 1978). Members of this elite group – which Hayek also refers to as the 'advance guard' of progress (Hayek 1960: 130) – can behave as sound, efficient maximizers, and thus are better suited to successful competition in the market. The process of free competition simply produces winners and losers; those on the losing side are solely responsible for their own fate because the resulting inequalities are an outcome of their inadequacies *vis-à-vis* impersonal market dynamics, and not because of another person's intention (Hayek 1977). Similarly, Friedman (1980) suggests that market outcomes are the fairest mode of distribution, since they represent a 'perfect' exchange of equivalents: one gets back the same proportion as one puts in. This position restates Smith's view that the free market is a 'natural system' of 'perfect justice', and further reinforces the naturalization of the free-market economy. In Hayek's words, the free-market economy is nothing less than 'a specific outcome of evolution itself' (Hodgson 1993: 176).

The most important principle for neoliberalism is freedom, formulated as negative, individualist and economic: 'liberty is not merely one particular value but … the source and condition of most moral values' (Hayek 1960: 6). Neoliberals reject any notion of social constraint beyond the minimal framework of a rule of law protecting contractual exchange and property rights. Freedom consists of the absence of arbitrary and unlawful state coercion, and its scope of exercise *par excellence* is the market. It consists of the choice to enter into trade relationships, and to buy or sell in the market. This purely negative or economic freedom must, Hayek observes, be distinguished from the many dimensions commonly yet mistakenly attributed to freedom today, such as 'spiritual' or 'psychological' freedom (since this may undermine belief in individual responsibility) and purely political freedom (since, as noted above, a person's negative freedoms are not thought to be restricted even when political inequalities exist). Any attempt by the state to reduce economic inequalities through social regulation merely limits and threatens economic freedom. Consequently, neoliberalism holds that, for the sake of freedom, both politics and law must be subordinated to the logic of the market. In terms of what Tullock (1982) starkly refers to as 'the imperialism of economics', all political behaviour is to be collapsed into rational economic self-interest. For neoliberalism, the market is held to be sacrosanct, to the extent that all other forms of human action no longer seem reasonable. The political itself, as a mode of action possessing its own specific meaning and autonomy, has been effaced as neoliberalism spreads across the globe.

Neoliberal ideology and the destruction of the political

Neoliberal globalization advocates a total extension of socioeconomic activity over the public realm, to the point of subsuming and therefore annihilating political life altogether. Arendt made clear that the 'end of the common world has come when it is seen only under one aspect and is permitted to present itself in only one perspective' (HC: 58). Arendt's diagnosis of the modern hegemony of the social – a hegemony which is not merely local or domestic in an increasingly consumerist, globalized world – compels us to consider the neoliberal impulse to depoliticize the public realm as a type of political evil of this global age. Under totalitarianism, the erasure of the boundaries between the public and the private led to the paralysis of action and freedom as a totalizing ideology of the social eclipsed the plurality of the political. The totalizing ideology imposed by regimes of domination annihilated joint action and critical deliberation, and multiplied a single perspective across the whole of the social field. Precluded from expressing their plurality on the public stage, individuals retreated towards the interiority of their intimate personal spaces. A similar dynamic through which the political becomes disposable from the perspective of a totalizing social ideology is one of the principal elements of the 'imperialism of economics' shaping neoliberal globalization.

Arendt's account of the distinction between the political and the social is meant primarily to publicize, as it were, the ways that powerful anti- or depoliticizing tendencies threaten the prospects for political action and, by extension, our freedom and capabilities to *become* human. For Arendt, it is crucially important to resist the annexation of political life to the means and ends of economic rationality. That is why she attempts to delineate that which differentiates the particular meaning and lived reality of the political from that of the social. Arendt has, however, been criticized on a variety of levels for this distinction, particularly in her treatment of it in *On Revolution*.[10] It has been argued, for instance, that whether or not it is explicitly recognized in classical thought, the social has political significance or, stated otherwise, that the essence of politics is to address social issues. It is implied, then, that Arendt's attitude to the 'social question' is marked by a profound insensitivity to the economically exploited and a lack of concern for poverty. The argument presented in Chapter 2 should serve to counter at least some of these types of criticism.

Nevertheless, to confront this criticism more directly, it must be recognized that Arendt considered the social question – or 'the terrifying predicament of mass poverty' (OR: 24) – deserving of serious attention. In *On Revolution*, she observes that liberation or emancipation from socioeconomic misery and deprivation 'is indeed a condition of freedom', that is, a condition of political action (OR: 32). Despite this interdependence of liberty and freedom, Arendt's point is that there is a relevant difference between the two. Whereas liberty is negative insofar as it refers to 'freedom from' want and economic deprivation, freedom is positive inasmuch as it refers to 'freedom to' initiate joint action with other individuals considered as political equals. Hence, as Sidonia Blättler and Irene Marti point out, Arendt 'certainly knows that freedom is incompatible with social misery, that freedom presupposes not only liberation from political domination but also from poverty' (Blättler and Marti 2005: 92). Arendt made clear that, apart from the misery of material deprivation, poverty is abject and dehumanizing because it places the human person under the permanent despotism of physical need (OR: 60). But it was more important for Arendt that the 'ignominy' of poverty and economic exploitation were not simply reduced to a matter of fact, such that how we respond to them 'politically' would similarly follow as an inevitable conse-quence of necessity. Doing so would render the political little more than adminis-trative handmaiden to the 'natural laws' and bureaucratic techniques of economic 'science'; freedom would succumb to necessity. In the dominant economic con-ception of political affairs, for instance, the aim of politics is the welfare of the greatest number. This view defines politics instrumentally and as subject to the predetermined end of utility; action is 'political' only insofar as it is 'useful' to *homo economicus*.[11] Hence the major problem for Arendt is not the social ques-tion as such, but the social realm from which it emerged and the consequent modern definition of politics as the functional struggle for economic power. We must then understand Arendt's critique of the social not as dismissing claims to socioeconomic equality but, on the contrary, as an 'attempt to defend the notion of political freedom against the usurpation of the public sphere by powerfully organized private interests' (Blättler and Marti 2005: 93).

Clearly, then, the question of the social – and the associated distinction between the public and the private – is indeed a complicated theme within Arendt's work. It is crucial, though, to recognize that Arendt's distinction between public and private 'is *not*', as Dana Villa points out, 'the same as that found in liberal theory' (Villa 1996: xii).[12] Arendt's motive in drawing this distinction is not to demarcate the boundaries of legitimate state or economic power, but rather to remind us of the phenomenologically unique realm of intersubjectively shared political action and judgement that is too easily extinguished when equated with either state or economy. In the Greek *polis* or even in the Roman republic, the social question was virtually absent from politics, but only because it was not the perceived pur-pose of the public realm to further the private interests of its individual members. Yet in modernity, 'society' has come to be defined precisely as the public realm where private interests are to be pursued, in particular through a form of 'political economy'. In this way, remark Michael Hardt and Antonio Negri:

[P]ublic spaces are increasingly becoming privatized. The urban landscape is shifting … to the closed spaces of malls, freeways, and gated communities … in such a way as to avoid the chance encounter of diverse populations, creating a series of protected interior and isolated spaces … and thus from this perspective our postmodern and imperial society is characterized by a deficit of the political. In effect, the place of politics has been de-actualized.

(Hardt and Negri 2000: 188)

Much of the difficulty surrounding the theme of the social question thus stems from the way that the social has been reified and, by extension, glorified in modernity. In other words, the properties of natural life and necessity, around which the social takes form, have been posited as the prepolitical reality that defines in advance the basis of human being and freedom. The social is the space in which natural life is inscribed as necessity, while society is the structure through which necessity maintains itself in its own privative character. The social can then be understood as the site of the repetitive production and reproduction of being, and social behaviour is effectively situated within the realm of causality and deterministic needs. Given the reification of the social – and thus its 'incontestable' status as the pre-eminent realm of life itself – the political as a realm with its own specificity and autonomy of action would no longer make sense, indeed it would no longer have any reason to exist. Because the artifice of the political is the antithesis of natural necessity, the political is in a sense the 'enemy' of the social, and must be eliminated. It is precisely this glorification or ideological certainty of the social that leads to political evil, in that it not only impoverishes our sense of reality, but also drastically restricts the scope of human freedom and action.

The Arendtian notion of the social and its extension throughout the modern age is partly connected to, and illuminated by, the situation that emerged in Europe following the First World War. The dissolution of political, national and religious ties generated a 'mass' society of individuals apathetic and indifferent to their rights and civic responsibilities. Oriented towards a life determined solely by commercial success or failure, the European population constituted a 'self-centred' mass of individuals characterized by 'monotonous but abstract uniformity', for whom 'the source of all the worries and cares which make human life troublesome and anguished' had disappeared (OT: 419–20). There developed a lack of interest in public affairs, solidarity and responsibility for the body politic. The reification of the social and a narrow focus on individual economic enrichment, Arendt suggests, come at the cost of trivializing the political.

Arendt finds that the trivialization or banalization of the political is a hallmark of modernity, or more particularly of modern ideological thinking, which subsumes the political to supposedly higher laws of historical and natural necessity. The nineteenth century introduced the grand ideologies of the modern era, especially those of nationalism, racialism and economism (in its capitalist and communist variants). While the specific substance of each of these ideologies is different, they each nevertheless claim to know 'the hidden truth about otherwise incomprehensible facts' (OT: 271). Whether this claim is couched as possession of 'the key to history, or the solution for all the "riddles of the universe", or the intimate knowledge of the hidden universal laws which are supposed to rule nature and man', all modern ideologies promise insight into an absolute truth that lies behind reality as a whole – the properties of which become visible only in light of the ideology itself (OT: 211). More pointedly, Arendt insists, ideological thinking assumes that 'one idea is sufficient to explain everything' by means of a logical deduction from this idea 'transformed into a premise' (OT: 605). In taking a single idea as an axiomatic premise from which all conclusions necessarily follow, ideo-logical thinking possesses a deceptively simple logical consistency that is thought to surpass experiential reality and establish its 'scientific' status. Once the prem-ise that there exists a hierarchy of 'superior' and 'inferior' races is accepted, for instance, logic demands that one also accept the conclusion that inferior races are 'unfit to live' and, further, that specific 'unfit races' may be exterminated for the benefit of the 'superior' race (OT: 608).

In Arendt's terms, ideological thinking exhibits three 'totalitarian elements', that is, elements that aim towards all-encompassing explanation based upon a single self-evident truth. First, ideological thinking 'promises to explain all historical happenings' – what becomes, what is born, and what passes away – by reducing history to knowable and predictable natural laws. Second, it claims understand-ing of a 'truer' reality hidden behind, and independent of, perceptible experience. Third, it orders all facts deductively in order to produce indisputable conclusions so that purposive action and its outcomes are determined by the necessity of logic rather than by choice (OT: 606–7). For Arendt, the combination of these three ele-ments exhibits a totalizing logic whereby the axiomatic idea serving as the ground of an ideology 'explains' the movement of history 'as one consistent process' (OT: 604). In other words, the historical development of social reality is pictured as cor-responding to the logic inherent in the idea given *a priori*. How conclusions within the logical system are reached by ideological thinking, and how historical events are produced within the social realm, are identical: history is not perceived or interpreted in light of an idea, but is that which is calculated by it, 'so that whatever happens, happens according to the logic of one "idea"' (OT: 605).

While the prescriptions derived from ideological thinking may themselves be violent, Arendt suggests that the coercive force of ideological thinking's logical process is violent as well. An ideology becomes total, she notes, when its content 'is no longer an objective issue about which people may have opinions, but has become as real and untouchable an element in their lives as the rules of arithmetic', thereby organizing 'the entire texture of life' according to its scientific exposition of historical–natural laws (OT: 476). Under these conditions, ideology possesses an instrumental character in the sense that all human beings, and even reality itself, are subject to the determinate laws of the 'gigantic movement of History or Nature' (OT: 610). The 'inner compulsion' of logicality supplies a consistency, certainty and security that actual experience cannot provide, and relieves those who accept the ideology of the need to think: once again, the themes of thoughtlessness and the abdication of responsibility loom large for Arendt. Further, the instrumentality of ideological thinking translates politically into the public realm as the superior force of an incontrovertible truth that destroys all other 'mere' opinions. Ideology is, in other words, a form of violence that is used for the purpose of decisively defeating other competing ideas. Ideological thinking is, in short, the affirmation of the forceful imposition of historical or natural necessity upon human action. By implication, those who resist thinking and acting in accordance with this 'strident logicality' are deemed expendable enemies of necessity (OT: 608).

Following Arendt's analysis of the nature of ideological thinking, I contend that neoliberalism is not simply an enthusiastic yet otherwise benign endorsement of the role of the free market within social relations. It is rather a determinate construction of social reality which claims 'to possess the key to reality' (OT: 229) and as such is the hegemonic ideology aligned with the exercise of contemporary politico-economic or 'social' power.[13] It provides a discourse of social relations which legitimizes inequality, naturalizes exclusion, and subordinates the political to the all-encompassing logic of economic necessity. Neoliberal economism does not simply make 'scientific' statements about the idea of the free-market system, but uses the idea of a free-market system in order to explain the course of the world on the basis of that idea's inherent logic. Neoliberalism therefore can, like other modern ideologies, 'pretend to be scientific philosophy' (OT: 604) inasmuch as it employs logical deduction from self-evident axioms regarding the 'laws' of human nature and the free market itself, as constituting the objective foundation of social order. Its overall aim is the economization of public life, the global colonization of the political by the social. Of course, as David Harvey points out, although presented as the unfolding of the logical necessity of an inevitable process, neoliberal economic globalization would not have been possible without undemocratic and unaccountable forms of coercive state intervention (Harvey 2005: 69).

Fundamental to this aim is the positing of the principle that the social possesses its own law of motion, requiring the insulation of the social from the political. Neoliberalism views economics as the expression of the laws of nature in the social. On this point it follows 'the glorification of labor ... and the elevation of the *animal laborans*' advanced by both Adam Smith and Karl Marx, and embraced by modern economism (HC: 85). For neoliberalism, in other words, the social represents the outward expression of labour power as a hidden 'natural–biological force' (OT: 598). Similarly, economics represents the scientific formulation of the free market's 'invisible hand' as a natural inclination to maximize self-interest. Ideally, such natural forces should remain 'unhindered by any spontaneous human action'; instead, economic and state policies would help translate into social reality the free movement of these forces in accordance with their inherent law (OT: 599). The idea of the free market is treated as possessing its own transcendent logic and motion, and the process of its realization is thought to best unfold the less it is 'interfered' with by the application of political laws extraneous to its logic.

These assumptions illustrate a general feature of neoliberalism that becomes increasingly apparent when viewed through the lens of Arendt's conception of modern ideology. Arendt remarks that one of the distinctive traits of modern ideology is that the 'idea' of the ideology becomes less important than 'the logical process which could be developed from it' (OT: 608). The fact that in the 'stringent logicality' of modern ideology, the 'real content of the ideology' is 'devoured' by the self-generated processes inherent in historical or natural necessity is of considerable importance (OT: 608–9). Under the plausible cover of conforming to necessity's law-like logic, modern ideology subordinates the ends of politics to the means of a force anterior to all experience. If we turn to neoliberalism as an ideology in Arendt's sense of the term, we can discern the specificity of its rationalization of its own overriding aim and course of development. Somewhat contradictorily, with neoliberalism the idea of the satisfaction of necessity via the free-market system is less important than the 'logical' process of neoliberal economic globalization, understood as an 'irresistible force' of global expansion, the movement of which is inherent in the idea of the self-regulated satisfaction of needs from which it develops. When conceived as an irresistible force, neoliberal globalization is, on the one hand, driven by an 'inner compulsion', as Arendt refers to the 'tyranny of logicality' (OT: 609), and on the other hand it exerts a formidable coercive pressure on those over whom, willingly or unwillingly, it holds sway.[14] As an irresistible force, one must either surrender to neoliberal globalization or be defeated by it; the logic of the process is indifferent to either fate. The modern society of neoliberal globalization is then divided into either executioners (successful capitalist globalizers) or victims (unsuccessful/inefficient/uncompetitive non-globalizers) – not, it is implied by advocates of neoliberalism, by any specific persons or human choices to which responsibility can attach, but by the inherent logicality that compels the neoliberal system and imposes the 'needs' of the economy.[15]

Against the compulsion of neoliberalism's 'tyranny of logicality' there stands, we can say in line with Arendt, only 'the great capacity of men to start something new', that is, the political (OT: 609). It is because of this very capacity that the coercive force of neoliberalism's logicality must be directed at the political; the political must be made powerless in the face of a greater necessity. Consequently, neoliberal globalization must aim to *depoliticize* the public realm in order to emancipate not human beings, but the metahistorical 'laws' of free-market capitalism, from the hindrance of diverse and potentially oppositional political opinions and action. The strength of neoliberalism is constituted by the appearance that there is no recognized alternative conceptualization of the political structure of the global socioeconomic system. In seeking to overtake the political by the globalization of the social, the principle of motion trumps the principle of action: the predictability of economic laws exerts a stranglehold on the unpredictability of the political capacity to 'start something new'. As a result of the depoliticization of the public realm, the 'space freedom needs for its realization is transformed into a desert' (EU: 344). Within the 'desert' of the social, predictability replaces unpredictability, logicality replaces thinking, necessity replaces freedom, isolation replaces solidarity, and loneliness replaces the sense of sharing a common world with others. In a global order 'whose chief values are dictated by labor', human beings not only have lost their 'place in the political realm of action', but even more significantly, the 'political sphere of their lives, where they act together in the pursuit of a common concern, is destroyed' (OT: 611–12). Superfluousness,

the 'experience of not belonging to the world at all' (OT: 612), becomes a characteristic feature of a global order dominated by neoliberalism because the common
world is itself rendered increasingly superfluous.

Arendt finds, then, that modern ideological thinking is especially pronounced
'when the world and life of human beings are indeed primarily determined by
economic factors and when the reality to which mental life is bound has become
fundamentally alien to thought and meaning' (EU: 42). If there is no political
space within which individuals can act freely in concert with others – creating a
common world or contributing to its creative regeneration through debate, deliberation and experimentation – then the world and the reality of experience cease
to make sense. We are of the world and belong to a common world, a world that
presents itself in the condition of human plurality, only insofar as we are guaranteed the opportunity to appear to each other as equals within the public realm.
A life without a political sphere devoted specifically to the appearance of human
plurality through the communicative and performative interaction of equals 'has
ceased to be a *human* life because it is no longer lived among men' (HC: 176;
emphasis added). Arendt does not mean that there is no human contact at all when
the public order is primarily defined socioeconomically. Rather, it is that the character of these associations is reduced to something less than distinctively human,
that is, political. Neoliberalism's insistence on a single overarching truth eliminates the need to exchange and confirm perspectives about reality. Its ideological
certainty suspends the action of subjecting our globalized world to the political
contestability of different opinions and judgements, leading to a 'private' reality that is no longer 'intersubjectively grounded' and thus humanly meaningful
(Parekh 1981: 88).

In terms drawn from the discussion of biopolitics in the previous chapter, in
the neoliberal social realm, individuals are subject to ideological thinking that
depoliticizes their agency and casts them as 'bare life'. Within the social realm,
in other words, individuals do not come together on the basis of their uniqueness
and their 'political capacities' (OT: 612), but come into contact on account of
their uniformity as 'natural' (apolitical) producers and consumers whose 'profitable' capacities are to be maximized through various optimizing technologies.[16]
It is the anonymous needs we share as members of the species, and the private
satisfaction of those needs, that bind us together through economic interdependence. As our economic interdependence becomes global, so too the 'life processes' of production and consumption displace political action on a global scale.
The main tenet of neoliberalism is simple: economics unquestionably must take
precedence over the political since, as Arendt realized, the political is thoroughly
unnatural. This single tenet sounds so plausible because it echoes commonly held
assumptions about the permanence, naturalness and inevitability of economic
'development' or 'growth', and that the conduct of human affairs is therefore predominantly about the means and techniques of commercial relations unimpeded
by state intervention. The ultimate purpose of neoliberal ideological thinking is
to convince us that things cannot be otherwise, and therefore we are left with
placid acceptance of (or submission to) the logic of the system: we labour in order

to consume, and consume in order to labour. The question of alternatives to this logic, and of the meaning of human existence beyond economy and society, is simply redundant from the neoliberal point of view. Thus the space for genuine political thought and action is all but closed.[17]

All of this suggests that neoliberalism as ideology – or, as Peter Baehr puts it, 'an all-encompassing ideological framework that abridges the complexity of life in a single, axiomatic, reality-resistant postulate that allows no cognitive dissonance' (Baehr 2002: 811) – exerts such a baleful influence on the world because it promotes a widespread attitude of worldlessness, of being without a sense of shared place or reality. The paradox of neoliberalism is that its drive to globalize the socioeconomic order as a space of uniformity and conformity effectively denies the plurality and spontaneity that defines a properly human world, thereby still leaving individuals fundamentally isolated from one another in the age of the 'global village'. Neoliberal globalization drives human agency from the world, pushing us towards a worldlessness that is inimical to an authentic, meaningful and dignified human existence. This leads to a kind of global privation that progressively erodes and even annihilates the political, perpetrating a large-scale political evil against both vast numbers of the world's people and the notion of humanity itself. The one-dimensional logic of neoliberal globalization signals the banalization of political action and the superfluousness of that worldly space between individuals in which the human condition is fully actualized.

Conclusion

Freedom, Arendt writes, 'is actually the reason that men live together in political organization at all' (BPF: 146). Put differently, only 'love of the world' and not the satisfaction of private needs and interests furnishes proper grounds for political life. Political action and speech comprise the highest potentiality of human existence, surpassing the fulfilment of basic physical needs (labour) and the technical fabrication employed for the production of material goods directed at gratifying social and economic needs or desires (work). In the public realm, as Arendt so strikingly portrays it, the specifically political character of human existence is affirmed: it is here that we *become* and disclose who we are as politically embodied persons. In recognizing each another as political equals – as free actors capable of developing our humanness or *humanitas* – through co-creation of the world that we share together, we simultaneously draw upon, validate and renew the human condition of plurality (MDT: 73–75). A shared and meaningful world is forged through dialogue and joint political action – which, by definition, includes diversity, contestation and a 'fiercely agonal spirit' (HC: 41) – in the public realm as a space for the articulation of human freedom and plurality. In contrast, neoliberal globalization as ideology and political economic practice exhibits contempt for central aspects of the human condition – natality, plurality, freedom and worldliness – that make possible the humanization of human beings. This is because neoliberalism substitutes 'society' for the world and, in the name of an absolute truth, conceives of society as something to be moulded from above in accordance with metahistorical economic laws and the logic of necessity. As Arendt puts it, such logic 'and all self-evidence from which logical reasoning proceeds can claim a reliability altogether independent of the world and the existence of other people' (EU: 318). It is a totalizing ideology that aims to make the world over in its image: the public becomes little more than the private writ large. In this way, Arendt insists, private interests have intruded upon the public realm 'in the most brutal and aggressive form' (Arendt 1977: 108).

As with the other forms of contemporary political evil examined in this book, neoliberalism's ideological thinking contains an element of violence (direct, structural and symbolic), since it must necessarily do violence to the world in order to achieve its end. Turning the world and its inhabitants into a means to an end, neoliberalism makes superfluous the particularities of actual human beings, their plurality, and their active agency. In the neoliberal vision, human agency and plurality are radically depoliticized. As a result, neoliberalism also makes superfluous the political public realm that both joins and separates diverse individuals in a common world, eroding their sense of shared reality and endangering their capacity to act together in politically meaningful ways. Neoliberal globalization therefore represents an acutely antipolitical orthodoxy that darkens the humanity of political agents, neutralizes the public realm, and fosters the conviction that no other worldly reality is possible. In short, it consigns the political, and the freedom to act in ways that disclose our very humanness to others, to oblivion. Sounding a similar theme, Perry Anderson argues that the ideological core of neoliberalism is the message that capitalism is the universal and permanent fate of humankind. In Anderson's words, neoliberalism 'is the most successful ideology in world history' which 'as a set of principles rules undivided across the globe' (Anderson 2000: 17). Neoliberal ideology might then be read in light of Arendt's warning that, with the increasing submergence of the political under the social, 'the modern age – which began with such an unprecedented and promising burst of human activity – may end in the deadliest, most sterile passivity history has ever known' (HC: 322).

Anderson also notes, however, that limitations persist to neoliberalism's practice. In Arendtian terms, it seems that, neoliberal domination of the global socioeconomic order notwithstanding, the absolute depoliticization and 'de-worlding' of public life seems impossible. This impossibility rests upon natality, the power to begin and to act that is part of the human condition. Action, Arendt argues, is 'ontologically rooted' in 'the fact of natality' (HC: 247). As long as human beings exist and continue to be born into the world, the 'faculty of interrupting' the 'automatic necessity' that structures socioeconomic life and 'beginning something new' in conjunction with other people remains alive and makes politics possible (HC: 246). Indeed, this power to act and begin something new, which is coextensive with the capacity for freedom, arguably can be seen in the recent rise of a global civil society framed as 'a heterogeneous political force that is opening up new political possibilities' (Patomäki and Teivainen 2004: 13).

Many parts of global civil society, especially those often labelled collectively as the 'alternative globalization movement', have shared interests in opposing neoliberalism, contesting capitalist domination, and democratizing economies

(*ibid*.: 2004: 112; el-Ojeili and Hayden 2006: ch. 5). While not opposed to globalization as such, the alternative globalization movement does challenge the
reductive neoliberal vision whereby human beings and their activities would
be increasingly determined by economic decisions and processes. Global civil
society in general, and the alternative globalization movement in particular, are
characterized by a strong cosmopolitan or transnational orientation that links the
local and the global, the creation of alliances on the basis of diverse experiences
and issues (the debt crisis of Southern countries, the rights of indigenous peoples,
environmental degradation), and the aim to open up a pluralist discussion about
change and the shape that the world might take. The World Social Forum (WSF),
for example, is frequently taken to be a promising initiative of the alternative globalization movement. Conceived as a response to the World Economic Forum, an
annual meeting of leading (neoliberal) economic and political figures in Davos,
Switzerland, the first WSF was held in January 2001 in the city of Porto Alegre,
Brazil. The focus of the WSF – the main slogan of which is that 'another world is
possible' – is to promote participatory forms of democratic dialogue and debate
beyond the confines of formal governmental institutions, and to facilitate building
progressive alternatives to neoliberalism (see Seoane and Taddei 2002; Teivainen
2002). Since the first meeting in Porto Alegre, hundreds of thousands of people
have participated in national, regional and international WSF gatherings.

Recall the discussion of the International Criminal Court in Chapter 1. There
we saw that Beck underlines the point that states are no longer 'the' actor in the
global system, but one actor among others, whose viability and legitimacy are
enmeshed within a dynamic network of power and counter-power (Beck 2005:
9). The outlook of cosmopolitan realism is fundamental to understanding the new
dynamic of global power relations, especially in light of the plurality of resistances
and emancipatory aims of the 'advocatory strategies' pursued by the diverse social
movements rooted in global civil society (*ibid*.: 13–14). Thus the establishment of
the ICC can be situated within this logic of power and counter-power at the heart
of cosmopolitanization, which itself is a manifestation of the post-Second World
War human rights movement viewed as a new cosmopolitan counter-power that
rejects the state's traditional claim to the domestic monopoly of power and the
inviolable autonomy associated with external sovereignty (see Sorenson 1999).
Occupying various strategic situations, human rights activists have had to resort
to both defensive and constructive modes of resistance, drawing together the local
and the transnational in their struggles against statist and corporatist powers (see
Risse *et al.* 1999). In many instances, the primary modes of struggle have been
mass demonstrations, disruptions of services, hunger strikes, and tactics such as
'naming and shaming' those suspected of atrocities. In other cases, modes of resistance have included public education, participating in multi-party dialogues, and
helping to craft policies and procedures for institutional reform. The combined
effect of these modes of political action has been to influence issue-creation and
agenda-setting, to transform (or subvert) the discourse of global politics, to rein-
vigorate public life, and to prompt institutional changes – with varying degrees of
success, of course. In the case of the ICC, for example, a coalition of nearly 1000

NGOs exerted a considerable influence during the negotiation process between states' representatives that led to the Rome Statute. This coalition convened working groups, provided information and analyses, fostered discussion and debate, promoted education and awareness, and participated with delegates at the Rome Conference in 1998. This influence was so significant that some commentators have suggested 'the ICC treaty might not have been concluded' without the actions of the NGO community (Chayes and Slaughter 2000: 241).

While the existence of a diverse and vigorous alternative globalization movement provides one indication that free action undertaken in concert with, and in relation to, other people still remains a possibility, we must also be cautious in reading global civil society and the alternative globalization movement as exemplifying the notion of the political as staked out by Arendt. This is primarily because the sphere of global civil society is, in keeping with both Arendt's distinction and the global entrenchment of the neoliberal socioeconomic structure, more aligned with 'the social' than 'the political'. In other words, global civil society is underpinned by the particular concepts, values and philosophies associated with (neo) liberalism's ascendance, and concomitant depoliticization of the public realm. Civil society and, by extension, global civil society are constituted by being 'outside' the formal political realm, at least as the latter is defined by neoliberalism as the admixture of states and markets. In the liberal sense, civil society is an 'intermediate' sphere of voluntary associations that is between the state and household (see Habermas 1989; Seligman 1992; Diamond 1999; Kaldor 2003; Keane 2003). In this conception, civil society matches up well with Arendt's characterization of the social as a public–private hybrid. The implication here is that global civil society is not only often tolerated by neoliberalism, but is even actively encouraged, inasmuch as civil society activities may support and reproduce neoliberal hegemony; for example, through the work of some development NGOs that functionally and symbolically legitimate neoliberal state-market reforms packaged as 'good governance' policy.[18] Indeed, Sklair (2001) argues that the most powerful social movement in the world is the one in favour of global neoliberal capitalism.

This is not the complete picture when it comes to global civil society, especially the alternative globalization movement. Many global civil society actors and social movements are quite explicitly oppositional and counter-hegemonic, seeking ways to publicize and rectify basic structural inequities, advocate for political change, and constitute alternative forms of interaction to achieve collective or common purposes. Furthermore, such social movements aim to draw people out of the private and into the public, focusing on creating a 'space of appearance' within which people may seek out recognition, shape new identities, attain distinction, and cultivate the kind of meaning that cannot be provided by the routinized economic necessities of production and consumption. In this light, global civil society can be said to be agency-oriented, protecting and advancing the possibility of action 'from below' and calling attention to the capacity for initiatory political action independent of the logic of neoliberal profit maximization imposed 'from above' (Falk 2000). At least some elements of global civil society may then support the political – as the possibility for new deeds and speech beyond the private sphere of the market – and illuminate our ability to resist the complete depoliticization of the public realm.[19] However, it is equally important not to romanticize global civil society, to recognize its contradictory nature due to its being deeply imbricated with the social, and to acknowledge that its overtly political significance is particularly vulnerable to being undermined by the geopolitical expansion of neoliberalism. An Arendtian cosmopolitan realism would demand nothing less of us than an ambivalent attitude towards global civil society as a site of the political. It is only in this cautious hope – inspired by natality, plurality and the capacity for freedom on the one hand, tempered by the forbidding tragedy of unmitigated human catastrophes on the other – that we might persevere against the absolute negation of worldliness and thus 'the end of all political life as we know it' (MDT: 81).

Notes

Introduction

1 Important instances of such work include Beitz (1999); Rawls (1999); Sen (1999); Pogge (2002); Singer (2002); Nussbaum (2006). The global justice literature is vast and is still growing rapidly.

1 Violating the human status

1 There is a vast literature on the concept of juridification and the various possible forms it may take. In this chapter, I assume that juridification (or judicialization) basically refers to processes of creating, expanding and modifying the formal norms, rules, agents and competencies of legal systems and the political orders associated with them, typically through the strategic interactions of state and non-state actors. My thinking on juridification has been informed primarily by Habermas (1987, 1996), but see also Della Carpini and Trägårdh (2004).

2 To avoid any confusion and to anticipate the discussion ahead, it should be noted that the human capacity for evil is not the same as an innate or 'natural' predisposition to evil: the former is located in the realm of action, while the latter would be inscribed within human nature.

3 While I cannot examine their similarities and differences on the topic here, Theodor Adorno has also developed a powerful postmetaphysical perspective on evil 'after Auschwitz'; see Adorno (1983, 1994, 2003). Adorno is more sceptical than Arendt about the possibility of making sense of extreme evil, although he does state that 'Perennial suffering has as much right to expression as a tortured does to scream', and his position on aesthetic experience and autonomous judgement via Kant opens the door to some potentially interesting parallels with Arendt. See Lara (2007) for an excellent discussion of postmetaphysical conceptions of evil.

4 The USA declined to join the declaration, for the reason that it wished to maintain its 'neutrality' in the war at this time. See Power (2002: 13); Bass (2000: 108–10).

5 The Charter of the International Military Tribunal for Nuremberg, in Article 6(c), defines crimes against humanity as: 'murder, extermination, enslavement, deportation, and other inhumane acts committed against any civilian population, before or during the war, or persecutions on religious, racial or political grounds in execution of or in connection with any crime within the jurisdiction of the tribunal, whether or not in violation of the domestic law of the country where perpetrated'. The other crimes within the jurisdiction of the tribunal were war crimes, crimes against peace (especially planning or waging a war of aggression), and conspiracy to engage in the aforementioned crimes. See International Military Tribunal (1948: 11).

6 On the notion of 'bare life', see Agamben (1998). For discussions of ways to think of 'rooted' versions of cosmopolitanism, see for example Appiah (1997); Beck (2002a); Erskine (2002); Szerszynski and Urry (2002).

7 Beck's characterization of 'zombie categories' bears a striking resemblance to Arendt's assertion in 1945 that 'national sovereignty is no longer a working concept of politics' yet it still 'leads the life of a walking corpse, whose spurious existence is artificially prolonged by repeated injections of imperial expansion' (EU: 143).

8 Arendt's very limited remarks on world federalism can also be found in 'The Nation' (EU: 206–11) and in 'Thoughts on Revolution and Politics' (CR: 199–233), where she remarks provocatively on the possible role of the council system leading to a 'new concept of the state' situated horizontally within a worldwide federated system. In *On Revolution* (166), she refers to the federal system as 'the sole alternative to the nation-state principle'.

9 In her 1945 essay 'Approaches to the "German Problem"', Arendt approvingly refers to the European resistance as an example of a postnational cosmopolitan movement, whose 'new appetite for responsibility', 'new feeling of European solidarity' and 'defense of human dignity' led them to recognize the 'crisis of state sovereignty' and raise the central issue that a 'good peace is now inconceivable unless the States surrender parts of their economic and political sovereignty to a higher European authority' (EU: 112–17).

10 One of the arrest warrants was subsequently terminated in July 2007, due to the death of the accused (ICC 2007).

11 In this respect, cosmopolitan realism connects up well with the notion of 'cosmopolitan memory'; see Levy and Sznaider (2002).

12 A variation on this theme appears in the writing of Jacques Derrida, who suggests that all decisions of responsibility involve ambiguities, paradoxes or contradictions that cannot be resolved logically into a dialectical third term. For Derrida, responsibility cannot rid itself of this double bind, for to do so would be to eradicate the plurality and alterity of human beings, which opens up the call of responding to the other and the political experiences of the twentieth century in the first place. Derrida's writings on this topic are voluminous, but some of the more relevant ones include (Derrida 1991, 1992, 1995, 1996).

13 Here cosmopolitan realism parts ways with John Rawls's 'realistic utopia', which contends that 'the great evils of human history' will '*eventually disappear*' once 'the gravest forms of political injustice are eliminated by following just (or at least decent) social policies and establishing just (or at least decent) basic institutions' (Rawls 1999: 6–7).

2 Superfluous humanity

1 For applications of Arendt's work to the related issue of violence in international politics, see Young (2003); Owens (2005).

2 Several prominent studies of Germany and the Holocaust have followed on from Arendt's ideas about the banality of evil, specifically the notion that ordinary people committed extraordinary crimes. Christopher Browning (1992) has focused on the roles of ordinary men within the context of a specific unit of the German Order Police operating in occupied Poland – many of whom chose to participate in the mass murder of Jews, even when given the opportunity to opt out. Daniel Goldhagen (1996) has concentrated on a comprehensive assessment of German society as whole, and of how many ordinary Germans deliberately supported the Nazi regime's campaign of extermination against the Jews. Goldhagen's work has attracted a great deal of criticism because many detractors believe it overgeneralizes in its indictment (or, for some, demonization) of the German public, and exaggerates the influence of what Goldhagen refers to as an 'eliminationist' variant of anti-Semitism that he believes was widely adhered to in German society. Arendt argues, in contrast, that anti-Semitism cannot

adequately account either for the specific political phenomenon of genocide, or for the actions taken by Eichmann and others in support of the project to exterminate European Jews. For more on the debate surrounding Goldhagen's work, see Eley (2000).

3 To clarify, what makes the case of Eichmann so terrifying is not that he was a good person who turned into an obviously bad one, or that he was innately bad; rather it was the particular notion of 'goodness' subscribed to by Eichmann (and apparently widely shared by others throughout European society) that enabled him to participate in administrative murder while possessing a sense of continuing moral rectitude. No matter what he did, he was convinced that it was unquestionably 'right' according to widespread social convention.

4 To avoid misunderstanding, it should be noted that I am not claiming any kind of moral equivalence between genocide (or the Holocaust in particular) and extreme global poverty; one is not 'as evil as', or simply analogous to, the other. Rather, they are different forms or orders of political evil imposed on human beings treated as thoroughly superfluous, although they may overlap or be mutually reinforcing.

5 The preceding data are from UNDP (2002, 2003, 2004, 2005); Nesiba and Burton (2004).

6 For further discussion of the multifaceted (economic, environmental, cultural, social and political) nature of vulnerability confronting poor societies and individuals therein, see Kirby (2006).

7 Interestingly, although Bales does not refer to Arendt, his observations on contemporary slavery and slaveholders suggest that the practice of new slavery can be characterized aptly in terms of the banality of evil. While many people would describe a slaveholder as evil in a traditional sense – as diabolical and 'not like us' – Bales notes that, on the contrary, his extensive interactions with slaveholders show them to be no 'different from a "normal" human being' and that they generally 'were family men who thought of themselves as businessmen' and 'pillars of the local community', engaged in a practice that 'is simply a small variable among many in a much larger economic equation' (Bales 2005: 24–25, 27). This reveals how the normalization or banalization of modern slavery has become globally spread across many different social and political contexts.

8 Pogge argues for a cosmopolitan approach to redistribution by focusing on the extent to which individuals are interdependent within the global economy. One of the shortcomings of this argument is that it places too great an emphasis on some notion of reciprocal advantage. I would suggest instead that all individuals should be considered the proper subjects of distributive justice regardless of their contribution to the global political economy, given the large numbers of global poor who are made 'redundant' by that very economic system. While a number of important questions about distributive justice connect with the overall discussion here, it is beyond the aim of this chapter to discuss them directly. Suffice it to say that charity cannot satisfy the demands of justice: 'Charity is an option, that is true, *but charity does not touch the sources of evil*. For that it would take political measures' (Bittner 2001: 30; emphasis added).

9 For a thoughtful discussion of Arendt and the relation between political injustice and invisibility, see Danielle Allen (2005).

10 Bauman refers to this condition as the social nature of evil, in *Modernity and the Holocaust* (1989: 166–68).

11 For an excellent treatment of Arendt on this point see Nedelsky (2001).

12 Singer notes that Bush mentioned evil in 319 speeches between 20 January 2001 and 16 June 2003. This same stark dichotomy is, of course, employed by militant Islamic extremists convinced that the USA is 'the' evil enemy. An exhaustive analysis of the Manichaean rhetoric of demonization in US presidential discourse, especially that of George W. Bush, is provided by Ivie and Giner (2007).

13 Arendt notes in her essay 'On Humanity in Dark Times: Thoughts about Lessing' that counteracting the 'worldlessness' that results from persecution and exploitation cannot

be achieved simply by having compassion for 'the unfortunate', but only by establishing 'justice for all' (MDT: 14).

3 Citizens of nowhere

1 The formal name of the Enabling Act, passed on 23 March 1933, was 'Law to Remedy the Distress of the People and the Nation'.
2 Although much of what is said in this chapter can be applied to immigration generally, the specific focus here is on stateless persons and refugees as particularly emblematic of the problem of rightlessness. Because refugees can be both *de facto* and *de jure* stateless, as discussed below, I refer to both stateless persons and refugees as exemplifying the condition of statelessness.
3 Following customary practice guided by contemporary international law, the terms 'citizenship' and 'nationality' are here used synonymously.
4 See also Batchelor (1995: 91–92). Arendt points out (EJ: 239–40) – with some irony, given his role in the denationalization and extermination of German Jews – that it was Adolf Eichmann's *de facto* statelessness that enabled the Israeli government to kidnap him in Argentina and transport him to Israel for trial, since neither Germany (his country of legal nationality) nor Argentina (where he was a resident alien) offered to extend Eichmann legal protection.
5 Jean-François Lyotard (1993) provides a thoughtful gloss on Arendt's notion of the right to have rights, framed as the 'right of interlocution' by which each individual 'whose right to address others is recognized by those others'.
6 For a now classic analysis of the development of nationalism and the nation-state that bears similarities to Arendt's critique, see Anderson (1983).
7 Arendt makes this point in reference to race conceived as a type of 'difference in general', that is, as the basis for reducing humanity from equal legal–political status to the 'natural' inequality of 'species' differentiation. She writes: 'If a Negro in a white community is considered a Negro and nothing else, he loses along with his right to equality that freedom of action which is specifically human; all his deeds are now explained as "necessary" consequences of some "Negro" qualities; he has become some specimen of an animal species, called man' (OT: 383).
8 I borrow the term 'imperial nation-state' from Wilder (2005). Wilder's book provides an exceptionally detailed analysis of the structural contradictions embodied in a specific European nation-state, in many respects helpfully illuminating some of Arendt's earlier claims.
9 For an excellent analysis of the link between European biopolitical racism and imperial regimes, that builds on Foucault's work, see Stoler (1995).
10 In *Remnants of Auschwitz: The Witness and the Archive*, Agamben (1999) explores the indistinction between the human and inhuman that occurs through the experience of abandonment in the concentration camp.
11 Through an analysis of sovereignty via the works of Hans Kelsen and Carl Schmitt, Hidemi Suganami (2007: 529, 530) concludes that because 'the practice of sovereignty is a *sufficient condition* of the *possibility* of arbitrary violence (and its actualisation under relevant conditions), it follows, by the force of logic, that the *possibility* of arbitrary violence (and its actualisation under those conditions) is a *necessary condition* of the practice of sovereignty'. Thus, within the global system of nation-states, 'the underlying practice of sovereignty' appears 'inescapably to be intertwined with the *possibility* of arbitrary violence'.
12 The UNHCR often assists governments in refugee status determination or, in about 9 per cent of cases, even undertakes this determination itself (UNHCR 2007a: 48). For a penetrating critique of the way the figure of the 'refugee' is constructed as a necessarily 'fearful' and passive subject, see Nyers (2006).

13 Six UN bodies have been established to monitor the principal international human rights treaties.

14 Some recommendations in this direction include Sassen (1999); Cohen (2006); Moses (2006).

15 As President *and* Commander-in-Chief of the US armed forces, President Bush was, conveniently enough, constitutionally empowered to decree the sovereign power of exception by means of his own authority. See the 'Military Order' on the 'Detention, Treatment and Trial of Certain Non-Citizens in the War Against Terrorism' (13 November 2001), available at www.state.gov/coalition/cr/prs/6077.htm.

16 Available at www.comlaw.gov.au/ComLaw/Legislation/Act1.nsf/ framelodgmentattachments/A475B9194F726EF8CA25741E00783CFB.

17 This is what happened to Peter Qasim, who was born in the disputed territory of Kashmir, India but fled to Australia as an asylum-seeker in 1998 because of fears of political persecution. Qasim arrived in Australia without identity documents, and India refused to acknowledge that he was an Indian citizen. As an 'illegal' stateless person, Qasim was placed in mandatory detention where he remained for seven years. In July 2005 he was released and given a 'Return Pending Bridging Visa', which allowed him to remain in Australia temporarily until he could be deported to another country. See BBC News (2005).

18 'Home Secretary Statement on Zones of Protection' (27 March 2003), available at www.ncadc.org.uk/archives/filed%20newszines/oldnewszines/newszine32/zones.html.

19 Human Rights Watch (2007b) reports that more than 900 unaccompanied children from Africa arrived in the Canary Islands by boat in 2006. In response, the Spanish government opened four new 'emergency centres', in which the majority of the children are being detained for indefinite periods and, according to HRW observers, are regularly subjected to abuse and ill-treatment by staff. The children have also been denied the opportunity to apply for asylum, as required by the 1989 Convention on the Rights of the Child (ratified by Spain in 1990).

20 As a reality check, it should be noted that despite the alarmist rhetoric that Western states are being overrun by a massive influx of displaced persons, the vast majority of the world's refugees and stateless persons, who are concentrated in Africa, Asia and Latin America, end up in neighbouring countries. Thus the world's poorest countries actually assume the most responsibility for refugees. In 1999, for example, Tanzania received more refugees than the whole of Europe put together, and currently hosts 400,000 refugees from neighbouring states. In 2005, the main countries of asylum for the ten largest refugee movements in the world all were in Africa and Central Asia (see UNHCR 2006).

21 It is worth recalling that in 1973, the United Nations qualified apartheid as a crime against humanity in the International Convention on the Suppression and Punishment of the Crime of Apartheid. While motivated directly by the policies and actions of the apartheid regime in South Africa, the Convention and its corresponding qualification of apartheid as a crime against humanity is not limited to that specific context, but is articulated as a fundamental principle of international and human rights law.

22 Having said that, it is not my intention here to engage with various normative arguments for (and against) freedom of movement within the literature on the ethics of immigration, as doing so would carry this chapter too far afield from its purpose of making the case that statelessness is a type of political evil. These types of debate are important, but they are secondary to Arendt's phenomenological point about movement and the human condition. For an excellent collection of articles on the ethics of movement and migration, see Barry and Goodin (1992); Seglow (2005).

23 It is extremely telling that there remains no right to freedom of movement across borders in international human rights law.

24 Jacques Derrida (1997) offers a similar critique of the concept of fraternity as predicated on the assumption of 'filiation' (or a model of lineage and descent that parallels the

jus sanguinis mode of acquiring citizenship) and thus of a metaphysics of identity that excludes those who do not share a presumed 'being-common' or 'being-in-common' (such as race, nationality, ethnicity, religion and class). For an excellent discussion of Arendt's conception of solidarity as requiring respect for 'strangerhood', see Hansen (2004).

25 Arendt's argument obviously draws on Kant's notion of universal hospitality and the 'right to visit' that he makes a cornerstone of his cosmopolitanism. Arendt never explores the Kantian notion of hospitality in any depth (see, for instance, the brief reference at the conclusion of her *Lectures on Kant's Political Philosophy*), although she strongly identifies with it through her reading of Jaspers' conception of world citizenship grounded on 'limitless communication' between the diversity of human beings who inhabit the earth (see 'Karl Jaspers: Citizen of the World?' in MDT). Seyla Benhabib (2004a) has probably most systematically examined the link between Kant and Arendt on the imperative of hospitality. Bonnie Honig (2006) provides a vigorous though sympathetic challenge to Benhabib's arguments.

4 Effacing the political

1 The three modes of the *vita activa* are mirrored by the three modes of the *vita contempletiva*: thinking, willing and judging.
2 For an illuminating discussion of Arendt's early (pre-*The Human Condition*) accounts of society and the social, see Pitkin (1998: 19–68).
3 The rise and expansion of the social as diagnosed in *The Human Condition* should be understood in light of Arendt's analysis of bourgeois capitalism and imperialism in *The Origins of Totalitarianism*, discussed in Chapter 2.
4 While my emphasis in this chapter is on Arendt's diagnosis of the progressive privatization and thus depoliticization of the public realm, it is important to realize that Arendt regarded this process as being disastrous for the private realm as well. For Arendt, the private realm provided a 'reliable hiding place from the common public world', for a life spent entirely in the public realm would 'lose its depth' and become 'shallow'. Some 'place to hide in', a home away from the glare of the public eye, is vital to protecting and nurturing personal relationships, love, childhood, and one's hopes, dreams and thinking (HC: 73). As Seyla Benhabib points out, the public and private realms should be conceived as interdependent: 'the public is inconceivable without the private, and vice versa' (Benhabib 2000: 211). Phenomenologically, Arendt suggests, the 'most elementary meaning of the two realms indicates that there are things that need to be hidden and others that need to be displayed publicly *if they are to exist at all*' (HC: 73; emphasis added). Consequently, we can understand the full extent of Arendt's critique of the social only by recognizing that it makes public what should remain private, and makes private what should be made public – thereby destroying both.
5 In a letter to Karl Jaspers (dated 6 August 1955), Arendt wrote: 'I've begun so late, really only in recent years, to truly love the world. … Out of gratitude, I want to call my book on political theories [*The Human Condition*] "*Amor Mundi*"' (AJ: 264).
6 Outside the Anglo-American context, the TINA claim is often referred to by the expression *pensée unique* ('single thought'); see Touraine (2001).
7 It should be noted that Smith also believed that the free market economy, as it develops through increasing division of labour, required certain initiatives on the part of government, particularly publicly funded education, in order to counteract the potential deterioration of intellect and cultural values within the mass labouring class. Neoliberals tend to ignore Smith's concerns about the degenerative effects of the free market system (although such concerns might be only an expression of Smith's desire to ensure the continued improvement of the free market system through successive generations).
8 See the group's 'Statement of Aims', www.montpelerin.org/mpsGoals.cfm.

9   *Ibid.*

10   See, for instance, Bernstein (1986); Dietz (1991); Wellmer (1996); Benhabib (2000: ch 5).

11   The Marxist view is similar in the sense that politics (and the struggle for political power) derives from socioeconomic needs. Such conceptions of political life reduce politics to solving the social question and tend, at best, to relegate political freedom to the background and, at worst, to resort to tyranny and terror.

12   For a similar point see, for example, Canovan (1994: 180).

13   For a trenchant critique of neoliberal globalization as ideology, see Touraine (2001). Manfred Steger (2005) refers to neoliberal ideology as 'globalism' and suggests that it entails the following propositions: globalization equals the liberalization and global integration of markets; globalization is inevitable and irreversible; nobody is in charge of globalization; globalization benefits everyone; and globalization furthers the spread of democracy.

14   Similarly, Pierre Bourdieu (1998: 96) refers to neoliberalism as a 'logical machine, which presents itself as a chain of constraints impelling the economic agents'.

15   I borrow the trope of executioners and victims from Albert Camus' prescient and powerful 1946 essay 'Neither Victims nor Executioners' in Camus (1991).

16   For an extensive treatment of the biopolitical dimensions of global neoliberalism, see Ong (2006).

17   See Bourdieu (1998: 29 ff.) for a similar critique of how 'neo-liberalism comes to be seen as an *inevitability*'.

18   David Harvey (2005: 117) notes that 'NGOs have in many instances stepped into the vacuum in social provision left by the withdrawal of the state from such activities. This amounts to privatization by NGO' and, in the words of Tina Wallace, 'NGOs thereby function as "Trojan horses for global neoliberalism"'.

19   For a fuller discussion of the relationship between the alternative globalization movement and Arendt's conception of political action, see Lang (2005).

Bibliography

Adorno, T. (1983) *Prisms*, Cambridge, MA: MIT Press.
——(1994) *Negative Dialectics*, New York: Continuum.
——(2003) 'Education after Auschwitz', in R. Tiedemann (ed.) *Can One Live after Auschwitz? A Philosophical Reader*, Stanford, CA: Stanford University Press.
Agamben, G. (1998) Homo Sacer: *Sovereign Power and Bare Life*, Stanford, CA: Stanford University Press.
——(1999) *Remnants of Auschwitz: The Witness and the Archive*, New York: Zone Books.
Allen, D. (2005) 'Invisible Citizens: Political Exclusion and Domination in Arendt and Ellison', in M. S. Williams and S. Macedo (eds) *Political Exclusion and Domination*, New York: New York University Press.
Allen, T. (2005) *War and Justice in Northern Uganda: An Assessment of the International Criminal Court's Intervention (Draft)*, London: Crisis States Research Centre, London School of Economics, www.crisisstates.com/download/others/AllenICCReport.pdf.
——(2006) *Trial Justice: The International Criminal Court and the Lord's Resistance Army*, London: Zed Books.
Altman, A. and Wellman, C. H. (2004) 'In Defense of International Criminal Law', *Ethics* 115: 35–67.
Anderson, B. (1983) *Imagined Communities: Reflections on the Origin and Spread of Nationalism*, London: Verso.
Anderson, P. (2000) 'Renewals', *New Left Review* 1: 5–24.
Appiah, K. A. (1997) 'Cosmopolitan Patriots', *Critical Inquiry* 23: 617–39.
Arendt, H. (1958) *The Human Condition*, 2nd edn, Chicago, IL: University of Chicago Press.
——(1963) *On Revolution*, New York: Penguin.
——(1965) *Eichmann in Jerusalem: A Report on the Banality of Evil*, revised edn, New York: Penguin.
——(1968) *Between Past and Future: Eight Exercises in Political Thought*, New York: Penguin.
——(1968) *Men in Dark Times*, San Diego/New York/London: Harcourt Brace & Co.
——(1970) *On Violence*, San Diego/New York/London: Harcourt Brace & Co.
——(1972) *Crises of the Republic*, San Diego/New York/London: Harcourt Brace & Co.
——(1977) 'Public Rights and Private Interests: In Response to Charles Frankel', in M. Mooney and F. Stuber (eds) *Small Comforts for Hard Times: Humanists on Public Policy*, New York: Columbia University Press.
——(1978a) *The Jew as Pariah: Jewish Identity and Politics in the Modern Age*, edited by R. Feldman, New York: Grove Press.

——(1978b) *The Life of the Mind*, San Diego/New York/London: Harcourt Brace & Co.

——(1992) *Lectures on Kant's Political Philosophy*, edited by R. Beiner, Chicago, IL: University of Chicago Press.

——(1994) *Essays in Understanding 1930–1954*, edited by J. Kohn, New York: Schocken Books.

——(1998) *Love and Saint Augustine*, edited by J. V. Scott and J. C. Stark, Chicago, IL: University of Chicago Press.

——(2003) *Responsibility and Judgment*, edited by J. Kohn, New York: Schocken Books.

——(2004) *The Origins of Totalitarianism*, revised edn, New York: Schocken Books.

——(2005) *The Promise of Politics*, New York: Schocken Books.

——(2007) *The Jewish Writings*, edited by J. Kohn and R. H. Feldman, New York: Schocken Books.

Arendt, H. and Jaspers, K. (1992) *Hannah Arendt/Karl Jaspers: Correspondence 1926–1969*, edited by L. Kohler and H. Saner, New York: Harcourt Brace Jovanovich.

Arrighi, G. (2002) 'The African Crisis: World Systemic and Regional Aspects', *New Left Review* 15: 5–36.

Augustine (1972), *City of God*, London: Penguin.

Australian Government (2007) *Annual Report, 2004–5*, Department of Immigration and Citizenship, www.immi.gov.au/about/reports/annual/2004-05/pdf.htm.

Axtmann, R. (2006) 'Globality, Plurality and Freedom: The Arendtian Perspective', *Review of International Studies* 32: 93–117.

Baehr, P. (2002) 'Identifying the Unprecedented: Hannah Arendt, Totalitarianism, and the Critique of Sociology', *American Sociological Review* 67: 804–31.

Bales, K. (2004) *Disposable People: New Slavery in the Global Economy*, revised edn, Berkeley, CA: University of California Press.

——(2005) *Understanding Global Slavery: A Reader*, Berkeley, CA: University of California Press.

Balibar, É. (2004) *We, The People of Europe? Reflections on Transnational Citizenship*, Princeton, NJ/Oxford, UK: Princeton University Press.

——(2005) 'Difference, Otherness, Exclusion', *Parallax* 11: 19–34.

Bass, G. (2000) *Stay the Hand of Vengeance: The Politics of War Crimes Tribunals*, Princeton, NJ: Princeton University Press.

Bassiouni, M. C. (1999) *International Criminal Law*, Ardsley, NY: Transnational Publishers.

Batchelor, C. A. (1995) 'UNHCR and Issues Related to Nationality', *Refugee Studies Quarterly* 14: 91–112.

Barry, B. and Goodin, R. E. (eds) (1992) *Free Movement: Ethical Issues in the Transnational Migration of People and of Money*, New York/London: Harvester Wheatsheaf.

Bauman, Z. (1989) *Modernity and the Holocaust*, Ithaca, NY: Cornell University Press.

——(1998) *Work, Consumerism, and the New Poor*, Buckingham: Open University Press.

——(1999) *Globalization: The Human Consequences*, New York: Columbia University Press.

——(2004) *Wasted Lives: Modernity and its Outcasts*, Cambridge: Polity Press.

BBC News (2005) 'Australia Frees "Indian" Migrant', 17 July, http://news.bbc.co.uk/1/hi/world/south_asia/4690423.stm.

Beck, U. (1992) *Risk Society: Towards a New Modernity*, London: Sage.

——(1997) *The Reinvention of Politics: Rethinking Modernity in the Global Social Order*, Cambridge: Polity Press.

——(1999) *World Risk Society*, Cambridge: Polity Press.

——(2002a) 'The Cosmopolitan Society and its Enemies', *Theory, Culture & Society*, 19: 17–44.

——(2002b) 'The Terrorist Threat: World Risk Society Revisited', *Theory, Culture & Society* 19: 39–55.

——(2003) 'Toward a New Critical Theory with a Cosmopolitan Intent', *Constellations* 104: 453–68.

——(2005) *Power in the Global Age: A New Global Political Economy*, Cambridge: Polity Press.

——(2006) *The Cosmopolitan Vision*, Cambridge: Polity.

Beiner, R. (2000) 'Arendt and Nationalism', in D. Villa (ed.) *The Cambridge Companion to Hannah Arendt*, Cambridge: Cambridge University Press.

Beitz, C. (1999) *Political Theory and International Relations*, 2nd edn, Princeton, NJ: Princeton University Press.

Benhabib, S. (2000) *The Reluctant Modernism of Hannah Arendt*, Lanham, MD: Rowman & Littlefield.

——(2002) 'Political Geographies in a Global World: Arendtian Reflections', *Social Research* 69: 539–66.

——(2004a) *The Rights of Others: Aliens, Residents, and Citizens*, Cambridge: Cambridge University Press.

——(2004b) *Reclaiming Universalism: Negotiating Republican Self-Determination and Cosmopolitan Norms*, The Tanner Lectures on Human Values, University of California at Berkeley, March 15–19, 2004, www.tannerlectures.utah.edu/lectures/documents/volume25/benhabib_2005.pdf

Bernstein, R. J. (1986) *Philosophical Profiles*, Philadelphia, PA: University of Pennsylvania Press.

——(1996) *Hannah Arendt and the Jewish Question*, Cambridge, MA: MIT Press.

——(2002) *Radical Evil: A Philosophical Interrogation*, Cambridge: Polity Press.

——(2005) *The Abuse of Evil: The Corruption of Politics and Religion since 9/11*, Cambridge: Polity Press.

Bittner, R. (2001) 'Morality and World Hunger', in T. Pogge (ed.) *Global Justice*, Oxford: Blackwell.

Blättler, S. and Marti, I. (2005) 'Rosa Luxemburg and Hannah Arendt: Against the Destruction of Political Spheres of Freedom', *Hypatia* 20: 88–101.

Bourdieu, P. (1998) *Acts of Resistance: Against the New Myths of Our Time*, Cambridge: Polity Press.

Brakman, S., Garretsen, H., van Marrewijk, C. and van Witteloostuijn, A. (2006) *Nations and Firms in the Global Economy: An Introduction to International Economics and Business*, Cambridge: Cambridge University Press.

Branch, A. (2007) 'Uganda's Civil War and the Politics of ICC Intervention', *Ethics & International Affairs* 21: 179–98.

Browning, C. R. (1992) *Ordinary Men: Reserve Police Battalion 101 and the Final Solution in Poland*, London: Penguin.

Burton, M. and Nesiba, R. (2004) 'Transnational Financial Institutions, Global Financial Flows, and the International Monetary Fund', in P. O'Hara (ed.) *Global Political Economy and the Wealth of Nations: Performance, Institutions, Problems and Policies*, London: Routledge.

Camus, A. (1991) 'Neither Victims nor Executioners', in *Between Hell and Reason: Essays from the Resistance Newspaper Combat, 1944–1947*, Hanover, NH/London, UK: Wesleyan University Press.

Canovan, M. (1992) *Hannah Arendt: A Reinterpretation of Her Political Thought*, Cambridge: Cambridge University Press.

——(1994) 'Politics as Culture: Hannah Arendt and the Public Realm', in L. P. Hinchman and S. K. Hinchman (eds) *Hannah Arendt: Critical Essays*, Albany, NY: SUNY Press.

Castells, M. (1998), *The Information Age: Economy, Society and Culture*, Oxford: Blackwell.

Chayes, A. and Slaughter, A. (2000) 'The ICC and the Future of the Global Legal System', in S. B. Sewall and C. Kaysen (eds) *National Security and International Law: The United States and the International Criminal Court*, Lanham, MD: Rowman & Littlefield.

Cohen, R. (2006) *Migration and its Enemies: Global Capital, Migrant Labour and the Nation-State*, Aldershot: Ashgate Publishing.

Cole, P. (2006) *The Myth of Evil*, Edinburgh: Edinburgh University Press.

Cotter, B. (2005) 'Hannah Arendt and "the Right to Have Rights"', in A. F. Lang Jr and J. Williams (eds), *Hannah Arendt and International Relations: Readings Across the Lines*, Basingstoke: Palgrave Macmillan.

Craig, G., Gaus, A., Wilkinson, M., Skrivankova, K. and McQuade, A. (2007) *Contemporary Slavery in the UK: Overview and Key Issues*, York: Joseph Rowntree Foundation, www.jrf.org.uk.

Curtis, K. (1999) *Our Sense of the Real: Aesthetic Experience and Arendtian Politics*, Ithaca, NY: Cornell University Press.

d'Entrèves, M. P. (1994) *The Political Philosophy of Hannah Arendt*, London: Routledge.

Della Carpini, M. and Trägårdh, L. (2004) 'The Juridification of Politics in the United States and Europe: Historical Roots, Contemporary Debates, and Future Prospects', in L. Trägårdh (ed.) *After National Democracy: Rights, Law and Power in America and the New Europe*, Oxford: Hart Publishing.

Derrida, J. (1991) '"Eating Well", or the Calculation of the Subject', in E. Cadava, P. Connor and J. Nancy (eds) *Who Comes After the Subject?* New York and London: Routledge.

——(1992) 'The Force of Law: The "Mystical Foundation of Authority"', in D. Cornell (ed.) *Deconstruction and the Possibility of Justice*, New York: Routledge.

——(1995) *The Gift of Death*, Chicago, IL: University of Chicago Press.

——(1996) *Aporias*, Stanford, CA: Stanford University Press.

——(1997) *Politics of Friendship*, London/New York: Verso.

——(2001) *On Cosmopolitanism and Forgiveness*, London/New York: Routledge.

Diamond, L. (1999) *Developing Democracy: Towards Consolidation*, Baltimore, MD: Johns Hopkins University Press.

Dietz, M. G. (1991) 'Hannah Arendt and Feminist Politics', in M. Shanley and C. Pateman (eds) *Feminist Interpretations and Political Theory*, Cambridge: Polity Press.

——(2000) 'Arendt and the Holocaust', in D. Villa (ed.) *The Cambridge Companion to Hannah Arendt*, Cambridge: Cambridge University Press.

Eley, G. (ed.) (2000) *The Goldhagen Effect: History, Memory, Nazism – Facing The German Past*, Ann Arbor, MI: University of Michigan Press.

el-Ojeili, C. and Hayden, P. (2006) *Critical Theories of Globalization*, Basingstoke: Palgrave Macmillan.

Erskine, T. (2002) '"Citizen of Nowhere" or "the Point Where Circles Intersect": Impartialist and Embedded Cosmopolitanisms', *Review of International Studies* 28: 457–78.

Euben, J. P. (2000) 'Arendt's Hellenism', in D. Villa (ed.) *The Cambridge Companion to Hannah Arendt*, Cambridge: Cambridge University Press.

Falk, R. (2000) 'Resisting "Globalization-from-Above" through "Globalization-from-Below"', in B. K. Gills (ed.) *Globalization and the Politics of Resistance*, Basingstoke: Palgrave Macmillan.

Farmer, P. (2003) *Pathologies of Power: Health, Human Rights, and the New War on the Poor*, Berkeley, CA: University of California Press.

Finnström, S. (2003) *Living with Bad Surroundings: War and Existential Uncertainty in Acholiland, Northern Uganda*, Uppsala: Uppsala University Press.

Foucault, M. (1990) *The History of Sexuality, Volume 1: An Introduction*, New York: Vintage Books.

——(2003) *'Society Must be Defended': Lectures at the Collège de France, 1975–1976*, New York: Picador.

——(2007) *Security, Territory, Population: Lectures at the Collège de France, 1977–1978*, Basingstoke: Palgrave Macmillan.

Franceschet, A. (2005) 'Cosmopolitan Ethics and Global Legalism', *Journal of Global Ethics* 1: 113–26.

Friedman, M. (1962) *Price Theory: A Provisional Text*, London: Cass.

——(1980) *Free to Choose: A Personal Statement*, New York: Harcourt.

Friedman, T. L. (1999) *The Lexus and the Olive Tree*, New York: Farrar, Straus & Giroux.

Geddes, A. (2000) *Immigration and European Integration: Towards Fortress Europe?* Manchester, UK: Manchester University Press.

Gibney, M. J. (2006) '"A Thousand Little Guantánamos": Western States and Measures to Prevent the Arrival of Refugees', in K. E. Tunstall (ed.) *Displacement, Asylum, Migration: The Oxford Amnesty Lectures 2004*, Oxford: Oxford University Press.

Gill, S. (2005) 'Theorizing the Interregnum: The Double Movement and Global Politics in the 1990s', in L. Armoore (ed.) *The Global Resistance Reader*, London: Routledge.

Gilpin, R. (2001) *Global Political Economy*, Princeton, NJ: Princeton University Press.

Goldhagen, D. J. (1996) *Hitler's Willing Executioners: Ordinary Germans and the Holocaust*, London: Abacus.

Habermas, J. (1987) *The Theory of Communicative Action*, Vol. 2, Boston, MA: Beacon Press.

——(1989) *The Structural Transformation of the Public Sphere*, Cambridge, MA: MIT Press.

——(1996) *Between Facts and Norms: Contributions to a Discourse Theory of Law and Democracy*, Cambridge, MA: MIT Press.

Hansen, P. (1993) *Hannah Arendt: Politics, History and Citizenship*, Cambridge: Polity Press.

——(2004) 'Hannah Arendt and Bearing with Strangers', *Contemporary Political Theory* 3: 3–22.

Hardt, M. and Negri, A. (2000) *Empire*, Cambridge, MA: Harvard University Press.

Harvey, D. (2005) *A Brief History of Neoliberalism*, Oxford: Oxford University Press.

Hayek, F. A. (1952) *The Counter-Revolution of Science: Studies on the Abuse of Reason*, Glencoe, IL: The Free Press.

——(1960) *The Constitution of Liberty*, Chicago, IL: University of Chicago Press.

——(1967) *Studies in Philosophy, Politics and Economics*, London: Routledge & Kegan Paul.

——(1977) *Law, Legislation, and Liberty*, Vol. 2, Chicago, IL: University of Chicago Press.

——(1978) *New Studies in Philosophy, Politics, Economics and the History of Ideas*, Chicago, IL: University of Chicago Press.

Held, D. and McGrew, A. (1999) *Global Transformations: Politics, Economics and Culture*, Cambridge: Polity Press.

Herbert, G. B. (2002) *A Philosophical History of Rights*, Brunswick, NJ: Transaction Publishers.

Herman, E. (2002) 'Foreword', in D. Chandler (ed.) *From Kosovo to Kabul: Human Rights and International Intervention*, London: Pluto Press.

Herzog, A. (2004) 'Political Itineraries and Anarchic Cosmopolitanism in the Thought of Hannah Arendt', *Inquiry* 47: 20–41.

Hobbes, T. (1996) *Leviathan*, edited by R. Tuck, Cambridge: Cambridge University Press.

Hodgson, G. (1993) *Economics and Evolution: Bringing Life Back into Economics*, Cambridge: Polity Press.

Holsti, K. J. (2004) *Taming the Sovereigns: Institutional Change in International Politics*, Cambridge: Cambridge University Press.

Honig, B. (2006) 'Another Cosmopolitanism? Law and Politics in the New Europe', in S. Benhabib, *Another Cosmopolitanism*, R. Post (ed.), Oxford: Oxford University Press.

Howard, J. (2003) 'To Deter and To Deny: Australia and the Interdiction of Asylum Seekers', *Refuge* 21: 35–50.

Human Rights Watch (2006) 'Commentary on Australia's Temporary Protection Visas for Refugees', www.hrw.org/backgrounder/refugees/australia051303.htm.

——(2007a) 'The June 29 Agreement on Accountability and Reconciliation and the Need for Adequate Penalties for the Most Serious Crimes', http://hrw.org/backgrounder/ij/uganda0707.

——(2007b) 'Unwelcome Responsibilities: Spain's Failure to Protect the Rights of Unaccompanied Migrant Children in the Canary Islands', http://hrw.org/reports/2007/spain0707/spain0707web.pdf.

ICC (2004) 'President of Uganda refers situation concerning the Lord's Resistance Army (LRA) to the ICC', International Criminal Court press release, 29 January, www.icc-cpi.int/press/pressreleases/16.html.

——(2007) 'The Prosecutor v. Joseph Kony, Vincent Otti, Okot Odhiambo, Raska Lukwiya, Dominic Ongwen', 11 July, www.icc-cpi.int/library/cases/ICC-02-04-01-05-248_English.pdf.

ICMPD (2004) *Irregular Transit Migration in the Mediterranean: Some Facts, Futures and Insights*, Vienna: International Centre on Migration Policy Development.

Ignatieff, M. (2000) *The Rights Revolution*, Toronto: Canadian Broadcasting Corporation.

ILO (2006) *The End of Child Labour: Within Reach*, Geneva: International Labour Organization, www.ilo.org/public/english/standards/relm/ilc/ilc95/pdf/rep-i-b.pdf.

International Military Tribunal (1948) *Trial of the Major War Criminals before the International Military Tribunal*, Vol. 1, Nuremberg: Secretariat of the International Military Tribunal.

Isaac, J. C. (1996) 'A New Guarantee on Earth: Hannah Arendt on Human Dignity and the Politics of Human Rights', *American Political Science Review*, 90: 61–73.

Ivie, R. L. and Giner, O. (2007) 'Hunting the Devil: Democracy's Rhetorical Impulse to War', *Presidential Studies Quarterly* 37: 580–98.

Jeffery, R. (2005) 'Review Article: Beyond Banality? Ethical Responses to Evil in Post-September 11 International Relations', *International Affairs* 81: 175–86.

Judt, T (2008) 'The "Problem of Evil" in Postwar Europe', *The New York Review of Books* 55, 14 February, www.nybooks.com/articles/21031.

Justice and Reconciliation Project (2007) '"Abomination": Local Belief Systems and International Justice', www.ligi.ubc.ca/sites/liu/files/Publications/JRP/JRPFN5Sept2007.pdf.

Kaldor, M. (2003) *Global Civil Society: An Answer to War*, Cambridge: Polity Press.

Kant, I. (1960) *Religion within the Limits of Reason Alone*, La Salle, IL: Open Court.

——(1978) *Anthropology from a Pragmatic Point of View*, Carbondale, IL: Southern Illinois University Press.

——(1991) 'Perpetual Peace', in H. Reiss (ed.) *Kant's Political Writings*, Cambridge: Cambridge University Press.

——(1997) *Critique of Practical Reason*, Cambridge: Cambridge University Press.

Kateb, G. (1992) *The Inner Ocean: Individualism and Democratic Culture*, Ithaca, NY: Cornell University Press.

——(2000) 'Political Action: Its Nature and Advantages', in D. Villa (ed.) *The Cambridge Companion to Hannah Arendt*, Cambridge: Cambridge University Press.

Keane, J. (2003) *Global Civil Society?* Cambridge: Cambridge University Press.

Kekes, J. (1990) *Facing Evil*, Princeton, NJ: Princeton University Press.

Kelly, F. (2001) 'Tampa Asylum-seekers Caught in Political Deadlock', Australia Broadcasting Corporation, 30 August, www.abc.net.au/7.30/content/2001/s355371.htm.

Kennedy, P. (2002) 'Global Challenges in the Beginning of the Twenty-First Century', in P. Kennedy, D. Messner and F. Nuschler (eds) *Global Trends and Global Governance*, London: Pluto.

Kirby, P. (2006) *Vulnerability and Violence: The Impact of Globalisation*, London: Pluto.

Klusmeyer, D. (2005) 'Hannah Arendt's Critical Realism: Power, Justice, and Responsibility', in A. F. Lang Jr and J. Williams (eds) *Hannah Arendt and International Relations: Reading Across the Lines*, Basingstoke: Palgrave Macmillan.

Kohn, J. (1996) 'Evil and Plurality: Hannah Arendt's Way to The Life of the Mind', in L. May and J. Kohn (eds) *Hannah Arendt: Twenty Years Later*, Cambridge, MA: MIT Press.

——(2000) 'Freedom: The Priority of the Political', in D. Villa (ed.) *The Cambridge Companion to Hannah Arendt*, Cambridge: Cambridge University Press.

Lang Jr, A. F. (2005) 'Governance and Political Action: Hannah Arendt on Global Political Protest', in A. F. Lang Jr and J. Williams (eds) *Hannah Arendt and International Relations: Reading Across the Lines*, Basingstoke: Palgrave Macmillan.

Lang Jr, A. F. and Williams, J. (eds) (2005) *Hannah Arendt and International Relations: Reading Across the Lines*, Basingstoke: Palgrave Macmillan.

Lara, M. P. (2007) *Narrating Evil: A Postmetaphysical Theory of Reflective Judgment*, New York: Columbia University Press.

Lebor, A. (2006) *'Complicity with Evil': The United Nations in the Age of Modern Genocide*, New Haven, CT: Yale University Press.

Levy, D. and Sznaider, N. (2002) 'Memory Unbound: The Holocaust and the Foundation of Cosmopolitan Memory', *European Journal of Social Theory* 5: 87–106.

Liu Institute for Global Issues (2005) Roco Wat I Acoli*: Restoring Relationships in Acholi-land: Traditional Approaches to Justice and Reintegration*, Liu Institute for Global Issues, Gulu District NGO Forum, with the assistance of Ker Kwaro Acholi, http://www.liu.xplorex.com/?p2=modules/liu/publications/view.jsp&id=16.

Locke, J. (1989) *Two Treatises of Government*, edited by P. Laslett, Cambridge: Cambridge University Press.

Lu, C. (2000) 'The One and Many Faces of Cosmopolitanism', *Journal of Political Philosophy* 8: 244–67.

——(2004) 'Agents, Structures and Evil in World Politics', *International Relations* 18: 498–509.

Lyotard, J. F. (1993) 'The Other's Rights', in S. Shute and S. Hurley (eds) *On Human Rights: The Oxford Amnesty Lectures 1993*, New York: Basic Books.

Marfleet, P. (2006) *Refugees in a Global Era*, Basingstoke: Palgrave Macmillan.

May, L. (2005) *Crimes Against Humanity*, Cambridge/New York: Cambridge University Press.

Macpherson, C. B. (1962) *The Political Theory of Possessive Individualism: Hobbes to Locke*, Oxford: Clarendon Press.

McDonald, A. and Haveman, R. (2003) *Prosecutorial Discretion: Some Thoughts on 'Objectifying' the Exercise of Prosecutorial Discretion by the Prosecutor of the ICC*, Contribution to an Expert Consultation Process on General Issues Relevant to the ICC Office of the Prosecutor, International Criminal Court, www.icc- cpi.int/library/organs/otp/mcdonald_haveman.pdf.

Milborn, C. (2007) 'The Assault on Fortress Europe: Thousands are On Their Way, But Europe Doesn't Want Them', Goethe-Institut Report, www.goethe.de/ges/pok/prj/mig/mgr/en2358674.htm

von Mises, L. (1949) *Human Action: A Treatise on Economics*, Ludwig von Mises Institute, www.mises.org/humanaction.asp.

Morgenthau, H. (1946) *Scientific Man Versus Power Politics*, Chicago, IL: University of Chicago Press.

Morton, A. (2004) *On Evil*, New York/London: Routledge.

Moses, J. W. (2006) *International Migration: Globalization's Last Frontier*, London: Zed Books.

Munck, R. (2002) *Globalisation and Labour: The New 'Great Transformation'*, London: Zed Books.

Nedelsky, J. (2001) 'Judgment, Diversity, and Relational Autonomy', in R. Beiner and J. Nedelsky (eds) *Judgment, Imagination, and Politics: Themes from Kant and Arendt*, Lanham, MD: Rowman & Littlefield.

Neiman, S. (2002) *Evil in Modern Thought: An Alternative History of Philosophy*, Princeton, NJ: Princeton University Press.

Nesiba, R. and Burton, M. (2004) 'Transnational Financial Institutions, Global Financial Flows and the International Monetary Fund', in P. A. O'Hara (ed.) *Global Political Economy and the Wealth of Nations: Performance, Institutions, Problems and Policies*, London: Routledge.

Nino, C. S. (1996) *Radical Evil on Trial*, New Haven, CT/London, UK: Yale University Press.

Northern Uganda Peace Initiative (2005), *Report on Acholi Youth and Chiefs Addressing Practices of the Acholi Culture of Reconciliation*, Kampala: NUPI/USAID.

Nussbaum, M. (1996) 'Patriotism and Cosmopolitanism', in J. Cohen (ed.) *For Love of Country*, Boston, MA: Beacon Press.

——(2006) *Frontiers of Justice: Disability, Nationality, Species Membership*, Cambridge, MA: Harvard University Press.

Nyers, P. (2006) *Rethinking Refugees: Beyond States of Emergency*, New York/London: Routledge.

Ohmae, K. (1995) *The End of the Nation State: The Rise of Regional Economies*, New York: Free Press.

——(1999) *The Borderless World: Power and Strategy in the Interlinked World Economy*, New York: HarperCollins.

Osiel, M. (2001) *Mass Atrocity, Ordinary Evil, and Hannah Arendt: Criminal Consciousness in Argentina's Dirty War*, New Haven, CT: Yale University Press.

Owens, P. (2005) 'Hannah Arendt, Violence, and the Inescapable Fact of Humanity', in A. F. Lang Jr and J. Williams (eds) *Hannah Arendt and International Relations: Reading Across the Lines*, Basingstoke: Palgrave Macmillan.

——(2007) *Between War and Politics: International Relations and the Thought of Hannah Arendt*, Oxford: Oxford University Press.

Oxfam Australia (2002) 'Adrift in the Pacific: The Implications of Australia's Pacific Refugee Solution', www.lib.washington.edu/southeastasia/Adrift.html.

Ong, A. (2006) *Neoliberalism as Exception: Mutations in Citizenship and Sovereignty*, Durham, NC/London, UK: Duke University Press.

Parekh, B. (1981) *Hannah Arendt and the Search for a New Political Philosophy*, London: Macmillan.

Parekh, S. (2004) 'A Meaningful Place in the World: Hannah Arendt on the Nature of Human Rights', *Journal of Human Rights* 3: 41–53.

——(2008) *Hannah Arendt and the Challenge of Modernity: A Phenomenology of Human Rights*, New York/London: Routledge.

Patomäki, H. and Teivainen, T. (2004) *A Possible World: Democratic Transformation of Global Institutions*, London/New York: Zed Books.

Patterson, O. (1982) *Slavery and Social Death*, Cambridge, MA: Harvard University Press.

Phillips, J. (2004) *Temporary Protection Visas*, Research Note 51 2003-04, Canberra: Parliament of Australia, www.aph.gov.au/library/pubs/RN/2003-04/04rn51.htm.

Pitkin, H. F. (1998) *The Attack of the Blob: Hannah Arendt's Concept of the Social*, Chicago, IL: University of Chicago Press.

Pogge, T. (1998) 'A Global Resources Dividend', in D. A. Crocker and T. Linden (eds) *Ethics of Consumption: The Good Life, Justice, and Global Stewardship*, Lanham, MD: Rowman & Littlefield.

——(2002) *World Poverty and Human Rights*, Cambridge: Polity Press.

——(2005a) 'World Poverty and Human Rights', *Ethics & International Affairs* 19: 1–8.

——(2005b) 'Recognized and Violated by International Law: The Human Rights of the Global Poor', *Leiden Journal of International Law* 18: 717–45.

Power, S. (2002) *'A Problem from Hell': America and the Age of Genocide*, New York: Basic Books.

Ralph, J. (2003) 'Between Cosmopolitanism and American Democracy: Understanding US Opposition to the International Criminal Court', *International Relations* 17: 195–212.

Ratner, S. S. and Abrams, J. (2001) *Accountability for Human Rights Atrocities in International Law: Beyond the Nuremberg Legacy*, 2nd edn, Oxford: Oxford University Press.

Rawls, J. (1999) *The Law of Peoples*, Cambridge, MA: Harvard University Press.

Refugee Law Project (2005) *Whose Justice? Perceptions of Uganda's Amnesty Act 2000: the Potential for Conflict Resolution and Long-Term Reconciliation*, Working Paper No. 15, www.refugeelawproject.org/resources/papers/workingpapers/RLP.WP15.pdf.

Rengger, N. and Jeffery, R. (2005) 'Moral Evil and International Relations', *SAIS Review* 25: 3–16.

Richmond, A. H. (1994) *Global Apartheid: Refugees, Racism, and the New World Order*, Oxford/New York: Oxford University Press.

Ricoeur, P. (1965) *History and Truth*, Evanston, IL: Northwestern University Press.

Risse, T., Ropp, S. C. and Sikkink, K. (eds) (1999) *The Power of Human Rights: International Norms and Domestic Change*, Cambridge: Cambridge University Press.

Roach, S. C. (2005) 'Value Pluralism, Liberalism and the Cosmopolitan Intent of the International Criminal Court', *Journal of Human Rights*, 4: 475–90.

——(2006) *Politicizing the International Criminal Court: The Convergence of Politics, Ethics, and Law*, Lanham, MD: Rowman & Littlefield.

Robertson, G. (1999) *Crimes against Humanity: The Struggle for Global Justice*, London: Allen Lane.

Rome Statute of the International Criminal Court (1998), www.icc-cpi.int/library/about/officialjournal/Rome_Statute_120704-EN.pdf.

Sassen, S. (1999) *Guests and Aliens*, New York: The New Press.

Schaap, A. (2005) *Political Reconciliation*, London/New York: Routledge.

Schabas, W. A. (2001) *An Introduction to the International Criminal Court*, Cambridge: Cambridge University Press.

Schirato, T. and Webb, J. (2006) *Understanding Globalization*, Thousand Oaks, CA: Sage.

Schmitt, C. (1985) *Political Theology: Four Chapters on the Concept of Sovereignty*, Cambridge, MA: MIT Press.

Schuster, L. (2005) *The Realities of a New Asylum Paradigm*, Working Paper No. 20, Centre on Migration Policy and Society, Oxford University, www.compas.ox.ac.uk/publications/papers/Liza%20Schuster%20wp0520.pdf.

Seglow, J. (2005) 'The Ethics of Immigration', *Political Studies Review* 3: 317–34.

Seligman, A. B. (1992) *The Idea of Civil Society*, Princeton, NJ: Princeton University Press.

Sen, A. (1999) *Development as Freedom*, New York: A. A. Knopf.

Sennett, R. (2006) *The Culture of the New Capitalism*, New Haven, CT: Yale University Press.

Seoane, J. and Taddei, E. (2002) 'From Seattle to Porto Alegre: The Anti-Neoliberal Globalization Movement', *Current Sociology* 50: 99–122.

Singer, P. (2002) *One World: The Ethics of Globalization*, New Haven, CT: Yale University Press.

——(2004) *The President of Good and Evil: The Ethics of George W. Bush*, New York: Dutton.

Sklair, L. (2001) *The Transnational Capitalist Class*, Oxford: Blackwell.

——(2002) *Globalization: Capitalism and its Alternatives*, Oxford: Oxford University Press.

Smith, A. (1976) *The Wealth of Nations*, Oxford: Clarendon Press.

Smith, J. (2008) *Social Movements for Global Democracy*, Baltimore, MD: Johns Hopkins University Press.

Sorenson, G. (1999) 'Sovereignty: Change and Continuity in a Fundamental Institution', *Political Studies* 47: 590–604.

Spirtas, M. (1996) 'A House Divided: Tragedy and Evil in Realist Theory', in B. Frankel (ed.) *Realism: Restatements and Renewal*, Portland, OR: Frank Cass.

Steger, M. (2003) *Globalization: A Very Short Introduction*, Oxford: Oxford University Press.

——(2005) *Globalism: The New Market Ideology*, Lanham, MD: Rowman & Littlefield.

Stevens, J. (2006) 'Prisons of the Stateless', *New Left Review* 42: 53–67.

Stoler, A. L. (1995) *Race and the Education of Desire: Foucault's 'History of Sexuality' and the Colonial Order of Things*, Durham, NC/London UK: Duke University Press.

Suganami, H. (2007) 'Understanding Sovereignty through Kelsen/Schmitt', *Review of International Studies* 33: 511–30.

Szerszynski, B. and Urry, J. (2002) 'Cultures of Cosmopolitanism', *Sociological Review* 50: 461–81.

Taminiaux, J. (2000) 'Athens and Rome', in D. Villa (ed.) *The Cambridge Companion to Hannah Arendt*, Cambridge: Cambridge University Press.

Teivainen, T. (2002) 'World Social Forum and Global Democratization', *Third World Quarterly* 23: 621–32.

Thatcher, M. (1987) 'Interview with *Woman's Own* Magazine', 31 October, www.margaretthatcher.org/speeches/displaydocument.asp?docid=106689.

Thomas, L. (2003) 'Forgiving the Unforgivable?', in E. Garrard and G. Scarre (eds) *Moral Philosophy and the Holocaust*, Aldershot: Ashgate Publishing.

Tormey, S. (2004) *Anti-Capitalism: A Beginner's Guide*, Oxford: Oneworld Publications.

Touraine, A. (2001) *Beyond Neoliberalism*, Cambridge: Polity Press.

Tsao, R. T. (2002a) 'The Three Phases of Arendt's Theory of Imperialism', *Social Research* 69: 579–619.

——(2002b) 'Arendt against Athens: Rereading *The Human Condition*', *Political Theory* 30: 97–123.

Tuck, R. (1993) *Natural Rights Theories: Their Origins and Development*, Cambridge: Cambridge University Press.

Tullock, G. (1982) 'Economic Imperialism', in J. Buchanan and R. Tollison (eds) *Theory of Public Choice*, Ann Arbor, MI: University of Michigan Press.

Turner, R. S. (2008) *Neo-liberal Ideology: History, Concepts and Policies*, Edinburgh: Edinburgh University Press.

UNAIDS/WHO (2005) *AIDS Epidemic Update 2005*, United Nations Programme on HIV/ AIDS and World Health Organization, Geneva: UNAIDS/WHO.

UNDP (2002) *Human Development Report 2002*, United Nations Development Programme, Oxford: Oxford University Press.

——(2003) *Human Development Report 2003*, Oxford: Oxford University Press.

——(2004) *Human Development Report 2004*, Oxford: Oxford University Press.

——(2005) *Human Development Report 2005*, Oxford: Oxford University Press.

UNHCR (2006) 'Refugees by Numbers 2006 Edition', United Nations High Commissioner for Refugees, www.unhcr.org/basics/BASICS/4523b0bb2.pdf.

——(2007a) *2005 Statistical Yearbook: Trends in Displacement, Protection and Solutions*, www.unhcr.org/statistics/STATISTICS/464478a72.html.

——(2007b) *Global Trends 2006: Refugees, Asylum-seekers, Returnees, Internally Displaced and Stateless Persons*, www.unhcr.org/statistics/STATISTICS/4676a71d4.pdf.

UNHSP (2006) *State of the World's Cities 2006/7*, United Nations Human Settlement Programme, www.unhabitat.org/mediacentre/sowckit2006_7.asp

US Department of State (2008) *Trafficking in Persons Report 2008*, Washington DC: Office of the Undersecretary for Democracy and Global Affairs, www.state.gov/g/tip/ rls/tiprpt/2008.

Vernon, R. (2002) 'What is Crime against Humanity?', *Journal of Political Philosophy* 10: 231–49.

Villa, D. (1996) *Arendt and Heidegger: The Fate of the Political*, Princeton, NJ: Princeton University Press.

——(1999) *Politics, Philosophy, Terror: Essays on the Thought of Hannah Arendt*, Princeton, NJ: Princeton University Press.

——(ed.) (2000) *The Cambridge Companion to Hannah Arendt*, Cambridge: Cambridge University Press.

Weber, M. (2000) 'The Profession and Vocation of Politics', in P. Lassman and R. Speirs (eds) *Political Writings*, Cambridge: Cambridge University Press.

Weissbrodt, D. and Collins, C. (2006) 'The Human Rights of Stateless Persons', *Human Rights Quarterly* 28: 245–76.

Wellmer, A. (1996) 'Hannah Arendt on Judgment: The Unwritten Doctrine of Reason', in L. May and J. Kohn (eds) *Hannah Arendt: Twenty Years Later*, Cambridge, MA: MIT Press.

Wilder, G. (2005) *The French Imperial Nation-State: Negritude and Colonial Humanism between the Two World Wars*, Chicago, IL: University of Chicago Press.

World Bank (2004) *Global Development Finance 2004*, Washington, DC: The World Bank.

WHO (2004) *World Health Report 2004*, Geneva: World Health Organization.

Wright, M. (1982) 'An Ethic of Responsibility', in J. Mayall (ed.) *The Community of States*, London: Allen and Unwin.

Wynter, A. (2006) 'Deadly Passage', *Red Cross Red Crescent* 2, www.redcross.int/EN/mag/magazine2006_2/12-14.html.

Young, I. M. (2003) 'Violence against Power: Critical Thoughts on Military Intervention', in D. K. Chatterjee and D. E. Scheid (eds) *Ethics and Foreign Intervention*, Cambridge: Cambridge University Press.

Young-Bruehl, E. (2004) *Hannah Arendt: For Love of the World*, 2nd edn, New Haven, CT/London, UK: Yale University Press.

——(2006). *Why Arendt Matters*, New Haven, CT: Yale University Press.

Index

absolute evil 13
accountability 10, 15, 28, 30, 34
Acholi 27–9
action 7, 10, 11, 14 18–21, 23–31, 34, 36, 45, 48, 52, 65, 66, 69, 70–1, 88–9, 91, 92, 93, 94, 95–101, 110–18, 120
Adorno, Theodor 122 n. 3
Africa 39, 40, 41, 74, 85, 86
Agamben, Giorgio 30, 75, 77–9, 82
agency, 25, 29, 37, 45, 50, 65–6, 70, 82, 87–8, 96, 116, 117, 118, 120
alternative globalization 92, 118, 119, 120;
    see also: global civil society
ambivalence 7, 10, 12, 15, 20, 24, 25, 27, 37
amor mundi 100
Anderson, Perry 118
animal laborans 94, 96, 98, 114;
    see also: labour
anti-Semitism 34, 123
apartheid 16, 126 n. 21;
    global 57, 80, 86–7, 90
appearances, space of 27, 95, 99, 116
Aquinas, Thomas 97
Aristotle 66, 96
asylum 56, 64, 80–7, 90, 126
atrocities 1, 5, 9, 10, 12, 13, 15, 17, 19, 26, 29, 33, 37, 54, 92, 119
Augustine, Saint 5
Auschwitz 12, 13, 125 n. 10
Australia 40, 83–4, 126 n. 17
authority 58, 60, 68, 69, 73, 83, 84, 86, 126
autonomy 96, 100, 110, 112, 119

Bales, Kevin 40–1, 53, 124 n. 7
Balibar, Étienne 86–7
banality of evil 3–4, 14, 36–8, 46, 52, 74, 123 n. 2, 124 n. 7
Bauman, Zygmunt 42–3, 50, 102, 124 n. 10
Beck, Ulrich 11, 22–4, 26, 119, 123 n. 7

behaviouralism 97
Benhabib, Seyla 30, 33, 54, 82, 89, 91
Benjamin, Walter 73
Bernstein, Richard J. 4, 12, 38
biopolitics 68, 75–8, 82, 116
biopower 75–8
birth 14, 71;
    see also: natality
Blücher, Heinrich 55
Bourdieu, Pierre 128 n. 14
bourgeoisie 34–5
Browning, Christopher 123 n. 2
bureaucracy 43, 51, 52, 74, 75, 97
Burke, Edmund 72–3
Bush, George W. 1, 49, 124 n. 12, 126 n. 15

Cambodia 9
Camus, Albert 128 n. 15
capitalism 36, 39, 51, 53, 98, 102, 103, 105, 115, 118, 120, 127 n. 3
catastrophes 46, 53, 55, 99
citizenship 21, 26, 35, 56, 60–1, 63, 64–5, 67, 73, 80, 81, 86–7, 91
civil society 28, 118, 120
Cold War 11, 102
collective guilt 51–2
colonialism 73, 74, 76;
    see also: imperialism
common sense 15, 17, 29, 47;
    see also: sensus communis
common world 14, 43, 46, 56, 66, 88, 90, 91, 96, 100–1, 102, 110, 116, 118
communication 27, 104
communism 98, 105
community 14, 17, 21, 22, 24, 25, 29, 31, 34, 35, 47, 52, 58, 60, 63–7, 69, 74, 75, 78–9, 82, 85, 87, 88, 90–1
concentration camps 13, 32, 44
conscience 16, 47–8

contingency 24, 31, 71, 88
cosmopolitan realism 8, 9–10, 11, 15,
    20–1, 24, 26, 29, 30, 31, 57, 119, 121,
    123 n. 13
cosmopolitanism 9, 10, 11, 17–18, 21, 23,
    24, 26, 30, 47, 127 n. 25
crimes against humanity 9, 10, 12, 15–16,
    17, 22, 27–31, 122 n. 5
critical theory 23
cruelty 18
Curtis, Kimberley 29

Darfur 9, 11
Declaration of the Rights of Man and
    Citizen 58–60
dehumanization 2, 3, 6, 7, 13–14, 36, 39, 48
demonization 1, 4–5, 12–14, 32, 36–7, 50,
    124 n. 12
denationalization 63–4, 67, 78, 80
Derrida, Jacques 30, 123 n. 12, 126 n. 24
dialogue 50, 95, 100, 101, 117, 119
Dietz, Mary 93
difference;
    see: plurality
disclosure 27, 30, 89, 95, 117–18
discrimination 40, 42, 74, 75, 80
domination 18, 70, 74, 96, 110, 111, 118
durability, of world 94, 102

economics 97, 106, 107, 114, 116
economism 98, 112, 114
Eichmann, Adolf 3, 6, 13, 14, 22, 36–7, 48,
    51, 52, 74, 124 n. 3, 125 n. 4
emancipation 34, 35, 58, 59, 99, 111
enlarged mentality 28, 47–8, 50–1;
    see also: representative thinking
Enlightenment 17, 19, 23
equality 7, 17, 21, 34, 59, 60, 66, 67, 70,
    75, 91, 95, 96, 100–1, 109, 111, 125 n. 7;
    see also: isonomia
ethics 11, 22, 30
ethnic cleansing 38, 49
exception 67–8, 75, 77–8, 79, 84, 103
exclusion 3, 13, 53, 54, 56, 57, 60, 62,
    66–9, 72, 82, 90, 91, 114;
    inclusive 57, 77–80. 84–88
extermination camps;
    see: concentration camps
extreme evil 4, 6, 10, 11, 12– 17, 19, 21,
    22, 26, 37, 49, 122 n. 3

federalism 26, 123 n. 8
First World War 44, 57, 61, 112
forgiveness 29

Fortress Europe 84
Foucault, Michel 75, 76, 77, 79, 82, 86
frailty of human affairs 5, 14, 19, 20, 22,
    27, 36, 54, 101
free–market theories 35, 103, 106–7, 108,
    109, 114–15, 127 n. 7
freedom 1, 2, 8, 17, 21, 26, 31, 62, 65,
    68–73, 93, 95, 96, 97, 100, 101, 102,
    106, 108–12, 115, 117, 118, 121;
    and sovereignty 68–73;
    of movement 87–91, 126 n. 22, 126 n. 23
French Revolution 59
Friedman, Milton 106, 107, 109
Friedman, Thomas 107
friendship, civic 89–90

genocide 5, 9, 10, 11–17, 19, 20, 21, 22,
    23, 24, 25, 26, 27, 28, 29, 30, 31, 32–3,
    38, 49, 54, 73, 79, 94, 123 n. 2, 124 n. 4
global civil society 92, 104, 118–21;
    see also: alternative globalization
globalism 128 n. 13
globality 23
globalization 39–45, 50, 53, 75, 92–3,
    102–5, 107, 110, 114–15, 117–18, 119,
    120, 121, 128 n. 13;
    see also: alternative globalization
Goldhagen, Daniel 123 n. 2
Greece, ancient 19, 69, 93–5, 97
guilt 22, 26, 52

Habermas, Jürgen 122 n. 1
Hardt, Michael 111–12
Harvey, David 103, 105, 107, 114, 128 n. 18
Hayek, Friedrich 106, 107, 109
Held, David 102
history, laws of 18, 21, 73, 112–13
Hitler, Adolf 48, 55
Hobbes, Thomas 35–6, 58–9, 71, 72–3, 108
Holocaust 9, 11, 12, 13, 15, 17, 21, 32, 93,
    123 n. 2, 124 n. 4
homelessness 7
homo faber 94–6;
    see also: work
homo sacer 78–9
Honig, Bonnie 127 n. 25
hope 8, 20, 121
horror 5, 9, 19, 32
hospitality 89, 127 n. 25
human dignity 8, 20, 57, 65, 70, 91, 100
human nature 4, 14, 18, 37, 58, 67, 100,
    108, 114, 122 n. 2
human rights 3, 7, 20, 21, 22, 24, 26, 27,
    28, 30, 32–, 43, 44, 49–51, 53, 56–70,

72, 73, 79–80, 82, 85–88, 90, 119;
  see also: right to have rights
human status 3, 7, 9, 10, 13, 14, 16, 18, 19,
  21, 22, 25, 26, 33, 37–8, 46, 48, 54
human trafficking 42
humanism 19
humanitas 89, 100, 117
humanity, historical 19–22, 24, 25, 31

idealism 2, 7, 9, 10, 19, 20, 25, 57, 66
identity 69, 73, 75, 81, 86, 87, 90, 126 n. 24
ideology 34, 50–2, 74, 93, 98, 102, 105,
  110, 113–18, 128 n. 13
imagination 23, 27, 28, 46–7
impartiality 17, 47
imperialism 12, 18, 33–7, 57, 62, 72–5,
  110, 125 n. 8
inequality 32, 38–41, 44–6, 51, 53, 86, 88,
  96, 97, 114
injustice 1, 2, 3, 28, 31, 44, 123 n. 13, 124
  n. 9
International Criminal Court (ICC) 9–11,
  15, 21–31, 119, 120
International Labour Organization (ILO)
  41, 42
international law 9, 16, 27, 28, 65, 67, 72,
  80–3
intersubjectivity 15, 21, 69, 70, 99
Iraq 1
Isaac, Jeffrey C. 20, 54
isolation 65–6, 115
isonomia 96, 101

Jaspers, Karl 17, 19, 32, 127 n. 25
judgement 10, 15, 28–9, 46–8, 51, 111
judging 48, 52, 127 n. 1
Judt, Tony 1
juridification 10–11, 15, 16, 21, 22, 26,
  122 n. 1
justice 3, 10, 15–17, 20, 27–31, 75, 78, 96,
  124 n. 8, 124 n. 13

Kant, Immanuel, 4–5, 10, 13, 17, 47, 127
  n. 25
Kateb, George, 2, 3, 45, 84
Klusmeyer, Douglas, 18
Kohn, Jerome, 12, 94

labour 41, 42, 43, 94–6, 99, 104, 114, 116,
  117
Lebor, Adam 11
legalism 29–30
liberalism 58, 77, 106
liberty 58, 106, 109, 111

Locke, John 108
love 100, 117;
  see also: amor mundi
Lu, Catherine 1, 17–18
Lyotard, Jean-François 125 n. 5

Machiavelli, Niccolò 19
Marx, Karl 98, 102, 114
mass society 97, 98
May, Larry 16, 55
memory 51, 123 n. 4
metaphysics 57, 126 n. 24
minorities 61–3, 74
Minority Treaties 61–2
Mises, Ludwig von 106, 108
modernity 14, 17, 33, 36, 43, 53, 93–4,
  97–9, 102, 111, 112;
  first 23;
  second 23;
  reflexive 11, 23–4
Mont Pelerin Society 106–7
morality 5, 94
Morgenthau, Hans 18–19

natality 14, 70–1, 117–18, 121
nationalism 20, 23, 60, 62, 72, 103, 112
nationality 21, 26, 60–2, 64–5, 67, 69, 75,
  80–2, 87, 91, 125 n. 3, 126 n. 24
nation-state 23, 26, 59–63, 68–9, 73–6, 80,
  86, 88, 97, 98;
  decline of 34, 60
nature, laws of 94, 112–14
necessity 50, 74, 93–7, 100, 111–15, 118
Negri, Antonio 111–12
neoliberalism 35, 39, 51, 92, 93, 102, 103,
  105–10, 114–21, 128
nihilism 15
non-governmental organizations (NGOs)
  120, 128 n. 18
Nuremberg trials 9, 16, 22
Nussbaum, Martha 17

Ohmae, Kenichi, 104–5
opinion, 47, 51 65;
  see also: enlarged mentality
oppression, 1, 2, 3, 62

Patterson, Orlando 40
personhood 3, 13
Pitkin, Hanna 46, 48, 127 n. 2
Plato 69
plurality 6, 7, 14–15, 17, 25, 26, 27, 30–1,
  36, 47–8, 66, 69, 71, 88–9, 90, 94, 95,
  98, 99, 100, 110, 116, 117–18, 119, 121

Pogge, Thomas 32, 44–5, 46, 49–50, 51, 53, 122 n. 1, 124 n. 8
polis 77, 96, 97, 111
political evil 1–10, 12, 14–15, 18, 30, 32–3, 36–9, 42, 45–6, 49, 51–4, 67, 75, 80, 90–3, 110, 112, 117–18
political, the 1–3, 7, 18, 39, 68, 77–9, 90, 92–100, 102, 105, 110–18, 120–1
Popper, Karl 106
poverty 32–54, 79, 92, 110, 111, 124 n. 4; *see also:* social question
power 1–3, 7, 8, 11, 12, 19, 20, 22, 23, 24, 25, 30, 34–6, 45, 51, 53, 58, 66, 76–9, 96–8, 103, 104, 105, 107, 108, 111, 114, 118–19
praxis 96
private realm 95–6, 98, 120, 127 n. 4
progress 1, 9, 18–19, 23, 31, 42–3, 109
promises 9, 11, 27, 30–1, 87, 113
public affairs 35, 62, 93–4, 96, 99, 105, 112
public realm 27, 31, 34, 35, 38, 56, 65–6, 89, 91, 93, 95–102, 110–11, 115–18, 120–1

race thinking 72–4, 112, 125. n7
racism 18, 40, 57, 62, 75–7, 86–7
radical evil 3–6, 13, 48, 50
Rawls, John 122 n. 1, 123 n. 13
realism, political 18–19, 20, 22, 24, 71
truth 12, 29, 58, 112–14, 116, 117; *see also:* ideology
reality, sense of 10, 15–16, 27, 90, 99, 112; worldly 69, 70, 118
refugees 43, 55–7, 63–4, 75, 77, 79, 80–9, 125 n. 2, 125 n. 9, 126 n. 20
representative thinking; *see:* enlarged mentality
resistance 15, 26, 119, 123 n. 9
respect 4, 25, 26, 49, 67, 101, 126 n. 24
responsibility 10, 11, 15, 19, 20, 43, 46, 47, 48, 51–4, 86, 89, 100, 109, 112, 113, 115, 123 n. 10; collective 2, 7, 22, 52; common 25–7, 30–1; global 24–5
revolution 9, 63, 104
Richmond, Anthony 86
Ricoeur, Paul 1–3
right to have rights 21, 25–6, 54, 65, 68, 87–8, 90–1, 101, 125
rightlessness 53, 57, 64, 65, 66, 67, 76, 79, 88, 90, 91, 125 n. 5
Rights of Man 58–60, 66, 72
rights, human 17, 20–1, 26, 33, 49–50, 54–61, 63–7, 69, 72–5, 77–82, 85–91, 119

rootlessness 7, 21
Rousseau, Jean-Jacques 59
Rwanda 9, 11, 15

Schmitt, Carl 68, 77
Scholem, Gershom 3–4
Second World War 3, 22, 25, 27, 38, 44, 48, 54, 103
self-determination 59, 61–2, 69
Sen, Amartya 96
Sennett, Richard 104
sensus communis 47
slavery 40–2, 124 n. 7
Smith, Adam 103, 106, 114, 127 n. 7
social question 110–11
social, the 93–103, 106, 110–16, 118, 120–1, 127 n. 2
solidarity 7, 11, 20–1, 24–5, 34, 36, 89, 112, 115, 126 n. 24
sovereign power 55–7, 61, 63, 67–73, 75, 80, 82–86, 88, 90
sovereignty 7, 21, 23, 24, 26, 56–62, 67–73, 75–8, 80, 84, 86, 88–91, 105, 119, 123 n. 7, 125 n. 11
space of appearance 95, 120
speech 66, 88–9, 95–6, 98, 99, 117, 120
Spirtas, Michael 18–19
statelessness 21, 42, 55–92
Steger, Manfred 128 n. 13
structural conditions 18, 35, 39, 44–6, 48, 49, 51–4, 56, 63, 68, 72, 77, 87
suffering 2, 18, 25, 29, 32–3, 38, 46, 49, 53–4
superfluousness 3, 6, 24, 33, 36, 53–4, 68, 76, 82, 83, 84, 117

technology, 76, 103–4
terror, 25, 54
terrorism, 7, 38
Thatcher, Margaret, 103, 107, 108
theodicy, 12
Third World, 82
thoughtlessness, 4, 6, 33, 37, 48, 52, 54, 113
totalitarianism, 5, 6, 7, 12, 33–6, 38, 53, 54, 73, 74, 110
Touraine, Alain 127 n. 6, 128 n. 13
tragedy, 18, 40, 60, 67, 121
tragic, 8, 18–19, 33, 69
Tsao, Roy, 33, 93
tyranny, 75, 115

Uganda 11, 27–30
UN Convention Relating to the Status of Refugees 80–1, 84

UN Convention Relating to the Status of Stateless Persons 81–2
UN Genocide Convention 16, 22
United Nations 11, 16, 22, 39, 40, 56, 82, 126
United Nations High Commissioner for Refugees (UNHCR) 56, 82, 125, 126
Universal Declaration of Human Rights (UDHR) 16, 49, 58, 80
universalism 7, 27, 30, 73
unpredictability 8, 19, 24, 25, 27, 31, 71, 115
uprootedness 36

Villa, Dana 43–4, 111
violence 2, 18, 21, 33, 38, 40, 42, 49, 53–4, 68, 76, 78, 79, 95, 96, 105, 114, 118, 123 n. 1, 125 n. 11; structural 33, 38, 45, 48, 53–4, 79, 118
vita activa 94, 127 n. 1

War on Terror 1, 83
Washington Consensus 107
Weber, Max 68
work 94–5, 98–9, 104, 117
World Bank 40, 44, 45, 107
World Social Forum (WSF) 119
worldlessness 53–4, 101–2, 102, 117, 124 n. 13
worldliness 30, 89, 94, 102, 117, 121

Young-Bruehl, Elisabeth 3, 55, 74

eBooks – at www.eBookstore.tandf.co.uk

A library at your fingertips!

eBooks are electronic versions of printed books. You can store them on your PC/laptop or browse them online.

They have advantages for anyone needing rapid access to a wide variety of published, copyright information.

eBooks can help your research by enabling you to bookmark chapters, annotate text and use instant searches to find specific words or phrases. Several eBook files would fit on even a small laptop or PDA.

NEW: Save money by eSubscribing: cheap, online access to any eBook for as long as you need it.

Annual subscription packages

We now offer special low-cost bulk subscriptions to packages of eBooks in certain subject areas. These are available to libraries or to individuals.

For more information please contact webmaster.ebooks@tandf.co.uk

We're continually developing the eBook concept, so keep up to date by visiting the website.

www.eBookstore.tandf.co.uk